Acclaim for *Healing a Broken World*

"This remarkable book offers an astute analysis of the disabling realities of the global economy. It reflects concretely on the obligations of Christian obedience. And then, precisely to connect the analysis and the obligation, it pivots on the freedom and courage for serious moral agency. . . . The author mobilizes immense learning about global context and about Gospel tradition. . . . It is a book much needed now, surely to be well received."

—WALTER BRUEGGEMANN
McPheeters Professor of Old Testament,
Columbia Theological Seminary

"Moe-Lobeda shows that Luther specifically attacked the injustices of this economic system when it was in its infancy. We live when it is achieving its powerful domination, and her question is, how can we find the moral agency to correct it? She finds it in Luther's theme of the indwelling Christ, which I have long thought is the best way into Luther's theology and ethics."

—GLEN HAROLD STASSEN
Smedes Professor of Christian Ethics,
Fuller Theological Seminary

healing
a broken world

healing a broken world

Globalization and God

Cynthia D. Moe-Lobeda

Fortress Press
Minneapolis

Healing a Broken World
Globalization and God

Scripture quotations are from the New Revised Standard Version Bible, copyright © 1989 by the Division of Christian Education of the National Council of the Churches of Christ in the USA and used by permission.

The poetry of Emilie M. Townes on pp. 118–19 is reprinted from "Women's Wisdom on Solidarity and Differences (On Not Rescuing the Killers)," which originally appeared in the *Union Seminary Quarterly Review* 53:3-4 (1999). Used by kind permission of the author.

Cover art: Ben Shahn, *The Red Stairway,* 1944. Tempera on Masonite, 16 x 23 3/8 inches, collection of the St. Louis Art Museum. © Estate of Ben Shahn/Licensed by VAGA, New York, N.Y. Used by permission.

Cover and interior design: Zan Ceeley

Library of Congress Cataloging-in-Publication Data

Moe-Lobeda, Cynthia
    Healing a broken world: globalization and God / Cynthia D. Moe-Lobeda.
      p. cm.
    Includes bibliographical references and index.
    ISBN 0-8006-3250-8 (alk. paper)
    1. Globalization—Religious aspects—Christianity. 2. Economics—Religious aspects—Christianity. 3. Globalization—Moral and ethical aspects. 4. Economics—Moral and ethical aspects. 5. Christian ethics—Lutheran authors. I. Title.

BR115.E3 M64 2002
261.8'5—dc21   2002016369

Manufactured in the U.S.A.
07   06   05   04   03   02   1   2   3   4   5   6   7   8   9   10

To Ron, precious lifelong lover and friend.

To two splendid sons, Leif and Gabriel,
whom I love beyond measure and
who teach me daily the wonders of life on this good Earth.

To my parents—Lila, Richard, Marcia—and sister, Suzan,
spirited givers of steadfast love.

Contents

Part One
Economic Globalization: Disabling Moral Agency

Part Two
The Indwelling God: Enabling Subversive Moral Agency

Preface

❧

Our children die of hunger because our land, which ought to grow food for them, is used by international companies to produce strawberries for your tables.
— A Mexican strawberry picker

You shall love your neighbor as yourself.
— Mark 12:31

THIS STORY BEGINS in Honduras. As a healthcare missionary, I witnessed young children languish from malnourishment, children who could have flourished had their parents had access to a *pedacito de tierra* (small plot of land) on which to grow beans, corn, and vegetables. But the arable land was owned and used by transnational corporations that grew bananas and beef for North American tables. An attempt to organize for land reform could mean death by paramilitary forces, who were in league with wealthy landowners.

While leading groups of United States citizens to Central America during years of civil war and conflict, I came to know a spectrum of people in Central American societies: military generals and revolutionaries, wealthy landowners and landless peasants, country presidents and opposition leaders, street vendors and business leaders, pastors, mothers of the disappeared, day laborers, attorneys, lay church workers.[1] From these encounters, a stark reality emerged: global economic arrangements threaten the survival and dignity of many impoverished Central American people. Their request was always the same: "Go home and tell your people what you have seen here, so that they might change the economic and political ways of your country that threaten our very lives." In subsequent work with homeless women in Washington, D.C.; theologians from Africa, India, and Korea; women's network leaders from the Caribbean and Africa; and others, I learned that the ravaging effects of economic globalization are felt the world over.

Things once seen cannot be unseen. My faith journey has been altered irrevocably by living and working, laughing and crying with people on the underside of history. To be loved by these brothers and sisters and to love them is to become a divided person, tied inseparably to the world of privilege, yet grounded too in the world of the brutalized. Though I know this position as gift, it also is torment. To these people, I am accountable. Their stories of oppression, resistance, and faith compel this inquiry. They shape my conviction that the call to "love thy neighbor as thyself" includes a call to subvert structures of exploitation and to forge faithful alternatives.

A paradoxical union of two stories shapes this book theologically. One, rooted in my Lutheran heritage, claims that salvation is by grace alone. God's magnificent and mysterious saving love is given unconditionally to each, and to all of creation. We are beloved, now and forever, a truth that I have experienced at the deepest level of being, a truth upon which my life depends. The other is a feminist liberationist story, which fully affirms the first story, and claims that human beings who know the God whom Jesus loved are called to participate in creation's salvation.[2] We are called and empowered to be the body of Christ on Earth—to be beloved and lovers, recipients and agents of God's creating, healing, liberating love for the world.

That call, life-giving and frightening, is heard in Jesus' invitation, "follow me" (Mark 8:34). He, as we, lived in a time and place in which structures of domination excluded women, the poor, slaves, and many others from fullness of life. Jesus' faithfulness to God led him on a path of profound love that challenged those systems and inaugurated new ways of living. It was and is a dangerous path to "follow." Our overwhelming urge is to ignore it, bypass it, or distort it, and to assume we are powerless to heed the call to subversive love.

My insistent hunger to see North American Christians heed that call stirred me to this journey between worlds. I refuse to believe that we are called by God to paths of subversive faithful love without also being empowered by God for that walk. Seeking guidance toward that moral-spiritual power, I turned to faith forebears whose relationship with Christ and Spirit living in them empowered such love. They are many. This book unfolds my encounter with one, Martin Luther. God's power and presence, Luther insisted, "fills all things," and may be written as "a fiery flame on the heart, mak[ing] it . . . burn with love and delight in whatever pleases God . . . creat[ing] new courage so that [one] . . . serves the people" and this good Earth.[3]

Luther's words are stunning. For Luther, "serving the people" included exposing and theologically denouncing economic structures that oppressed the poor and forging creative neighbor-loving alternatives. The "new courage" to do so, born of Christ and Spirit living in us, is the mystery I pursue here.

Introduction

❧

Just as a continuously growing cancer eventually destroys its life-support systems by destroying its host, a continuously expanding global economy is slowly destroying its host—the Earth's ecosystem. . . . Reversing this trend calls for a restructuring of the global economy.
　　　　　　　　　　　　　　　　—State of the World, 1998

I have set before you life and death, blessings and curses. Choose life so that you and your descendants may live.
　　　　　　　　　　　　　　　　—Deuteronomy 30:19

THIS QUEST IS BORN of a contemporary moral crisis of profound and unprecedented dimensions. That crisis, elaborated in the first three chapters, is twofold. First, the reigning model of economic globalization threatens Earth's life systems, cultural integrity and diversity, and the lives of many who are poor in order that some might consume exorbitantly and a few accumulate vast wealth.[1] This way of life is a threat to life itself.[2] Second, as a society, we acquiesce to the prevailing form of globalization. We comply with its demands and accede to its truths, as if indeed, "There Is No Alternative." We fail to consider seriously the long-term social and ecological implications of economic globalization, resist it, and forge alternatives. This dearth of moral agency—and its reawakening—is the concern of this undertaking. It explores, first, the disabling of moral agency by the prevailing paradigm of economic globalization, and then, the enabling of moral agency by relationship with God indwelling creation.

Insistent hunches and a distrust of modern dualism moved me to consider the indwelling God as a source of moral-spiritual power. The intuitions that became integral to my theses and method were:

- The moral crises of global economic injustice today are integrally spiritual; they signal something terribly amiss in the relationship between human beings and God.

- Christian ethical reflection on "what we are to do" (normative and constructive reflection) is inadequate if it does not also address the question of moral agency, the power to "do what we ought."

- Where moral life and the mystery of God's presence are held in one breath—moral life understood as mystical life—moral agency may be found for forging paths toward more just, compassionate, and sustainable ways of living.

In contrast to these sensibilities, which wed spirituality with morality, stands modernity's persistent tendency to divorce the two, particularly to disassociate intimate "personal" relationship with an immanent God from public moral power. Traditions of moral agency grounded in relationship with God have been obscured by social constructions that present this relationship as distinctly inner, privatized, and apolitical.[3] This inquiry, then, reclaims an organic link between moral agency and relationship with God and is informed by a growing body of theological inquiry into that connection. I assert this link by interchanging the terms *moral agency* and *moral-spiritual agency*.

My primary aims are to: (1) demystify key dynamics whereby corporate- and finance-driven globalization disables the moral capacity to see it for what it is, resist it, and move toward alternatives; (2) uncover and explore ways in which relationship with God may kindle and sustain the moral-spiritual power needed for resisting the dominant model of economic globalization and forging alternatives; and (3) lay groundwork for further inquiry into divine immanence as source of moral agency and into faith forebears as guides toward that agency. The intended end point is an evolving and contextual morality-spirituality of resistance, revisioning, and rebuilding rooted in relationship with God "present in all places, even in the tiniest leaf."[4]

The undertaking is part of my larger desire to contribute theologically, theoretically, and practically to the emergence of North American Christian praxis in which intimate communion with God and critical analysis of globalization engender moral agency—the agency required to resist a dangerous form of globalization and live toward economic ways that support planetary flourishing and human dignity.

Questions Addressed

Many North American Christians are people of deep compassion and enormous heart, longing to love God by loving Her children, especially the most vulnerable. Presumably, we do not wish to buy shirts made in sweatshops, snow peas grown on land that should feed hungry children, or metal products from mines that have displaced thousands of people. Surely, we are not pleased to be culprits in "ecocide," pumping toxins into the Earth and destroying the systems upon which life depends. Yet many people, insulated by privilege, remain blind to the suffering and ecological devastation created by current global trade and investment regimes.[5] Others, while aware, feel muted, dwarfed by the situation, and powerless to change destructive lifestyles and economic structures. Whether in "cruel innocence" or informed despair, we acquiesce.[6]

The pathos of the situation is enormous. Christians are called, before all else except love for God, to love neighbor as self. This is our gift and calling, our primary lifework here on Earth, and we long to fulfill it. Yet, in tragic contrast, we find ourselves in an ungodly situation, locked into a global political economy that structures exploitation into the very fabric of our lives. In the dialectic of powerlessness and hope, it seems the former often prevails.

For followers of Jesus Christ, who is a source and model of life-transforming and life-giving love, two vexing theo-ethical questions emerge: (1) How is our moral agency so disabled that we acquiesce to global economic arrangements requiring us to exploit rather than to love both Earth and neighbor? and (2) How might faith in (and of) Jesus Christ enable moral agency to resist those arrangements and to forge alternatives? These questions are the motivating backdrop of this undertaking. My two theses respond to them.

Theses

Part 1 argues a thesis from which emerges a question. Part 2 responds with a related thesis. In part 1, I argue that the prevailing model of economic globalization normalizes and dictates political-economic relationships that cripple human capacity to make decisions and take actions other than those that serve the utility of the market. Globalization corrodes moral agency. This raises a question: in the face of a seemingly impenetrable model of globalization, what resources in Christian traditions might enable "subversive" moral agency—that is, agency for resistance, revisioning, and rebuilding alternatives to the dominant paradigm of globalization? In part 2, I examine how subversive moral agency may be enabled through relationship with the indwelling God, and I show that critical encounter with faith forbearers can provide examples of that agency and guidance toward it.

Note two important distinctions between what is argued and what is presupposed. I do not argue *that* Christian traditions include a historical trajectory in which divine immanence has underwritten moral agency.

I presuppose that trajectory and explore it in a historical instance. I use that inquiry to consider the interplay between moral agency and the indwelling God in a contemporary North American context.

Secondly, I do not argue *that* the reigning paradigm of economic globalization poses substantive threats. Others have done so, providing overwhelming evidence.[7] Nor do I address substantively the crucial question of alternatives to that paradigm. Alternatives are being developed, and brilliantly so, by people the world over, from Indian physicists and fisherfolk, to Caribbean women's collectives, to African economists and theologians, to North American ecologists and workers, to Mexican *campesinos* (rural farmers). They may be explored, assessed, and refined by any who would seek them.

This project presupposes both the threats posed by globalization and the availability of alternatives. I address instead the attendant questions of moral agency for resisting globalization and for moving toward alternatives, issues relatively ignored to date in theo-ethical discourse. To these questions of agency I speak, for the moral crisis in this culture of complicity is not lack of knowledge. It is the failure to get up and walk.

Mapping the Journey

Chapters 1 through 3 introduce the prevailing paradigm of economic globalization, begin to demystify it, and analyze two major dynamics whereby it undermines moral agency. "Economic globalization" has become so broadly and variously used in public discourse as to be meaningless unless clarified. Chapter 1 provides that clarification for the purpose of this inquiry. I summarize the specific trends to which the term refers in this project, the political-economic argument justifying globalization, the historical trajectories in which it stands, and the principal dangers it poses.

In chapter 2, I argue that the globalizing economy, in its current form, disables moral agency by disabling democracy.[8] Globalization subordinates democratic political power to unaccountable economic power. This subordination undermines citizens' political capacity to shape alternative economic policies, structures, and lifestyles that contribute to social justice and sustainability. The moral significance of this claim is great: globalization removes, from more or less democratically constituted and accountable political bodies, significant power to influence decisions that impact human and other well-being for generations to come and places that power into the hands of relatively few unaccountable economic players.

The second dynamic through which globalization cripples moral agency, the subject of chapter 3, is ideological. The ideology underlying the prevail-

Healing a Broken World

ing model of globalization undermines the capacity to imagine and perceive more socially just and ecologically sustainable alternatives to that model. Presuppositions of this ideology erase certain social sectors, historical struggles, possibilities, and consequences either by ignoring them or by treating them as insignificant. The resulting social amnesia reduces the capacity to critique globalization on moral grounds from historical perspectives.

These three chapters provide an illustrative, rather than exhaustive, treatment of globalization. I view globalization through a specific window that both provides manageable limits and illumines the whole. That window is the liberalization of transnational investment, the most recent and arguably most far-reaching development generated by the reigning paradigm of globalization. This development reveals key moral implications of economic decisions and illustrates the power dynamics by which a democratically unaccountable global power structure is emerging. To examine this movement's impact, I present a case study of the Multilateral Agreement on Investment (MAI). The MAI, initially a specific global investment agreement of unprecedented breadth through which investment liberalization became internationally well-known and contested, subsequently became a movement to incorporate the treaty's provisions in other multilateral institutions and instruments.

Chapters 4 through 6 respond to the preceding chapters with a highly focused and illustrative inquiry into the interplay between moral agency and relationality with the immanent God. Chapter 4 explores one instance of a historical trajectory in Christian traditions in which that relationality has generated "subversive" moral power in contexts of domination: the life of the sixteenth-century Protestant reformer Martin Luther. In what ways, I ask, did relationship with the indwelling God issue in ways of being and doing for Luther that unmasked and undermined structures and ideologies of domination? In the case of Luther, what theological and ideological factors disabled the faithful and subversive moral agency engendered by that relationality?

Chapter 5 brings Luther into dialogue with selected contemporary feminist theo-ethical voices to craft a constructive proposal. It considers theoretical, theological, and practical moves whereby relationship with God "present in all creatures . . . and in stone, in fire, in water . . ." may counter the morally disabling dynamics of globalization.

My overarching hope is that, empowered by God's indwelling presence, we might live differently. The vision of ordinary people resisting systemic economic brutality and crafting economic ways that enable the web of life on Earth to flourish guides my work. Thus, the closing, chapter 6, invites the reader to imagine what it might mean practically, in the everyday lives of materially privileged North Americans, to be habitation of God, who "fills all things."

An appendix elaborates the methodological framework informing the project and linking its two parts. I ask three sets of questions pertaining to the inter-discipline of Christian Ethics: What methodological fault lines in it truncate its capacity to respond adequately to the moral crises posed by the globalizing economy?[9] What criteria enable analyses of globalization to be accountable to the underside? How are we to draw upon distant faith forebearers to think critically about and recover subversive moral power? In response to the first question, I propose a substantive shift in Christian Ethics. The second question issues in principles of critical and feminist theory and theology shaping my method. In response to the final question, I present the conundrums inherent in an attempt to gain guidance from historical figures for faithful response to moral crises they did not face. Readers interested in negotiating the terms of engagement between two such unlikely conversation partners as Martin Luther and a contemporary feminist liberationist theological ethicist should consult this last portion of the appendix.

Faith Forebearers as Guides

The decision to journey into Christian ancestral terrain flows from my conviction that the moral capacity of Christian communities is grounded in the historical stories in which we locate ourselves. "We are heirs to revolutionary imaginations and songs," says biblical scholar Walter Brueggemann. Where we ignore, distort, or obscure stories of resistance in our heritage, moral formation toward faithful resistance is thwarted.

The move to hear faith forebearers reflects also my hunger for hope. Encountering women and men who went before, particularly voices domesticated or obscured, I found a contradiction that startles and whispers hope. While our tendency today may be toward acquiescence, we are descendants of a "cloud of witnesses," whose relationship with God disallowed acquiescence to powerful systems of domination, where those systems demanded betraying faith in Jesus Christ. We are well advised to seek the wisdom of these ancestors who drew no distinction between morality and spirituality. How did they come to embody the living Christ, and to drink the "dew of God's Spirit . . . diffused throughout all the earth," to such an extent that— despite many and sometimes terrible mistakes—they undermined systemic domination and lived toward more faithful alternatives?[10] On the other hand, what mistakes thwarted the subversive potential of relationship with the immanent God in their lives? We have before us in a constellation of faith stories—many silenced and yet waiting to be heard—guides who, although they did not face the crises with which we live, witness to the moral power offered by God's presence in every creature, "even in the tiniest leaf."[11] This project encounters one of those forebearers—Martin Luther, a leader of the Protestant Reformation.

Why Martin Luther? I sought a historical figure for whom a dominant political economy, its accompanying theology, and the practices it institutionalized shared the following characteristics of globalization today. It marginalized some to the extent that their lives were threatened; it was assumed, in the dominant public discourse, to be inevitable; it required practices seen by some as an affront to faith; and it undermined moral agency. I sought a figure for whom relationship with the indwelling God, wed to the experience of being loved by God, issued in "critical vision" and practices that undercut dominant belief systems, practices, and power alignments. Finally, I sought a figure who—grounded in her or his historical experience—posed a challenge not only to systems of domination but also to the social construction of Christianity in her or his time and place.

Situated in the Lutheran tradition, I feel obligated to challenge European and Euro-American Lutheranism's failure to take seriously the social justice effects and the moral agency effects of justification in Luther's thought. This pervasive misread of Luther bifurcates the person as justified individual from the person as historical social being and has tended to legitimate passivity in the face of social injustice. Lutheran tradition in the United States has leaned toward marginalizing the moral life as it pertains to bodies politic and the political body, where Luther held the moral life at the center of faith.

Challenging this misread entails recovering the significant role of the indwelling God in Luther's sense of moral agency. Luther's notions of the immanent God have gone underrecognized and undervalued. I find them particularly intriguing and fruitful for the task at hand. I reclaim this dimension of Luther, reading him in light of the globalizing economy and selected contemporary voices in theology and ethics.

Fascinating parallels exist between Luther's situation and ours. Luther's intense hermeneutic of suspicion was aimed at any authority or power that prevented Christians from living according to right relationships *coram Deo* and *coram mundo*.[12] He embodied a moral obligation to see, demystify, and subvert those powers.[13] In this sense, his task parallels ours in relationship to globalization where it prevents us from living according to "right relationships." Further, what was held to be natural, essential, and divinely ordained, Luther disclosed as human construct.[14] Today, globalization in its prevailing form is assumed to be natural, essential, and—by some—divinely ordained. Finally, Luther confronted the sins of dominant institutions; his "public theology" entailed seeking directly to influence the political-economic world—including its rulers—theologically and politically.

The liberative potential in Luther's sense of moral agency, however, was limited by his patriarchal, Constantinian, and anti-Semitic social theory. My constructive proposal also draws upon Luther to illustrate the limitations to moral agency imposed by positivist social theory, which reinscribes the power alignments it rationalizes.

A Broader Theo-Ethical Project

My focus on specific dynamics that disable and regenerate moral agency vis-à-vis economic globalization contributes to a broader project in Christian ethics. That project seeks to (1) help people of the "Global North" grasp the dynamics of globalization; (2) assist those who are Christians to drink deeply from the wellsprings of faith, there to find manifold resources for resistance and for rebuilding more just and sustainable economic ways; and (3) bring those resources to bear in broader publics.

Clearly, this broader project entails a more comprehensive Christian ethical engagement with economic globalization than is possible in a single book. The questions probed herein are one dimension of that more extensive treatment. It will include the spectrum of tasks noted below with the corresponding questions constitutive of Christian ethical inquiry. Taken as a whole, these tasks express the descriptive, critical, normative, constructive, and transformative dimensions of Christian Ethics.[15] They do not occur in a linear fashion but spiral around one another, deepening and changing in their interaction.

A first task of Christian Ethics vis-à-vis globalization is to describe, interpret, and analyze the globalizing political economy. *The overall question: What is going on and why?* What, for instance, are the power dynamics; theological, ideological, and social theoretical underpinnings; multiple long-term implications for human and other life; and historical precursors of corporate- and finance-driven globalization? A second task is to develop alternatives to the dominant paradigm and—yet more crucial—to bring into public discourse alternatives that already are being crafted but remain largely ignored by powerful leaders. *The question: What could be?* A third role of Christian Ethics is to assist in discerning which modes of global economic interaction (the current paradigm or diverse alternatives to it) are more consistent with the ways of God revealed in Jesus Christ and the Spirit. *The question: What ought be, and what norms guide discernment?* What, for example, ought be the purpose of economic life, and what paradigms best serve that purpose? A fourth and often overlooked role of ethical inquiry is to identify obstacles curtailing the power to live toward more faithful alternatives. *The question: What disables moral agency?* Included here would be identifying ways that Christian theologies have contributed to complicity with neo-liberal globalization. A fifth and equally ignored task is to recall and rekindle agency for overcoming those obstacles. *The question: What enables moral agency?* Finally, ethics will propose and define practical steps toward what ought and could be. *The question: What does this mean for everyday lives in terms of lifestyle, public policy, institutions, social systems, belief systems?* This book addresses the first, fourth, and fifth tasks and questions.

Situating the current undertaking in my broader theo-ethical agenda raises a number of important methodological issues. First, that I begin with the descriptive-interpretive task reflects my sense that crucial moral weight lies in perceptions of what *is*. What we see and refuse to see and *how* we see are morally loaded, bearing upon whether we foster or thwart liberative change. False sight cripples moral agency. That is, when good and compassionate people do not *see* and do not understand the consequences of our economic ways, we simply carry on with them. We need critical and morally responsible sight, and we need tools to cultivate political-economic literacy—a literacy that acknowledges the power of large corporations today in determining who has food and water and who does not, the terms of the human species' relationship to the planet, and the survival chances of endangered cultures. Furthering that "morally responsible sight" and literacy is part of my purpose in this project.

Second, the decision to probe issues of moral agency is unorthodox in an inter-discipline commonly held to be concerned primarily with normative and deliberative questions. That decision is integral to my critique of Christian Ethics developed in the appendix. I argue that sidelining questions of agency is a disciplinary fault line that thwarts Christian Ethics' capacity to address globalization adequately. Christian Ethics is more than a descriptive-interpretive, critical, normative, and constructive discipline. It is also transformative. Ethics must go beyond asking what is, why, what ought be, and what could be. For even when we see the destructiveness of globalization and know alternatives to it, the trajectory of our body politic is to continue according to that agenda. As a society, we are so morally *mal*-formed by and into ways of economic injustice that seeing critically, knowing alternatives, and discerning what is morally preferable are insufficient to *re*-form us. Christian ethics must consider also moral agency; that is, concerning economic life, we must ask not only "What is the case?" "What are economic alternatives?" and "How ought people of faith live in accord with faith?" but also "Wherein lies the power to so live?" and "What deadens and enlivens that moral power?"

Third, my responses to the questions of moral agency, while crucial, are of course partial. I consider only a few of the multiple psychological, sociological, theological, and structural dynamics undermining and generating the moral power to seek social justice and regenerative Earth-human relations in today's global economy. Clearly, my questions and responses alone will not enable North American Christians to overcome moral inertia and become builders of more just and sustainable economic ways. These contributions must work in concert with those of diverse people the globe over.

Finally, I note a few intended lines of inquiry for further work related to my broader theo-ethical agenda. One line would investigate the potential in other manifestations of Christian mysticism for moving people of faith toward ways of life that embody subversive love for self, neighbor, and the rest of creation.[16] Another would grapple with what I identify in the initial chapter as a defining trend of economic globalization: the commodification of life forms, of the elements that support life, and of experiences. I hope to use the commodification of water and of seeds as concrete and symbolic windows into the issue. Concretely, the marketing of both on a global level has life and death implications. Symbolically they are signs of God's presence on Earth, not least in the sacraments of Baptism and Eucharist. A third intention is to work constructively with understandings of salvation, creation, and spirit that might enliven moral power in the context of advanced global capitalism. I would again pursue my conviction that living roots of morally enabling theologies and practices are in faith forebearers and traditions long ignored or distorted.

Theological Starting Points

This work grows in theological soil. That ground is a constellation of christological, soteriological, and ecclesiological convictions. Suggested in the preface, they are noted more fully here. God embraces each of us and all of creation with unquenchable, intimate, and inconceivably splendid love. Human beings are invited into "lovership" with this God who seeks creation's liberation from all forms of oppression, exploitation, and exclusion; redeems humans from undermining the community of life; and breathes into us liberative, life-transforming love. We are personally, communally, and limitlessly loved by God, who has a special kind of caring for and presence with the most vulnerable.

Jesus of Nazareth embodied and made visible this God whose love is known in Her activity—in history and beyond—to restore the great community of life from all that thwarts its ongoing flourishing. By God's grace, we are to live in community, to be nurtured by and to nurture community. As beings-in-community, we are called to be bearers of God's love, to be bearers of the boundless and radiant love and life-power that is God. As such, we are called to liberative work guided by a theological vision of a world in which no one is oppressed, excluded, or exploited, and the sustainability of Earth's life systems is nourished. That vision entails a radical challenge to current global economic arrangements. We are called to a radically different way of living everyday life. Given that communities of faith are called to the seemingly impossible—called to justice-seeking love in a world of structured injustice—then life with God must offer the moral-spiritual power to heed the call. Many communities and figures throughout history have born witness to that moral-spiritual power. Their wisdom and witness is to be drawn upon by people of faith today.

These claims pertaining to Christian faith assume that other faith traditions also hold valid claims to relationship with God and to moral-spiritual wisdom and power. The moral crises of our day call people of varied faith traditions to plumb the depths of their traditions and to bring them into fruitful, mutually respectful dialogue with one another for the sake of abundant life for all today and for generations to come.

Presupposed Moral Norms

While no book may argue all of its presuppositions, key presuppositions must be stated explicitly and be defensible.[17] This project presupposes the aforementioned theological starting points, as well as two Christian moral norms stemming from them. One is love for neighbor. The other is sustainable and regenerative Earth-human relations. The moral weight of *neighbor-love* depends upon what is meant by the term.[18] In my use, *neighbor-love necessarily* bears the following qualifiers, which are grounded in my feminist-liberationist reading of the commandment to love neighbor as self.

First, love implies active commitment to the well-being of who or what is loved. While love at its best includes delight, tenderness, life-giving passions, compassion, and deep pleasure, the fundamental ingredient of love is steadfast enduring commitment to seek the good of who or what is loved. In biblically informed faith, "love is an energy that must be incarnated in action."[19]

Next, where systemic injustice exists, and it does in nearly every dimension of life, seeking the well-being or good of who or what is loved inherently entails seeking to undo injustice. That is, the norm of neighbor-love *includes* the norm of justice.[20] Because doing justice necessarily means active political engagement in challenging unjust social structures, neighbor-love implies that political engagement. Where injustice exists, then, neighbor-love entails seeing systemic injustice for what it is and naming it thus;

resisting it; envisioning alternatives more resonant with faith; and living toward them.[21]

Third, *neighbor-love* presupposes a valuation and norm of self-love. The biblical commandment to love neighbor is constructed brilliantly to assume the normativity of self-love: "You shall love your neighbor as yourself" (Lev. 19:18). Commonly held child development theory confirms that humans become able to love by being loved, and that healthy self-love is a requisite of mature capacity to love others. Feminist theory has exposed the damage done to women by the notion that "other-love" negates self-love, or at least supersedes it morally.

Finally, where faithful living requires knowledge and courage to forge unknown paths that transgress dominant cultural norms and disrupt dominant power structures, love is the epistemological partner of reason but has priority over it. Subversive knowledge and the courage to embody it are born of love. Regarding pioneers of justice from Isaiah through Martin Luther King Jr., Daniel Maguire notes that "their love capacities gave them powers of discernment, and so opened doors that merely brilliant minds never knew existed."[22]

Where I use the terms *love* or *neighbor-love* throughout this project, they always bear these four implications. To read these terms, herein, without holding these implications in mind is to misread what I have written and to miss its central implications for the lives of North Americans in the globalizing economy.

The norm of regenerative *Earth-human relations* extends the norm of neighbor-love to future human generations and to the other-than-human world. I understand these two norms to be at the heart of Christian moral life. According to Paul, "The whole law is summed up in love" (Rom. 13:10). Daniel Maguire says it well: "It is the biblical view that *being moral is loving well.*" "In fact, the whole thrust of biblical religion is toward the recovery of the broken human capacity to love. Its treatment of justice, of the reign of God, of prophecy, and of hope can be understood only within the felt need of this movement to 'revive the heart' (Isa. 57:15)."[23] All this said, love is a mysterious matter of the heart, body, and soul, and of the presence of God in them. It is magnificently beyond the capacities of reason to fathom. My reasoned use of *neighbor-love* as a moral norm is held in this light.

Key Concepts

Four concepts running through the inquiry require initial clarification and nuance here: *we-us, subversion* or *subversive, community,* and *immanence.*

We and Us

We and *us* are fraught with problems when the author is not "we" or "us," but "I" and "me." Potential problems include: (1) false universalization: speaking for others and assuming a commonality in perspective that may not exist; (2) false inclusion: assuming as "already existent the very relationship [we or us] constitutes"[24] and obscuring power differentials and other axes of difference within that relationship; (3) exclusion: implicitly excluding those on the outside of we and us and naturalizing that exclusion; and (4) confusion: failing to clarify a pronoun's referent.

Nevertheless, frequently I speak in the first person plural, and with good reasons. First, my constructive proposal for the quickening of moral agency calls for a reconstitution of moral identity; it calls for a movement from "self as autonomous individual agent" (self fundamentally as "I") to "self as woven into a 'cosmic communion'" (self as "we"). Second, I speak out of my experience, which is a collective experience of powerlessness and agency in a culture of powerlessness. I speak as a part of the people I address. My position within a culture of powerlessness and also within resistance movements exemplifies this work's overarching theme—moral agency's deadening and enlivening. I seek to practice the art of disciplined intellectual engagement not only as an observer, but as an integral thread in the fabrics of both social atrocity and transformation. Therefore, I retain we/us and attempt to mitigate against the problems by alerting the reader to them here, and by identifying the range of referents. We/us, herein, refers variously to the human species, North American people of consumer privilege, Christians among them, or the author and her readers. While the context clarifies the referent, I cannot as a rule address the infinite and potent differentiation within these categories.

Subversion or Subversive

Subversive is a loaded word, inviting varied and misleading interpretations. I refer not to *subversion* as an end in itself. I refer to subversion as a faithful dimension of neighbor-love and regenerative Earth-human relations in response to structures of domination that destroy or maim life, obscure the Word, or otherwise thwart God's gift of abundant life for all.[25] Those structures may be interpersonal or international. They may be political, economic, ecclesiastical, or other. Subversion, as used here, includes resistance but goes beyond it to signify also revisioning and the development of alternatives to what is resisted. Thus, I use "subversion" interchangeably with "resistance, revisioning, and rebuilding." Subversive moral agency undermines domination and injustice, forging more faithful ways of life.

Relationality with the indwelling God, as seen in Luther, had (and has) subversive social structural implications. Without the nuance I provide later, that claim would be suspect in two senses. First, it is anachronistic. Organized effort toward structural social change was not constitutive of reality in Luther's premodern world view. Luther sought to be faithful to God; he neither intended nor claimed to be subversive. Yet his faith and ways of embodying it became "subversive" to an established structure of domination, the reigning ecclesiastical power structure.[26] Second, Luther, as many figures and movements noted for undermining systems of domination, is riddled with paradox in relationship to systemic domination, in some senses undermining but in others underwriting it. My focus on his faith as subversive represents only one pole of that dialectic.[27] My intent is not to erase the opposite pole. Yet the confines of the project leave room to address it only briefly.

Community

Community currently is a popular and potent word both connoting and denoting varied phenomena, and it is invoked for contrasting purposes. Meaning almost anything, *community* means nothing unless nuanced and clarified.[28] Furthermore, the term is suspect for many feminists.[29] In this project, I presuppose the normativity of community. So doing requires both clarifying my use of the term and acknowledging the dangers it presents. My purposes, at this point, are to activate sensors mitigating the dangers inherent in appeals to community, and to prevent the reader from assuming meanings of community other than those intended in this study.

Community presents the dangers posed by *we*. That is, appeals to community tend implicitly to valorize unified, unchanging, heterogeneous social groups and exclusive identity. These appeals may legitimate dominant perspectives within the community without heeding the viewpoints of others (either within or outside) who may be marginalized by those perspectives.[30] Furthermore, community suggests intrinsically equitable or just internal relationships of power. The term, in this project, does not valorize, legitimate, or suggest the above.

Community herein has two referents, distinct but integrally related. *Earth community* connotes a biocentric and geocentric (rather than anthropocentric) web of life and life support systems comprised of the Earth, its elements and inhabitants (past, present, and future), and God.[31] *Earth community* assumes interdependence, astounding diversity, and regenerativity. The ethical import is the dislodging of anthropocentric boundaries around community, embedding human community in a broader community of life. The implications will play out both in terms of moral agency and in terms of relocating the global "economy" in the great "economy of life." *Community* also suggests human groups characterized by interdependence and action aimed at a "good in common" as well as at individual good. Both referents presuppose human life as ontologically communal, an assumption with theological foundations. They include the claim, first articulated in Christian theology by the Cappadocians, that the God in whose image human beings are created *is* a communion of beings.[32] Central also is the Hebrew Bible notion, expressed by Walter Brueggemann, that "life and death do not have to do simply with the state of the individual person, but with the relation between the person and the community which . . . gives the person personhood." Birth is the embrace of community, and death is "departure from that community either by force or by choice."[33]

Immanent God

Immanent comes from the Latin *immanere*—to remain within. I use the term as a rubric to signify a specific notion, the notion of God dwelling within creation. Historically, in Christian theology, God "within us" implies God "among us." I presuppose this two-dimensional sensibility and build on it.

God's immanence, as a concept and a faith claim, has a centuries-long and highly contested theological history. Sorting out the range of referents and contested issues in order to arrive at a normative theological meaning is not my purpose. I explore not the *concept* of "divine immanence," but rather its implications for moral agency. Thus, I do not engage centuries of theological and philosophical debate regarding the term and its referents. Below I briefly note its theological history—in terms first of contested areas and then of shifting position in modernity—only to situate the current project.

The "immanent divine" is a contested concept in at least four senses, expressed here as questions. First, what is the relationship of 'God immanent' to 'God transcendent'? Different schools of Christian theology have emphasized God's immanence or transcendence, or a balance between the two. That balance also has been understood in varied ways. Second, what is the relationship of God as immanent Jesus Christ on the one hand and God as immanent Spirit on the other?[34] Third, in what sense is God immanent? Is immanence a functional category, and if so, in what functions is God immanent (creator, redeemer, sustainer, transformer)? Or is immanence an ontological category? Does immanence begin with the incarnation or is it without beginning?[35] Finally, what are the implications of God's immanence for human relationship with God, one another, and the rest of creation?

This project concerns only the last of these questions. I do not grapple with the others but do assume a stance regarding the first and second. First, God immanent implies also God transcendent, and vice versa; I presuppose a dialectic. Second, I presuppose God immanent as both Jesus Christ and Spirit and do not address the relationship between the two.

A historical shift in modernity vis-à-vis the first of these contested areas lays groundwork for my thesis. Theological liberalism emphasized God's immanence. Neo-orthodoxy critiqued this emphasis and emphasized God's transcendence. More contemporary theologies, especially some feminist and eco-feminist theologies, have begun to reclaim an immanent God. They assert crucial moral import in the claim that God indwells bodies, relationships, and the Earth. This project explores that import.

In short, I do not start with the theological doctrine or concept of immanence and its conceptual genealogy and work deductively from them. Rather I start by probing the interplay between moral agency and the immanent God in Martin Luther, put my findings in dialogue with assumptions about moral agency emerging in some feminist theo-ethical thought, and then "mine" that interface for the purpose of my constructive project. This methodological move is considered further in the appendix.

In Sum

This constructive project in Christian socio-ecological ethics takes seriously the ancient theological claim that God indwells creation as unquenchable love and there works toward creation's flourishing. I explore that claim in one of many historical instances and use that exploration to think critically and constructively about how God's indwelling presence might issue in subversive moral agency in the context of economic globalization. So doing requires demystifying key dynamics whereby globalization undermines the moral agency to resist it and to move toward alternatives. This journey between worlds recovers a sense of sacred relatedness as a root assumption of the Christian moral life and reclaims the subversive moral power stemming from that root. That moral power works against complicity with global economic systems that thwart God's gift of abundant life for all and toward economic ways that sustain communities and the Earth community according to compassion and justice for generations to come.

Part One

Economic Globalization:
Disabling Moral Agency

1

Introduction to Globalization

❧

THE PREVAILING PARADIGM of economic globalization is "transforming the face of the earth" and impacting culture, consciousness, and material conditions of present and future life for all species.[1] Neither the structures of power emerging with globalization nor its ideological and theoretical underpinnings is addressed adequately from a critical perspective in the dominant public discourse. This and the following two chapters begin to demystify the reigning model of economic globalization.

Globalization involves a complex constellation of dynamics and players. To interpret and critique that complexity with integrity in just three chapters, I view globalization—following this chapter—through a specific window that provides manageable limits and illumines the whole. That window is the "liberalization of transnational investment," the most recent move in the "free trade and investment agenda."[2] To disclose the power dynamics at play in this move is to unravel the tangled web of globalization as a whole. Although trade and investment are inseparable, I focus on investment because the "freedom" of foreign investment from regulation arguably has more far-reaching, and less examined, implications than its precedents in "free" trade. Note that the adjectives *free, deregulated, open,* and *liberalized* with respect to trade and investment are used interchangeably.

In this chapter, I briefly sketch the main trends involved in globalization, the economic argument rationalizing it, the social-theoretical framework and ideological context of globalization, the historical trajectories in which the current wave of globalization stands, and threats it poses.

Seven Defining Trends

The term *globalization* has multiple referents. In this project it denotes only the dominant paradigm of economic globalization today. This model involves seven intimately related trends. One is a rapid increase in the movement of goods and services as well as capital—trade and investment, respectively—across international borders.[3] A second, the focus of chapter 2, is the subordination of democratic political power to unaccountable economic power in order to ease that movement. Third, a growing portion of the world's largest economies are planned and directed in ways unaccountable to the public as a whole. That is, comparing gross sales of a corporation to the Gross Domestic Product (GDP) of a nation, fifty-one of the world's one hundred largest economies are corporations.[4]

The privatization of public goods and services constitutes a fourth major trend in globalization. Privatization gives ownership of basic goods and services such as water, electricity, health care, and education to corporations or individuals usually not accountable to the communities impacted. To illustrate, the privatization of water allows a foreign corporation to purchase the water supply in an impoverished South American country and export it for sale at whatever price the market will bear in Seattle or San Francisco.[5] Original users of the water are left without. A fifth trend is an accelerating commodification of life forms and experiences. *Commodification of life* refers to placing a monetary value on life forms (for example, genetic material or seed strains developed over the centuries by indigenous people) and on life experiences (such as spiritual growth, happiness, cultural practices), and marketing them, often on a global level. A sixth and intimately related trend is the strategic marketing of western consumer-oriented ways of life around the world.

A final defining trend is the commodification of money. The *commodification of money* denotes the ascendence of "speculative" trade in money (for short-term gain) over trade in goods and services, and over investment in long-term production-oriented economic activity.[6] This development is documented by analysts from across the political spectrum.[7] The commodification of money, together with the revolution in communications and information technology, enables huge amounts of money to be bought and sold across national borders instantly by investors unaccountable for social and environmental impacts and unregulated by national or international entities. The impact, as seen in the Asian and Mexican financial crises of the 1990s, may be devastating; sudden shifts in capital may dramatically affect the well-being, even the survival, of millions. (If space allowed, we would note other dangers inherent in the commodification of money.)[8] This trend is central to the moral significance of globalization. Increasingly, trade in money for the purpose of maximum short-term profit dominates transnational economic activity. Thus, the finance and corporate sectors seek to "free" investment from regulations and other political constraints that might diminish profit.

Healing a Broken World

Transnational investment liberalization is at the intersection of these defining trends. Most simply stated, using the terms of its advocates, investment liberalization removes legal and regulatory barriers to the movement of capital and operations across borders by corporations and investment enterprises.[9] This latest dismantling of barriers is said to "crown" the dismantling of trade barriers achieved over the last fifty years under the GATT and, since 1995, by the World Trade Organization (WTO).

Investment deregulation is achieved through bilateral and multilateral investment agreements, which legally limit the right of governments to regulate cross-border corporate and other financial activity. Many opponents and advocates of these agreements consider the impact on human and other life to be more far-reaching than any other preceding steps in the globalization process. Some opponents argue that the impact on non-human life is catastrophic. Herein lies the "free" investment agenda and the enormity of its consequences for life on Earth. The "'free' market is given full rein to determine the course of human existence in most fields of endeavor—agriculture, industry, economics, science and technology, politics, culture"— and the impact of human life on the planet.[10]

These seven developments are historically situated. None is new. New is their global scale, the speed of financial and economic transactions enabled by high speed cyber-technology, the preponderance of multilateral agreements that free not only commerce but also currency from governmental regulations and political accountability, and the extent to which money is dissociated from the goods and services that once provided its value. For reasons that will become apparent, I use the terms *neo-liberal globalization* and *corporate- and finance-driven globalization*, as well as *globalization* and *economic globalization*, to indicate the economic model defined by these trends.

The Political-Economic Argument

The key economic argument underlying globalization and hence the "free" trade and investment agenda is this: deregulation of foreign trade and investment contributes to growth that "benefit[s] every citizen."[11] Regulations on trade and investment detract from growth, and thus from economic well-being. This theory is the bedrock of virtually all stances in favor of globalization—and particularly of investment liberalization.[12] The claim is grounded in neo-classical economic theory wed to laissez-faire political theory. The former entails the following key assumptions regarding moral anthropology and economic interactions. These assumptions are outlined below but are explored more fully in chapter 3.

The moral anthropological assumption holds that human beings are motivated primarily by individual self-interest. In economic life, the individual will seek what provides her/him the most good at the lowest cost. The intelligent pursuit of private economic gain is the most "rational" (and thus the most highly valued) behavior, implying that other modes of behavior (that is, behavior not resulting in private economic gain) are less rational (and thus less valued). This principle—rooted in utilitarian economic theory and philosophy—translates to a theory of consumption (satisfaction maximization), and of production (profit maximization). Consumption will be guided by the quest to "get the most for your money" and production by the quest to maximize profit. If each person takes care of her- or himself in this way, all will benefit.[13]

The assumptions regarding economic interactions are threefold. First, the market free from government regulation will result in optimal allocation of society's economic resources and in growth in wealth for individuals and nations. That is, choices freely made by individuals to buy and sell in the competitive and self-regulated market will result in the greatest good for the greatest number. Second, the theory of "specialization according to comparative advantage" will insure that countries specializing in and trading freely what they can produce at a lower cost than their trading partners will gain economically. Finally, economic units are equal in power, and competition among equals will maintain price and quality, and prevent exploitation.

These four assumptions are the "capitalist market rules of the game" according to neo-classical economic theory.[14] The benefits promised by the economy that plays by these rules include competitive prices, free choice, efficiency, economic growth, and maximum profit for producers. Theories regarding the extent to which failures in the market are considered aberrations (on the one hand) or inherent flaws (on the other), and regarding the degree and kind of government intervention that is beneficial, differentiate between two political ideological poles of the neo-classical economic paradigm. The "laissez-faire pole," in contrast to the "welfare liberalism pole," holds that most forms of government intervention will undermine the market's ability to serve the well-being of all, the "magic of the market."

Held together, these theories render the argument for "free" trade and investment: International trade and investment liberalization improves the well-being of all. Regulations on trade and investment detract from that well-being. More specifically, deregulation increases (and is necessary to increase) foreign trade and investment. Increased foreign trade and investment generates (and is necessary to generate) economic growth directly, and also indirectly by increasing competition, which increases efficiency. Increased efficiency lowers consumer prices and generates growth. Growth, as measured by GNP or GDP, increases (and is necessary to increase) prosperity, employment, and living standards for most people. The economic problems of "developing nations" are due to restrictions of market forces. Economic and other social problems are better solved by means of the market than by political processes. (The exception is problems arising from external shocks, such as natural disasters and war.) In sum, deregulation of foreign trade and investment contributes to growth that benefits all.

Some champions of globalization in its prevailing form appeal not only to neo-classical economic theory but also to the global corporation itself as a "social good that has served and will continue to serve social well-being."[15] Faced with evidence that corporate-driven economic activity has significantly damaged social and ecological health, this perspective tends to fault existing impediments to the free market, to call for business ethics, and to claim that the benefits of globalization will be evident for all in the long run.[16] Since the Asian financial crisis, some mainstream economists have begun to fault one dimension of globalization—unrestricted capital flows—and have called for capital controls. Regarding threats to environment and labor rights, advocates of corporate freedom suggest voluntary, but not obligatory, performance standards. I have found no adequate response to critiques that globalization endangers cultural diversity and democracy, and continues the legacy of colonialism, or that growth is limited by the constraints of the biosphere.

Social-Theoretical Framework and Ideological Context

Globalization—with free trade and investment at its center—is part of a larger ideological and social-theoretical framework known by many in Latin America, Africa, and elsewhere as neo-liberalism. Seen through the interpretive lens of "popular" movements in Central America and Mexico, neo-liberalism consists of a broad socio-political restructuring begun in the early 1980s and referred to interchangeably as the "neo-liberal agenda," the "free trade and investment agenda," the "corporate agenda," "the deregulation agenda," "neo-colonialism," and the "Washington consensus."[17]

Neo-liberalism has two basic premises. First, the freedom of markets from state intervention contributes to wealth-creation and social well-being. Second, the freedom of individuals to act in perceived self-interest in economic life is a moral right and contributes to wealth-creation and social well-being. In fact, self-interested economic activity is the highest form of rationality and is a moral obligation. The criteria for economic well-being, according to neo-liberal theory, are macroeconomic variables such as growth, investment rates, and inflation rates. Relatively ignored are power and wealth inequity, quality of life indicators, and environmental concerns. The neo-liberal paradigm presupposes that economic decisions are best made by economic and financial experts rather than by the people whose lives may be threatened by those decisions.

Two guiding policies for neo-liberalism are trade and investment deregulation, and Stabilization and Structural Adjustment Programs (SAPs). The latter are required by the International Monetary Fund (IMF) as prerequisites for World Bank, IMF, and other loans. Structural adjustment aims at restructuring economies to enable integration into the global free market economy and to create a trade surplus allowing payment on foreign debt.[18] Stabilization and Structural Adjustment Programs have helped to curb inflation and restart economic growth. Yet, in many countries they have proved devastating to the poor. UNICEF estimates 6 million children under age five have died each year since 1980 as a direct result of SAPs. Structural adjustment works hand in hand with trade and investment deregulation, which is one tool for "adjusting" nations toward export-oriented economies.

Historical Trajectories

The current wave of globalization is situated in at least three historical developments in which major U.S.-based corporations and finance institutions, especially since the Civil War, have gained power by (1) attaining the legal rights of citizens,[19] (2) uprooting themselves from accountability to communities and then to nations, and (3) progressively freeing themselves from both domestic and international regulation. Along with many Asian, African, Latin American, and indigenous American analysts, I locate the free trade and investment agenda also as a stage in the history of colonialism. Finally, the legacies of slavery and white supremacy, of the subordination of women, and of working-class exploitation are historical loci of globalization.

The first major development occurred in 1886 when the Supreme Court ruled that corporations are "natural person[s] under the constitution," and have all of the rights of persons.[20] The ensuing deregulation of corporate activity enabled corporate power to grow and consolidate. Oligopolies developed and wealth concentrated.[21]

Another historical development—the progressive uprooting of corporations and financial institutions in the United States in the twentieth century—entailed a shift from local operations to regional, then national, then international, and finally transnational operations. Links of accountability to local communities, bioregions, and workers were severed. New Deal legislation, intended to keep banks servicing and accountable to their own communities, was undone in this shift.

The third development, the progressive deregulation of United States banking and other financial services, largely was achieved by the 1980s, either by law or by creative corporate arrangements such as holding companies and mergers.[22] The result was financial services institutions operating not only across geographic boundaries, but also across service and institutional boundaries; one company, operating around the globe, could provide multiple financial services.[23] Undone here was New Deal legislation intended to prevent the domination of financial markets by single institutions and to prevent commercial banks from playing in the stock market rather than using depositors' money for loans toward productive activity.[24] Deregulation of banking in the United States was accompanied by deregulation of international monetary transactions, led by the United States.[25]

The legacy of colonialism is a longer-term historical trajectory in which many Two-Thirds World and indigenous analysts locate the free trade and investment agenda.[26] Some Latin American analysts identify the people suffering as a result of that agenda—or in resistance to it—with those who suffered at the hands of dictatorships supported by United States military and monetary support.[27] Different analysts characterize and periodize the phases of colonial history and their relationship to globalization differently. Vandana Shiva, one of India's leading physicists, identifies globalization as "the imposition of one culture on all others . . . the predation of one class, one race, and often one gender of a single species on all others . . . seeking control, freeing itself of responsibility for the limits arising from the imperatives of ecological sustainability and social justice."[28] The result is the destruction of cultural and biological diversity. She identifies three waves of globalization: the colonization of America, Asia, Africa, and Australia by European Powers; the imposition of a Western idea of "development" during the post–World War Two era; and recolonization by the unleashing of "free trade."[29] Chief Saul Terry of the British Columbia Council of Chiefs of Tribes testifies that the "colonial experience of indigenous peoples could be a 'template' for seeing and understanding what will happen to all peoples under corporate-driven globalization. There is a neo-colonial steamroller coming at us again."[30]

Martin Khor, political economist and president of the Third World Network, defines colonialism as the process by which Two-Thirds World economies "have fallen under the control of foreign corporations which have raided their resources and shipped them out to the point where they have little ability to resist further control and raiding, or to seek alternative economic strategies."[31] He describes a continuous process of colonialization from the era of colonial rule, which "changed the economic and social structures of

Third World societies" through the economic and financial arrangements whereby transnational corporations and banks aided by multilateral institutions such as the World Bank and IMF drew these countries into dependence and depleted and degraded their resources.[32] Many Central Americans identify two phases of colonialism: the era in which United States hegemony was maintained through support for military-oligarchy regimes; and the era, beginning in the early 1980s, of control through neo-liberal economic policy.

An era of "corporate colonialism" extended from decisions by the United States to gain control over foreign markets, resources, and economies following the Great Depression. In this era, former colonies of the United States and European nations gained formal political independence, but "in reality [their] economic system and thus political policy [was] directed from outside."[33] Debt dependency, structural adjustment, and free trade became means of control. This era moved toward a global economic order in which large "stateless cosmocorps"[34] are "free" to control raw materials and human resources and to develop markets in Two-Thirds World countries for profit. Until the recent international furor over the Multilateral Agreement on Investment (MAI) and the WTO ministerial meeting in Seattle, this corporate colonialism was carried forward largely outside of dominant public discourse.

The beginning of this phase is commonly identified with the financial arrangements institutionalized in the Bretton Woods decisions of 1944, which established the World Bank and the International Monetary Fund. However, I locate its inception over a decade earlier with a long-range planning process established by the U.S. Council on Foreign Relations in close collaboration with the State Department. The Council determined that to maintain prosperity and full employment at home—that is, to avoid another devastating depression—without major economic reforms such as increased government intervention in the market, the United States must have access to the raw materials and markets of a "grand area" including the Western Hemisphere, the former British Empire, and Asia.[35] The Council was an "incubator of leaders and ideas unified in their vision of a global economy dominated by United States corporate interests" aimed at shaping United States foreign policy toward those ends.[36]

These historical moves have in common one enormous and lethal blind spot: none locate human life and well-being within Earth's ecosystem and as dependent upon it. Maximized growth in production, consumption, and profit has been valued as a "good" without factoring in the long-term impact on Earth's capacity to sustain life as we know it. Human economies and the emerging global human economy have been dissociated from the biospheric economy of life. In economic and financial decision-making processes that determine the fate of many elemental resources necessary for life (decisions regarding production, consumption, trade, and investment patterns), the cost of destroying or degrading those resources does not count.[37] This fault line—the extractive human economy conceptually *extracted from* the greater planetary economy—is the deadly fault line, unacknowledged until recent years, of globalization throughout five centuries.

It is impossible here to adequately situate globalization in these and other historical loci. Yet the very act of historicizing globalization issues three challenges relevant to my thesis. First is the reigning assumption that globalization is inevitable and natural and hence above human agency. History reveals, to the contrary, that the deregulated global market is not "found in nature"; rather, it is the result of accumulated human decisions and actions. Hence, at least in principle, this form of globalization is responsive to human moral agency. As a historical phenomenon, globalization can be—and is—resisted, subverted, or changed.[38] Challenged also is the assumption that global capitalism is consistent with democracy. The progressive subordination of political power to unaccountable economic power suggests the undermining of "people's power." And finally, questions are raised regarding the concept of "freedom" when it is used to reinscribe the unregulated operation of economic powers.

Threats Posed by Globalization

Economic globalization brings economic growth and, with it, enormous economic benefits for many. Economic growth has lifted many out of poverty and has created an abundance of goods and services and soaring standards of living for many others. These are tremendous accomplishments. They are overshadowed by an almost limitless chorus of diverse voices documenting the threats that globalization poses to the web of life on Earth. That chorus includes prominent scientists; economists; Christian ethicists; the World Council of Churches; and hundreds of other NGOs or citizen's organizations throughout the globe including labor, environmental, anti-poverty, women's rights, and human rights organizations.[39] These voices represent multiple perspectives and address diverse threats. Taken as a whole, their message is that the prevailing model of globalization widens the gap between the wealthy and the rest of humanity and assaults Earth's life-support systems, democracy, human rights, cultural integrity and diversity, and the very lives of many who are poor. Human labor, creativity, and intelligence; land; and other natural resources are used for the profit of a few. Globalization, shaped by transnational corporations and finance enterprises to maximize profit, cannot serve the interests of the Earth and the majority of its inhabitants. These claims render globalization—and "free" trade and investment in particular—a burning moral issue.

Liberalized trade and investment, while generating economic growth, exacerbates poverty through a complex web of factors.[40] These include extraction of natural resources and destruction of ecosystems; profit repatriation by transnational corporations; terms of trade dominated by the richer nations; the reduction of jobs, wages, and labor protection standards; elimination of benefits; crippling of local and regional systems of agricultural and other production; external debt repayment; and Structural Adjustment Programs.[41] The combined impact is catastrophic. The "developing nations" transfer to the industrialized nations billions of dollars annually.[42]

For the very poor, globalization may be life-threatening.[43] The United Nations Development Programme reports that globalization "is concentrating power and marginalizing the poor, both countries and people. . . . During the last 10 years per capita income has decreased in 80 countries. . . . Ironically, those left behind are deeply integrated in world trade."[44] The reality, according to that Programme, is staggering: "In 1960 the 20 percent of the world's people who live in the richest countries had 30 times the income of the poorest 20 percent—by 1995, 82 times as much income. Consider the extraordinary concentration of wealth among a small group of the ultra-rich. . . . New estimates show that the world's 225 richest people have a combined wealth of over $1 trillion, equal to the annual income of the poorest 47 percent of the world's people (2.5 billion people). . . . The richest three people have assets that exceed the combined GDP of the 48 least developed countries. . . . It is estimated that the additional cost of achieving and maintaining universal access to basic education, health care, reproductive health care, adequate food, safe water and sanitation for all is roughly $40 billion a year. This is less than 4 percent of the combined wealth of the richest 225 people in world."[45]

Women in poverty pay a particularly high price.[46] They are central in the quest for cheap labor as seen in the *maquiladoras* (assembly plants owned by corporations based outside of the country) of Mexico and Central America, and the sweatshops of Asia and elsewhere. When SAPs reduce health care, education, food supplies, fuel, and other resources, women bear much of the burden for providing them and caring for people who are left without.

Economic growth, the aim and primary promise of globalization, has collided with the Earth's natural limits.[47] Global economic growth, together with population growth, threatens Earth's capacity to regenerate.[48] While human life depends upon the health of Earth's life-systems, "every natural system on the planet is disintegrating," and the human species is the cause of it.[49] Life according to the triune god of growth, profit, and consumption—

the gospel proclaimed by the prevailing model of globalization—is endangering life itself. [50] According to the *State of the World 1998*, reversal of this collision course requires restructuring of the global economy.[51]

While advocates of globalization portray it as facilitating cross-cultural interaction of diverse societies, critics see quite the opposite impact on cultural diversity. "Globalization is the imposition of a particular culture on all the others."[52] This perspective is born out in the words of Lee Bickmore, then-president of Nabisco in a 1968 *Forbes* magazine article in which he looks forward to "the day when Arabs and Americans, Latins and Scandinavians will be munching Ritz crackers as enthusiastically as they already drink Coke or brush their teeth with Colgate."[53] A recent Pepsi advertisement committed the company to making Pepsi more available than water the world over, and the ad depicts a smiling Japanese woman in traditional dress, pouring Pepsi at a tea ceremony. The threat to cultural diversity and integrity takes varied forms including the homogenization of human culture, the commodification of cultural wealth for the profit of people external to that culture, and the destruction of cultural practices integral to the survival of peoples. In the words of Esther Carmac Ramirez, an indigenous leader in Costa Rica: "To exploit our traditional knowledge is to cut the umbilical cord between our mother (Earth) and our peoples. To cut this cord is to threaten the survival and well-being of future generations and put an end to life."[54]

Leaders like Ramirez remind us of an important point: we must not face the power and dangers inherent in globalization without acknowledging that alternatives are unfolding, at both conceptual and practical levels. A most untold story of the last two decades is the visionary and practical organizing of little known groups throughout the world aimed at surviving, resisting, and transforming globalization and its effects. Including farmers and fisherfolk, economists, labor unionists, ethicists, scientists, students, business people, activist coalitions, and others throughout the globe, these groups develop and live toward alternative visions of a global economic order in which the wealth of a few is not bought by the impoverishment of the many and of the Earth.

2

Disabling Democracy:
Subordinating Democratic Political Power
to Economic Power

∼

THE PREVAILING MODEL of economic globalization dictates and normalizes political-economic relationships that cripple human capacity to make decisions and take actions other than those that serve the utility of the market. In other words, globalization corrodes the moral agency required to resist it and to move toward more just and sustainable alternatives. The preceding chapter introduced corporate- and finance-driven globalization. This chapter and the next examine a set of dynamics whereby that model of economic life undermines moral agency. Chapter 3 will expose ideological and theoretical underpinnings of globalization and their corrosive impact on the capacity to critique it on moral grounds and to move toward viable alternatives. In this chapter, I probe dynamics whereby globalization removes from the body politic the capacity for political participation on behalf of creation's well-being, effectively de-democratizing society. I argue that globalization subordinates democratic political power to unaccountable economic power. That corrosion of democratic power disables citizens' capacity to shape economic policies, structures, and lifestyles that contribute to social justice, and to a "sustainable relationship between the human species and the planet."[1]

The moral and theological significance of this assertion must be clear. Globalization removes from more or less democratically constituted and accountable political bodies the power to influence decisions that shape common life and places that power into the hands of relatively few unaccountable economic players. "Decisions that shape common life" refers to matters of enormous moral and theological weight, decisions determining the survival chances and quality of life for many today and for generations to come: Who will have the necessities for survival—food to eat, clean water, shelter? Which peoples have human rights and which do not? Will the Earth of our children's day be capable of sustaining life as we know it? Economic decisions bear tremendous moral weight.

Key Concepts and Premise

Political

The *political* may be understood narrowly as the functions of government or formal interest groups, or more broadly as the processes through which groups of people—be they households, institutions, localities, nations, international bodies, or other groups—determine the governing terms of life in relationship to one another, other groups, and the rest of creation.[2] My use of the term *political* refers to the latter. In line with the feminist argument that "the personal is political," the "political" here includes social practices typically excluded from public deliberation by liberalism's dichotomy between private and public.[3] Theologically considered, the "political," in this broader sense, is integral to human life and is positively valued. The biblical witness, as I understand it, holds that God created humans for community and that communities are to shape ways of life that praise God through active love for creation. The processes for shaping life in common are, by definition, political. Hence, humans are ontologically (fundamentally) political creatures, and this is good. Being political is a reflection of our createdness as beings-in-relationship.[4] The moral norm of active love for creation is established by God for humans to realize through political, though not only political, processes.

Democracy

My intent here is to establish the range of meaning to which *democracy* and *democratic* refer in this project. I draw from three intellectual trajectories —classical liberalism's constructions of democracy, feminist critiques of those constructions,[5] and other recent or mid-century radical democratic theory[6]—as well as from North and Latin American "popular" movements for economic democracy.

I presuppose that democracy is normative for Christian Ethics. That is, what corrodes democracy is suspect from a perspective of Christian Ethics. Presuming the normativeness of democracy raises complex problems for both conservative and progressive theorists. I share progressive critiques of liberal democracy and thus do not uphold democracy uncritically as the goal of public life. Contemporary feminist theorists, for example, challenge fundamental presuppositions and categories of democratic theory. They argue that liberal constructions of democracy have (1) erased the public agency of women, people of color, and people without property by constructing a "universal" citizen that is male, white, and propertied; (2) failed to expose and critique the government of women by men and; (3) ignored "the political implications of dividing the social order between private and public . . . which is also the division between sexes."[7] Yet, I contend that these and related critiques are not reason to dismiss democracy as a norm, but rather to take it more seriously. Thus, I do not argue *that* people ought to value democracy, but rather I suggest implications of doing so in the context of globalization. I assume, then, an audience that already considers democracy preferable to its alternatives and would be concerned about ways of life that undermine it.

Democracy has multiple valid (though contestable) meanings. In modernity, it "has been variously construed as a distinctive set of political institutions and practices, a particular body of rights, a social and economic order . . . or a unique process of making collective and binding decisions."[8] *Democracy* may refer to an ideal or to an actuality, and misleads when the former is mistaken for the latter.[9] Democracy's long history and multiple strains add to the confusion. The connotations of the term have developed over more than two millennia in highly diverse contexts and stem from a variety of sources. "Greek, Roman, medieval, and Renaissance notions intermingle with those of later centuries to produce a jumble of theory and practices that are often deeply inconsistent," writes Robert Dahl in *Democracy and Its Critics*. Applying ancient ideals to modern situations without acknowledging radical contextual differences furthers confusion.

In addition to arguably valid uses, democracy has been misused to justify military intervention, counterrevolution, and dictatorship, and has been refigured to imply free markets, anything but communism, development, or the right to do anything without considering the consequences to others. Misused and mythologized, the term can mean almost anything.[10]

My working concept of democracy rejects four common reductions. First, democracy often is reduced to the right to vote; if the right to vote (together with the formal freedoms of speech, press, and religion) exists, then democracy is present, and a political system is morally approved.[11] However, the vote, while crucial to democracy, is not sufficient; choosing between options that one has little power to establish does not necessarily imply voice and power in decisions shaping common life. Feminist theorists have explored ways in which the right to vote has helped women achieve "formal political equality without substantive political influence."[12] Furthermore, as suggested by some voices of the Two-Thirds World, democracy as the right to vote "becomes a moot point when the right to life itself is denied through economic, social, and political structures that serve only the interests of a . . . wealthy and powerful elite."[13]

Second, democracy may be reduced to a particular set of political institutions, which then become "sacred." Yet, when an imperfect and particular expression of democracy is made sacred, democracy is lost as a body of dynamic principles to be explored, debated, and refined in new contexts.[14]

The third is more a limitation than a reduction. Liberalism has limited democracy to the political sphere (defined as "the legal and administrative functions of the state") and has held that where market forces did not serve the common good, "political constraints would hold economic forces in check."[15] Limiting the scope of democratic accountability to exclude the economic sphere, however, has left its power for domination and exploitation insufficiently checked. As stated by one theorist, a defining limitation of capitalist democracy is the "invulnerability of economic to democratic power."[16] More on this later.

Fourth, common wisdom often presupposes a single universally held theory of democracy. Yet, as Carole Pateman argues, "the notion of one 'classical theory of democracy' is a myth."[17] That myth—a composite of many early modern theories—obscures classical and contemporary democratic theories and practices that challenge the fusion of democracy with capitalism and ground my thesis that the subordination of political power by unaccountable economic power today undermines democracy.

The role of participation in democracy is one relevant area of difference in theories of democracy. For some classical theorists, "the participation of the people has a very narrow function" restricted largely to the election of governing officials who compete for the (male) electorate's votes.[18] For other classical theorists, like contemporary theorists of participatory democracy, "participation has far wider functions and is central to the establishment and maintenance of a democratic polity."[19] They argue that democracy requires the development of politically relevant qualities in ordinary people and that such development occurs through practicing participation. "We learn to participate by participating."[20] In this sense, democracy is valued not only as a means of electing leaders or protecting individual rights or the common good, but also for its role in making citizens capable of political participation and in promoting "the development of a democratic culture."[21]

Participation—understood as functioning not only to ensure government by elected officials, but also to establish and maintain cultures of widespread democratic capabilities—as a condition of democracy does not imply participation per se.[22] It implies participation characterized by having impact and power to shape the socio-ecological good. The question of what conditions enable that kind of participation is beyond the scope of this study. Here we simply note the centrality of economic factors. Both classical and contemporary theorists of participatory democracy argue that substantive economic inequity works against widespread political participation in determining the terms of common life.[23]

The main point here, however, is to reject the uncritical reduction of democracy to a mythological single and universally normative theory and form. That reduction may obscure developments in democratic theory and practice that contest the conflation of capitalism with democracy and the elevation of economic power over democratic political power. Substantive variation in democratic theories' descriptive and normative accounts of participation illustrates the importance of this point.

These four reductions unearthed, we turn to a working concept of democracy for the current context of unprecedented corporate and financial power. *Democracy* joins the Greek *demos* (the people) with *kratia* (power, rule, or authority), rendering "people's power" or "rule by the people." Democracy implies rule by the many rather than by the few. Democracy exists where people have power—in terms of capacities, resources, and institutions—to participate with relative equality and liberty in governance, understood as decision making regarding the political, economic, and cultural life of the heterogeneous body(ies) politic.[24]

Democracy, then, implies a form of politically organized human community in which political power is exercised by, or accountable to, those who must live with the consequences of its exercise, and in which political power is distributed with relative equity.[25] Because economic power converts to political power, where democracy is valued, publicly unaccountable or concentrated economic power is suspect. That is, democracy implies that the norms of accountability to those affected and of equitable distribution apply also to economic power. Democracy, then, is relative, and the more accountability and equity in economic and political power that pertains among different social sectors, the more democratic the situation. To the extent that significant decisions about the shape of current and future life are removed from public deliberation and influence into the realm of an elite few, democracy is undermined.

This concept of democracy makes a claim regarding its relationship to economic power in the current context, in which many corporations represent larger economies than do many nation-states. The claim is this: The democratic nature of a society is compromised if economic power is exempt from the norms of democracy, or if the right to economic freedom is upheld uncritically where it generates extreme economic inequality.[26] Where economic power is concentrated in the hands of a few, democracy is undermined. Where democracy is strong, unaccountable economic power is undermined. This position has been on the table at least since theories of classical liberalism and democracy developed in the seventeenth and eighteenth centuries. I bring it to bear on the new context of globalization.

The theoretical genealogy of this claim is situated in at least four histori-cal debates: democracy vs. property rights,[27] democratic theory vs. neo-classical economic theory,[28] classical democratic theory vs. classical liberal theory,[29] and democracy vs. capitalism.[30] The contradictions made apparent by these debates suggest that where democracy is valued, unrestrained eco-nomic freedom is suspect. Economic freedom—*from* political accountabil-ity and regulation and *for* unconstrained wealth concentration—works against the democratic norms of accountable and distributed power. This emerging account of democracy is not new but rather hearkens back to con-cepts of democracy since obscured by the ideological fusion of democracy with capitalism and with liberalism.

Moral Agency

Clarity with regard to the term *moral agency* is necessary.[31] I do not, at this point, argue a thesis regarding agency but rather construct a conceptual framework from which to begin.[32] A preliminary caveat is in order regarding *the common good,* a problematic term integral to my concept of moral agency. Uncritically suggesting a *singular* common good, it may become a "veneer for the legitimation of elite interests," excluding the voice and interests of some.[33] Where "unequal access to the common good and the effective forging of it" is not acknowledged, a presupposed common good perpetuates that inequality by obscuring it.[34] Anthropocentrically con-ceived, "the common good" tends to exclude non-humans. Yet, it is crucial to speak of a "common good" that encompasses the whole social-ecological order, as distinct from the "individual good." For want of a better definition, I understand *common good* as a "pluralistic socio-ecological common good" that seeks the good of all and is arrived at through public interaction that expresses difference and seeks to include the perspectives of the more vulnerable.

Thus, my response to the problem of elitist claims to a singular or uni-versal common good is not the extreme postmodernist position. That posi-tion renounces a common good in the form of universally normative aspects of social life. In contrast, I affirm universally normative aspects of morality but challenge processes that enable an elite few to determine them. While I agree with the postmodernist critique of universalizing *descriptive* accounts of human reality, I distinguish between *descriptive* and *normative* accounts.

Moral agency, for the purposes of this project, is understood in moral-philosophical terms as the power to serve the "pluralistic socio-ecological common good." In theological terms, it is the power to embody a funda-mental moral norm of Christian life. That norm is active love for creation where creation includes self, others, and the rest of nature, and where love implies serving the well-being of the beloved, which may call for challenging systemic injustice.[35]

The generality of the terms need not detract from the concrete implications for economic and political life. To "embody active love for creation" in economic life is to live in ways that promote social and ecological well-being, prioritizing the concerns of the most vulnerable. It is to move toward economic lifestyles, relationships, policies, and structures that build communities characterized by social justice, ecological sustainability, and compassion. Moral agency, then, is the power to live—in life's multiple dimensions—in ways that serve not only the needs of self and family but also the ongoing well-being of the larger Earth community, and in ways that do not contribute to unnecessary suffering and do not threaten Earth's capacity to sustain life for generations to come. In the context of economic arrangements that thwart the survival or dignity of many, the call to "embody active love for creation" is a call to subvert those arrangements. Moral agency, then, is the power to subvert, that is, to resist and to live toward alternatives. That subversive and multifaceted activity is political, according to my definition above—that is, it constitutes participation in the shaping of public life. The moral norm of active, embodied love is a call to political participation on behalf of life and against what destroys it. In relatively democratic societies, moral agency, thus conceptualized, entails the exercise of democratic political power to shape just and sustainable communities. This notion of moral agency undergirds this project.

Key issues regarding moral agency that bear upon this project are raised by two intellectual trajectories. First are accounts of moral agency in liberal philosophical and theological perspective, and second are feminist and postmodernist challenges to those accounts. Diverse concepts and theories of moral agency are found within and between the discourses of moral philosophy, political philosophy, Roman Catholic moral theology, and Protestant ethics. The different notions have differing implications for constructive ethics. Our primary concern here is moral agency in theological terms. Any theological concept and theory of agency presupposes a perspective on the theological categories of moral anthropology, soteriology (theology of salvation) and christology, revelation, grace, law, sin, and the divine-human encounter.[36] Notions of moral agency also entail assumptions regarding free will, accountability, autonomy, rationality, motivation, conscience, responsibility, subjectivity, and political community. Of particular relevance for this project are questions of political community and the theological categories of divine-human encounter and soteriology as related to moral agency.

Until challenged by second-wave feminist theory, womanist theory, and postmodernist theory, liberal notions of moral agency referred to the power or potential of individuals to act freely, autonomously, and rationally—and hence responsibly—in accord with moral norms. In theological ethics this became the power or potential to make free and rational choices in response to God's invitation, call, or being. According to liberal political theory, moral agency is located in the autonomous individual subject. Agency stems from the rational application of universal abstract principles and is made possible by independence of will from emotional factors. The aims of agency are associated with the responsible use of power. Agency is inseparable from, but not synonymous with, subjectivity, the former associated more with doing and the latter with being or the qualities of selfhood.[37] These accounts respond to questions of: What grounds the possibility of moral agency? Where is agency located? What are the aims of and constraints on agency? What is the relationship of moral being to moral doing?

Agency is "a central problem in feminist theory" in part because the liberal Western tradition has constructed women as passive rather than as agents in the public sphere and has suspected women who act as agents.[38] Agency becomes a highly contested category in feminist theory when the deconstruction of liberalism's gendered (male) subject leads to the deconstruction of subjectivity altogether. That move, argue some theorists, threatens "what is fundamental to the feminist struggle: agency."[39]

Notions of agency have been recast in the last two decades by the postmodernist insistence on the social construction of knowledge and by diverse womanist and feminist challenges to theological and philosophical categories, theories, and methods—especially as they underwrite dualistic anthropologies and universal abstract moralities. Notions of agency produced by patriarchy and colonialism are suspect. The concerns inherent in liberal theories of agency remain but are interrogated, answered differently, and present new possibilities.[40] For example:

- Individual autonomy is held in tension with relationality to self, other, God, Earth, and community.[41] The site of agency shifts partially or entirely from individual autonomy to relationality, community, or alliance.[42] Community extends beyond its human members.

- Moral reasoning is embodied, that is, inseparable from rather than independent of emotion, sensuality, spirituality, and practice.

- Moral agents are embedded in socio-ecological contexts and thus are historically contingent, rather than abstract and universal. Agency is formed in a historical matrix of structural factors and power relationships and is shaped by continuing legacies of oppression and survival. Constraints to agency include the matrix of oppression and domination in which the agent is formed. Agency is viewed through an interstructural lens. Memory, vision, imagination, and hope form and mal-form moral agency.

- Recast, especially by womanist perspectives, agency is less defined by the responsible use of power than with survival and dignity in the face of powerlessness and with demystifying and dismantling situations of oppression.[43]

- The moral self as thinker is dethroned from elevation over self as doer.[44] Moral knowing and being arise from doing, from experience rather than thinking alone. Doing and being are treated not as polarities but as mutually informing.

Having identified these issues, I revisit my working concept of moral agency in light of them. Moral agency, for the purposes of this project, is understood as the power to embody active love for creation including self, other, and other-than-human creation. Moral agency suggests the power to orient life around the long-term well-being of communities and the Earth, prioritizing the concerns of the most vulnerable.

This concept of agency is enhanced by feminist, womanist, and postmodernist interrogation of liberal thought regarding agency. The power to "embody active love for creation" is disabled and enabled in a complex weave of reason, emotion, sensuality, and spirituality. At play in that power are imagination, vision, memory, hope, modeling, and more. Practice is a shaper of moral agency. The power to "embody active love for creation" is the purview of both community and individual where the latter is understood as being-in-relationship.[45] Human agents are part of a larger-than-human community of life. Moral power is corroded and enlivened "in a field of power relations" spanning generations.[46] This power entails being, knowing, and doing, none of which necessarily precede the others. Moral agency is, by definition, political; it is manifest in processes whereby people make decisions regarding the terms of their life in common. In a relatively democratic society, moral agency entails the exercise of political power to shape just and sustainable communities.

A Premise Arising from the Three Concepts

From these three concepts—the political, democracy, and moral agency—a premise arises: What disables the capacity for democratic political participation disables moral agency.

Healing a Broken World

The Main Argument:
The Dominant Paradigm of Globalization
Disables Democracy

The remainder of this chapter argues its thesis: Corporate- and finance-driven globalization disables moral agency by disabling democracy. More specifically, globalization subordinates democratic political power to unaccountable economic power. This corrosion of democracy undermines citizens' capacity to shape economic structures, policies, and lifestyles that will build social justice and establish regenerative Earth-human relations.

As detailed in chapter 1, the window through which we view globalization is the movement to "free" transnational investment from public regulation and accountability. This movement is one arm of the free trade and investment agenda. This agenda seeks an open, liberalized, deregulated, or "free" global system of trade, investment, and financial services. The aim is to remove obstacles to the "free" operation of transnational corporations and finance enterprises across international borders. The investment liberalization movement provides a useful window, for it reveals in blazing colors the moral implications of economic and financial decisions; it is the most recent and arguably most far-reaching development of globalization; and it illustrates the power dynamics by which a democratically unaccountable global power structure is emerging.

To examine this movement's impact on democracy in limited space, I use a case study of the Multilateral Agreement on Investment (MAI), a global investment treaty of unprecedented power, through which investment liberalization became internationally well-known and contested. The case study illumines the central dynamics at play in the movement to "free" transnational financial and economic activity from public accountability. These dynamics, in turn, illumine the larger issues of moral agency: Who has the power and the right to make decisions that impact the possibility of life with dignity for millions today and in the future? Are those decisions to be made by the body politic(s) or by large transnational corporations and finance enterprises? If those decisions are removed systematically and legally from the hands of the people and into the hands of a small elite whose power lies in control of capital, then democracy is undermined, and with it the moral agency to shape economic ways that serve the well-being of Earth and its inhabitants.

The Multilateral Agreement on Investment (MAI): A Case Study

The MAI was negotiated in the Organization for Economic Cooperation and Development (OECD) from May 1995 through late 1998, in relative secret until early 1997.[47] Its purpose, according to both supporters and detractors, was to make it easier for individual and corporate investors to move assets— whether money or production facilities—across international borders. The MAI would accomplish this goal by limiting the legal ability of governments (at all levels, including local, state, provincial, and subnational [for example, Native American]) to regulate both foreign investment and the activities of foreign-based corporations. The MAI was permanently halted in the OECD by coalitions of civil society groups—led by Canadians and the French— who brought under scrutiny the alarming impact the agreement could have on environmental protection, cultural integrity, and human and labor rights.

While the MAI per se was one specific agreement, the term is widely used to denote the investment liberalization agenda currently pursued in other venues, most visibly in the World Trade Organization (WTO).[48] A primary aim of the WTO 1999 ministerial in Seattle was to establish a round of negotiations that would expand the WTO's authority over investment and finance related services, essentially incorporating the MAI into the WTO.[49]

Among the agreement's most visible supporters are the OECD, composed of the twenty-nine most industrialized nations of Europe, North America, and the Pacific region; the International Chamber of Commerce (ICC); and the ICC's U.S. affiliate, the U.S. Council for International Business (USCIB). The power and role of large corporations—represented by the two business coalitions—in promoting MAI-like agreements is central to the question of who has power to make decisions shaping life today.[50]

Opponents of investment deregulation include a long list of environmental, labor, family farmer, human rights, women's rights, anti-poverty, and other organizations (both religious and secular) representing a spectrum of civil society.[51] Also opposed are numerous Canadian and U.S. local, provincial, and state governments—many of which declared themselves MAI-Free Zones—and associations of local and state officials.[52]

Proponents of liberalization claim that it will increase the prosperity of nearly everyone (see chapter 1). In short, they argue that deregulation increases foreign trade and investment and competition. These increases generate economic growth, which translates to increased prosperity for all. The intent, proponents claim, is to provide a "level playing field" for investors worldwide.

Opponents refer to the MAI as "a corporate bill of rights"; "NAFTA on steroids"; an "exercise in neo-colonialism"; and a threat to the environment,

Healing a Broken World

human rights, and democracy. They contend that MAI-like agreements "would give private corporations . . . not only the legal status of nation-states, but also such powerful tools to enforce their newly acquired 'rights' that governments would be compelled by law to safeguard corporate interests over those of their own citizens."[53] MAI-like agreements would disempower citizens and governments, undermining the legal authority of governments to regulate economic activity in the public interest. Political power, opponents argue, would be shackled by the economic freedom of large corporations and finance enterprises.

My study of provisions central to MAI-like agreements confirms this argument. Here we consider six provisions. The implicit query regarding each is, "Does it enable or disable democratic political participation on behalf of the 'pluralistic socio-ecological common good'?"

The MAI's "most favored nation treatment" provision would require governments to treat all foreign investors the same, regardless of investments they have made in other countries with unacceptable human or labor rights standards. This may sound innocuous, but play it out. Dictatorships and other governments abusing human rights are propped up by foreign investment. In the pre-MAI world, investment sanctions may be used to discourage foreign investment in those regimes. Sanctions may be primary (refusing to invest in the offending country) or secondary (prohibiting government from doing business with foreign companies invested in the country). This provision of the MAI bans secondary investment boycotts. That is, governments could not limit business with foreign corporations that invest in dictatorships. For example, many of the investment sanctions aimed at overturning apartheid in South Africa would be forbidden under MAI-like agreements. Screening corporations for poor environmental or labor rights records would be forbidden. This provision is referred to by MAI supporters as "eliminating discrimination."[54] At this moment in history, when citizens around the world are "discriminating" against sweatshops, child labor, and environmentally destructive business practices, investment deregulation threatens that impulse, erecting a wall between social and economic policy.[55]

According to the MAI "national treatment" provision, governments (at all levels) must treat foreign investors as favorably as domestic. In the pre-MAI world, laws distinguishing between local and foreign business enable governments to promote small local business and business owned by economically marginalized people and to protect scarce natural resources. This provision of MAI-like agreements would allow foreign corporations to sue governments—including local governments—for those laws on the grounds that they discriminate against foreign business. This provision clashes with the move toward a more sustainable future, which many believe will be built on small-scale enterprise and local control of resources.

Consider two examples: First, this provision would give foreign mining companies equal access to resources on indigenous lands—that is, permission to own 100 percent of a mining operation and to repatriate 100 percent of its profit—with no obligation to employ local people in management, reinvest in the community, or repair environmental damage. According to one indigenous spokeswoman, Victoria Tauli-Corpuz, leaders of indigenous communities in the foothills of the Andes are threatening mass suicide if Shell Oil takes control of their lands. A second example: as water becomes increasingly scarce, commodified, and privatized, this provision would give foreign corporations equal right to own and export water and sell it to those with buying power. Already in 1998, under the North America Free Trade Agreement (NAFTA) investment clause, the Alaska-based Sunbelt Water Company sued the Canadian government for $400 million because British Columbia enacted a moratorium on the export of fresh water.[56]

A third provision would ban restrictions on the movement of capital across national borders. Rapid inflows and outflows of money pose serious risks to a national economy and may mean death for people with no guaranteed economic security net. The Mexican peso crisis of 1994 and the Asian financial crisis are prime examples. In the words of South Korean theologian Yoon-Jae Chang, "Suddenly in November 1997, . . . foreign investors, panicked by the Asian currency crisis, demanded their dollars back, and lenders called in their short-term loans. . . . Koreans say that this is the most tragic event ever since the Korean War. . . . Korea is now plunged into a stormy night of company bankruptcies (more than 1,000 in December, 1997), mass layoffs, [and more]. . . . A layoff in a household means a death sentence to one's family in Korea. Those who have found no way out of the swamp have committed suicide—sometimes a familial suicide. . . . The only winners in Korea are the foreign banks, who will get their money back and then some."[57] Currently, nations—at least theoretically—may guard their economies by placing controls on speculative foreign investment. The MAI would eliminate the right and obligation of nations to protect against speculative threat; the MAI would outlaw capital controls, requiring that a government allow foreign investors to transfer unlimited amounts of capital "into and out of its territory without delay."[58]

Another provision would limit or ban many performance requirements. Under this provision, governments could not require foreign companies to meet certain performance standards—such as environmental, labor, and consumer protection standards—even if they are required of domestic companies. Prioritizing companies with high environmental standards, a public policy mechanism for preventing environmental degradation, would be undone. Policies, such as credit programs, designed to address women's poverty could be attacked. Performance requirements are referred to, by

Healing a Broken World

MAI supporters, as "market distorting measures" from which freedom is sought.

The MAI's "investor-to-state dispute resolution" provision, contradicting most previous international agreements, would enable private international investors and corporations to sue governments—including local governments—directly for regulations or practices that undermine profits.[59] Governments, including local governments, could be required to pay monetary compensation and to overturn existing regulations. Disputes would be judged by a tribunal of trade experts in which proceedings would be secret, records not publicly accessible, and decisions legally binding.

A provision banning uncompensated expropriation of assets would enable corporations to legally challenge local, state, or federal laws that might diminish corporate profit. Governments would be required to compensate corporations monetarily and to overturn laws, or face severe trade sanctions. In August of 1998, under a similar provision in NAFTA, the Ethyl Corporation of Virginia sued Canada for $251 million for prohibiting the import and transport of an ethyl product considered a dangerous toxin and already banned in Europe and California.[60] Canada paid $13 million and lifted the ban. Even the threat of costly lawsuits or trade sanctions may lead governments to weaken social and environmental protections. Consider, for example, the case of Guatemala and Gerber. According to UNICEF, 1.5 million infants die yearly due to breast milk substitutes that are frequently mixed with unclean water. Seeking to reduce infant mortality, Guatemala in 1983 passed a law to encourage breast-feeding. The law, based on a UNICEF regulation for marketing infant formula, prohibited graphics idealizing the use of infant formula. Gerber refused to comply, claiming expropriation of its trademark. By 1995, threatened by the newly formed WTO's support for Gerber's claim, Guatemala backed down and exempted imported infant formula from its labeling policy. The internationally respected UNICEF code, protecting infants of Two-Thirds World nations, was undone in the name of corporate profit.

While these provisions pertain to the content of MAI-like agreements, the process of establishing them also circumvents democratic political processes. Consider this statement by then–Director General of the WTO Renato Ruggiero regarding the MAI: "We are writing the constitution of a single global economy."[61] What does it mean for the "constitution of a single global economy" to be negotiated by unrepresentative officials of the twenty-nine most industrialized nations, in a process relatively secret until citizens' groups disclosed it on the Internet? What is the implication when a "constitution" designed by a powerful few transgresses other international agreements established by the United Nations? For example, the 1974 Charter of Economic Rights and Duties of States declared that all nations have the "inalienable right to regulate and exercise authority over foreign invest-ment"; "no state shall be compelled to grant preferential treatment to foreign investment"; and national governments have the right and responsibility to "regulate and supervise the activities of transnational corporations" in order to serve the basic economic, social, and environmental priorities of their countries. All three rights are betrayed by investment deregulation in general and by MAI-like agreements specifically.

The content of multilateral agreements to deregulate transnational investment, and the process of establishing them, discloses a defining aim of globalization: large transnational corporations and finance enterprises are to "dictate their rules to society, rather than the other way around."[62] Democ-racy is at risk where the power to make decisions shifts from citizens and democratically constituted governance institutions to a relatively few supra-national, publicly unaccountable, and undemocratically constituted eco-nomic players.[63]

Implications

Globalization contradicts the democratic norms of accountable and distrib-uted power, promotes antitheses of democracy (unaccountable and concen-trated power), and defies liberalism's premise that "political constraints would hold economic forces in check."[64] Globalization removes from citi-zens the means for political participation in shaping economic arrange-ments that may determine life and death for many, Earth-human relations, and relationships between people the world over. The exclusion of citizens from the creation of social policy renders actual and perceived powerless-ness. However, Christians (and others) are called to serve the well-being of Earth and its inhabitants, not to advance destruction and exploitation. To that end, we are called to seek lifestyles, public policies, and social struc-tures that enable social justice and sustainability. The concrete implications are manifold. To illustrate, heeding this call might lead us to advocate for public policies that fine the production and transport of toxins rather than fining governments that discourage those activities; prohibit sweatshops rather than prohibiting labor protection laws; and curtail excessive financial speculation and give vulnerable peoples control over the terms of foreign investment and corporate activity in their lands. Heeding that call, we might embrace economic principles and lifestyles aimed at equitable distribution of wealth and power.

In a relatively democratic society, these are works of political participation and are integral to the Christian moral-spiritual life. They are manifestations

Healing a Broken World

of moral agency, understood as power to embody active love for creation, including self, other, and the rest of nature. The dominant paradigm of globalization undermines democracy, and with it our moral agency manifest in democratic political participation toward just and sustainable communities. Perhaps the impetus against this disabling of democracy is democracy itself, where it holds to a vision of equitable and accountable economic power as well as political power.

We are left with more questions than answers. What would it mean for moral agency in the context of globalization if democracy were to extend to the economic sphere so that, there, people identified themselves more as citizens than as consumers? What worldview allows us to tolerate the contradiction between valuing democracy and accepting its corrosion? What ideology abdicates corporations from accountability? What perceptions of human being and freedom, the *telos* (end) of economic life, and the possibility of substantive social change rationalize the dominant paradigm of globalization and breed moral passivity in the face of its threats?

3

Ideological Underpinnings:
Neo-Liberalism and Social Amnesia

∾

Man [sic] *is a creature who makes pictures of himself* [sic] *and then comes to resemble the pictures.*

—Iris Murdoch, *Metaphysics and Ethics*

There are times in life when the question of knowing if one can think differently than one thinks, and perceive differently than one sees, is absolutely necessary if one is to go on looking and reflecting at all.

—Michel Foucault, *The Use of Pleasure*

RECALL THE MOTIVATING QUESTION for this project: How is the moral agency of relatively economically privileged people in the United States so disabled that we acquiesce to a model of economic globalization that undermines democracy, threatens Earth's regenerative capacity, and requires the exploitation of other human beings? In partial response, my thesis is this: the prevailing model of globalization cripples human capacity to make decisions and take actions other than those that serve the utility of the market. This "crippling" disables moral agency—the capacity to embody active love for creation. In economic life, to "embody active love for creation" is to move toward economic practices, policies, and structures that enable ecologically sustainable, socially just, and compassionate communities.

This chapter examines the ideological and social-theoretical underpinnings of globalization and their corrosive impact on moral agency. I identify four key theoretical and ideological presuppositions underlying corporate- and finance-driven globalization. Uncritically accepted, these presuppositions, or "market myths," shape a "way of perceiving" human existence and moral power (moral anthropology), the dynamics and consequences of globalization (what is), social and ecological history (what has been), what is morally normative and acceptable (what ought be), and the (im)possibility of alternative economic arrangements (what could be), which coheres with

46

the mandates and mores (moral attitudes) of the global free market. The theoretical and ideological presuppositions identified here tell people not only how to perceive the world and make sense of it, but also what to forget. Market myths erase certain people, historical struggles, and consequences by either ignoring them or claiming them to be insignificant. The resulting social amnesia breeds acquiescence to current global economic arrangements. I refer to the "way of perceiving" shaped by these four presuppositions as "global free-market ideology" or as "neo-liberal ideology." In accord with this worldview, society places human life and the rest of nature in the service of the global free market rather than maintaining the market as servant of society and the broader community of life. In the words of Indian Christian ethicist M. P. Joseph, we "become a market society instead of a society with a market."

An ideology—that is, an underlying worldview, partially conscious and partially not—shapes our interpretation of socio-ecological reality and history; our vision of what ought be; and our stance regarding the possibility of substantive social change. It molds our sense of who we are and ought be in relationship with God, one another, and the rest of creation; our purpose; what is worth living and dying for; our sense of who counts; and our moral power. Global free market ideology distracts and deceives on all these accounts. The need is to uncover, probe, scrutinize, and clearly assess the key ideas or presuppositions composing neo-liberal ideology.

Other critics of globalization point, in similar terms, to the importance of this exposé. David Korten asserts, "One important step will be to free ourselves from the illusions of the ideology that legitimates the policies that are freeing the corporation as an institution from human accountability."[1] Frances Moore Lappé, struggling—as am I—to untangle forces allowing complicity with deadly economic arrangements, arrives at a similar conclusion. "What," she queries, "could be powerful enough to allow us to tolerate, to accept, to acquiesce to, these millions of silent deaths [by hunger] every year? What could possibly explain our ability to condone such a status quo? I've finally come to believe that there is only one thing powerful enough. It is the power of ideas—the ideas we hold about ourselves and our relationships to one another. It is these ideas that allow us to condone or even to support with tax dollars, that which we as individuals abhor—and somehow to tolerate the discomforting contrast."[2]

The word *ideology* has multiple connotations. In very general terms, the meaning of *ideology* falls into one of two categories or, as Janet Jakobsen suggests, "slips between" the two categories.[3] One is pejorative and the other neutral. In the former, *ideology* implies false consciousness or a set of ideas, beliefs, and analyses of social relations that helps to mystify them or to "produce acceptance of existing power relations as 'natural.'"[4] In this sense an ideology distorts thought or consciousness through misleading ideas perpetrated by the people and power structures that stand to benefit. In the neutral sense, *ideology* refers to any pattern of concepts, theories, beliefs, and values—conscious and not—that link a human group together, interpret power relations and other socio-ecological phenomena both historical and current, and shape normative sensibilities. An ideology is shaped by and shapes social structures and may "motivate people to defend a given status quo or subvert it."[5] In this sense, ideology is not inherently false, yet any given ideology may function in the pejorative sense, that is, as a tool for mystification and production of false consciousness. The meaning I intend in using the term is the neutral sense, although the ideology that I uncover functions, I argue, in the pejorative sense.

Market Myths

The ideological underpinnings of globalization are many. We examine not all but four of the most powerful and inextricably linked market myths. The guiding questions regarding each myth are two: What claim is made? How does that claim contribute to the dominant paradigm of globalization and our complicity with it? The second question focuses on the deceptive and distracting power of these myths.

Market Myth #1: Growth Benefits All

Growth in a nation's economy, as measured by the Gross Domestic Product (GDP), refers to an increase in the amount of services and goods produced and paid for. As measured by per capita or per household income or wealth, growth refers to growth in average income or wealth. Growth, then, means rising national income, wealth, production, and consumption. As noted by Carol Johnston, in the twentieth century, growth has shifted from its classical meaning of increase in commodities produced and sold to increase in economic activity defined as "any activity that draws a money price, whether or not any actual material item is involved."[6]

The Claim

Free trade and investment lead to growth, which translates to greater economic well-being for all. Regulations on trade and investment detract from growth, and hence from economic well-being. The argument, as elaborated in chapter 1, is recapped here: deregulation increases (and is necessary to increase) foreign trade and investment. Increased foreign trade and investment generates (and is necessary to generate) economic growth directly, and as well as indirectly by increasing competition, which increases efficiency. Increased efficiency lowers consumer prices and generates growth. Growth increases (and is necessary to increase) prosperity, employment, and living standards for most people.

This theory is the bedrock of arguments for trade and investment liberalization.[7] Advocates of liberalization insist that it fosters growth, which is the key to economic well-being for all. As stated repeatedly by the Organization for Economic Cooperation and Development (OECD), "The efficiency benefits of an open trade and investment regime contribute to economic growth and hence rising incomes. . . . Market openness brings real, direct economic gains to *all* consumers—whether firms or individuals"; "Trade and investment have become major engines of growth. . . . Increased trade and investment and the greater prosperity it brings, are a win-win proposition."[8] The International Chamber of Commerce summarizes, "Wealth creation is the intended and actual consequence of liberalization . . . [of] deregulation."[9]

Deception and Distraction

Without a doubt, liberalization generates economic growth, which has reaped incredible bounty for a good many and has enabled many others to escape poverty. The claim's first clause—"trade and investment liberalization generates growth"—is true. Deception lies in the second clause— "growth translates to greater economic well-being for all." A crucial fault line running through this theory is its dependence upon the false presupposition that economic growth is an accurate and adequate indicator of economic well-being; that is, more economic activity necessarily means a healthier economy.

The presupposition is invalid today for at least four reasons.[10] First, growth as measured by GDP counts as a *gain* for humanity, socially and environmentally destructive activity. Second, growth theory does not account for distribution of wealth and income. Next, the goal of unlimited growth is invalidated by its failure to recognize Earth's natural limits. Finally, growth, as measured by GDP, is an inadequate measure of economic well-being because GDP attributes to a host country profits made in other countries. We look, in turn, at each problem:

Growth as measured by GDP fails to account for the social and ecological costs of growth and to distinguish between destructive and sustaining economic activity. All economic activity is measured as a "gain for humanity." For example:

- The more consumptive a lifestyle the better, for consumption translates to growth. That is, the more a household buys, throws away, and replaces, the more good it is doing.

- Indicators of breakdown in families, communities, and health count as growth. Ten-year-olds purchasing cigarettes, alcoholics feeding their addiction, and the sale of pornography all contribute to growth.

- The GDP treats the extraction of natural resources as income rather than as the depletion of an asset. Former president of the World Bank Barber Conable states: "GDP figures . . . are generally used without the caveat that they represent an income that cannot be sustained. . . . [They] ignore the degradation of the natural resource base and view the sales of nonrenewable resources entirely as income."[11] When a forest is cut down in the mountains of the Philippines, destroying sustenance for indigenous peoples, the deforestation registers as growth.

- Growth figures fail to consider the costs born by the larger society and future generations as a result of a business transaction. These costs are called "externalities." Examples of externalities include water pollution, disease, injury due to workplace hazards, and toxic waste.[12]

- Growth figures do not account for the implications of economic or financial activity beyond the period to which the figures pertain. Thus the speculative activity that contributed to the Asian financial crisis registered as a social good, as growth. Likewise, the short-term growth derived from shifting to export-oriented agriculture does not account for the dramatic commodity price fluctuations that might occur in subsequent years.

Second, growth theory does not take distribution of wealth and income into account. Thus, growth in terms of GDP or average household income or wealth may obscure an accompanying increase in poverty. For instance, economists claim growth in the United States economy based upon an increase of 22.2 percent in average household net worth from 1983 to 1998 and a general upward trend of GDP during the same period.[13] Yet numbers of homeless people are increasing, more and more people are unable to obtain health care, and many citizens are experiencing severe economic insecurity and job loss. The contradiction is explained by the deceptiveness of growth indicators as measures of economic well-being. The GDP and 22.2 percent increase in *average* household net worth hide a 10 percent *decrease* in the *median* household net worth during the same period, the

Healing a Broken World

declining real wages of the middle class, and the shrinking after-tax income of the poorest 20 percent in contrast to the skyrocketing income of the wealthiest 1 percent.[14] Growth figures fail to acknowledge that in the United States, as stated in "The Eisenhower Report," "The rich are getting richer, the poor are getting poorer and minorities are suffering disproportionately."[15] According to a United Nations report, while liberalization has increased many countries' net income, in many nations "income distribution has worsened and poverty has increased during liberalization."[16]

Third, the presupposition that growth translates to economic well-being for all is invalidated by the claim's failure to recognize Earth's natural limits. According to free market theory, growth has no fixed limits,[17] and boundless economic growth will bring all people to a state of prosperity as defined by Western middle-class standards.[18] Yet, as many economists, scientists, environmentalists, and ethicists now point out, the human economy is part of a much larger planetary economy of life, and the economy's limits in both renewable and nonrenewable resources have been so pushed that unchecked growth now further destroys Earth's regenerative capacity. Economic growth, the aim and primary promise of globalization, has "collided with the Earth's natural limits."[19]

Finally, growth as measured by GDP is an inadequate measure of economic well-being because GDP attributes to a host country corporate profits that actually are repatriated (returned) to the company's host country. Hence, global corporate production in a Two-Thirds World nation falsely registers as growth for that nation.[20]

Clearly, growth is not an adequate and accurate indicator of economic well-being if we ask: "Growth for whom and at what costs?" The economic theory rationalizing globalization depends upon growth as the promise of globalization: liberalization renders growth, which benefits all. The second clause of that presupposition is undone in these four ways, and with it the primary theoretical rationale for globalization in its dominant form.

The faulty presupposition that growth is an adequate indicator of economic well-being and is beneficial to all is not the only fault line in the growth-based economic argument rationalizing liberalization. A second problem is the argument's explicit appeal to Adam Smith and David Ricardo, considered fathers of free market theory and free trade theory, respectively.[21] The appeal to Smith to justify investment deregulation is invalid because deregulation dismantles conditions that Smith presupposed or prescribed as necessary for his theory to work.[22] Note four of those conditions.[23]

First, Smith both assumed and prescribed the *rootedness* of capital. His discussion of the "invisible hand" is located in his assertion that capital invested *domestically* creates more wealth for individuals and nations.[24] In direct contradiction to Smith's rootedness of capital and domestic oriented economy, "free" trade and investment aims specifically at *uprooting* capital and at export-oriented economies. Second, Smith's theory presupposed a competitive market composed of buyers and sellers too small to significantly impact the market price of goods.[25] Global oligopolistic corporations defy that model. Deregulated investment further betrays it by jeopardizing the chance for survival of small business. Advocates of free trade and investment fail to disclose that "the global economic system they are creating in Smith's name bears a far greater resemblance to the monopolistic market he condemned than to the competitive market system that he theorized."[26] Third, Smith presupposed that as hourly productivity increased, wages would increase. This has not been the case in today's global economy.[27] Finally, Smith insisted that a worker's "wages must at least be sufficient to maintain him *[sic]*" and sufficient "for him *[sic]* to raise up a family."[28] As demonstrated earlier, deregulation in the global marketplace has allowed transnational corporations to chase the lowest labor costs, paying wages far from "sufficient to raise a family." The appeal to Smith is suspect because his primary goal for economic life—unlimited growth in the production of goods for consumption—neither *is* the primary goal of transnational investment today, nor is *viable* today as the primary goal of economic life. Using Adam Smith to rationalize today's global free market conceals conditions of the contemporary global market by implying that it mirrors the market Smith theorized.

The appeal to David Ricardo's theory of "specialization according to comparative advantage," to support trade and investment deregulation, also falls apart in the transnational corporate context.[29] Given the conditions it presupposes, the logic of Ricardo's theory works. However, in the contemporary context, crucial conditions are not met. For instance, the theory fails to account for the fact that many of today's traders (in both goods and capital) are not nations, but rather transnational corporations and finance institutions. Hence, although the traders benefit as the theory predicts, benefit to nations or national economies is not assured unless trade and investment are regulated to ensure that benefit. The theory also does not recognize the limits to growth imposed today by the biosphere.

As with the appeal to Adam Smith, the appeal to Ricardo is suspect if used to justify a contemporary policy that dismantles conditions he presupposed. Proponents of deregulated transnational investment and trade ignore "Ricardo's critical assumption that factors of production [including capital and labor, although here we look at capital] are internationally immobile."[30] The theory of comparative advantage, according to David Ricardo, requires a situation in which labor and capital do not move freely across national borders. According to Ricardo, if capital moves freely across borders, *wages will gradually decline to the level of wages in the least developed country involved.*

Healing a Broken World

Indeed such is proving to be the case, as corporations move production or assembly facilities to countries that keep wages (and environmental standards) low in order to attract foreign investment.[31] Supporters of liberalization appeal to a theory that hinges on the international *immobility* of capital to support agreements, such as the MAI, aimed at radically enhancing the *mobility* of capital. The human and environmental costs of applying the theory of comparative advantage to the context of internationally mobile capital are dramatic.[32]

A third fault line in the growth theory undergirding "free" trade and investment is that neo-classical economic theory claims to address the crises of economic life without addressing issues of power imbalance; social and economic inequity; ecological impacts; and historical sources of poverty such as colonialism and centuries of resource depletion. These are key factors in economic life. Yet, the theory considers them largely irrelevant to economic life, and thus obscures them.

Market Myth #2: Freedom Is Market Freedom

The Claim

A fundamental principle of global free market ideology is the "grounding of human freedom in private property" and, derivatively, in the freedom to do as one pleases in the marketplace with one's property.[33] A constellation of presuppositions links human freedom to private property and market freedom and renders the first dependent upon the latter two:

- The economic freedom enabled by global free trade and investment— freedom to consume and to accumulate wealth without limits, to use it as one chooses, and to have vast consumer choice—*is* integral to human freedom and is a necessary condition for human freedom to flourish. To obstruct the freedom of the global market is to obstruct human freedom.

- The human species is free to use the Earth's resources for the sake of profit. That freedom extends to those humans who can buy access to the Earth's resources.

- Tools for maintaining freedom include private property, consumer choice, and free trade and investment or free markets.

- Market freedom, as seen in capitalism, is a necessary condition for democratic freedom.

- Freedom is threatened by expanding government, especially through taxation and regulation, for these constrain people's freedom to use possessions as they choose.

- The operation of market forces free from regulation, while not aimed at the widespread good, inexorably will serve the well-being of a society that plays by free market rules. The more free the markets, the more prosperous the society, and hence the more free its members.

In sum, freedom is *for* doing as one pleases with one's money and property, and is therefore freedom *from* the demands of the widespread good and from public accountability, scrutiny, regulation, and responsibility. Market freedom is elevated de facto over other notions of freedom and is portrayed as if it nourishes the depths of human freedom. This notion of market freedom "is the supreme and universal value from which market theory and practice derive their ethical force and meaning."[34] It is supreme in that other values may be sacrificed to it, and universal in that it pertains to all people of all cultures. Contradictions between this notion of freedom and the cultural values of many non-Western peoples are ignored. This notion of freedom—classical liberalism's freedom taken to its extreme—has shaped economic theory and practice in the latter half of the twentieth century and undergirds globalization.

That market freedom is the grounding of human freedom is implied by the ideological weight of the word *free* attached to "trade and investment" and "markets." Labeling deregulated commerce as "free"—that is, with the terminology of inalienable moral rights—associates it with freedom of the human spirit, political freedom, moral freedom, and democracy. This notion of freedom is not only implicit, but also explicit in the discourse of free market advocates in varied contexts. The following excerpts—voices from international business coalitions, the OECD, the Christian Right, mainstream economics, and political theory—illustrate. Each excerpt, though brief, is consistent with the larger treatises and bodies of literature from which it is drawn.

- The International Chamber of Commerce: "Deregulation and improvement of market access . . . fosters competitiveness and prosperity as the most reliable basis for individual freedom and dignity."[35]

- The OECD: "The case for open markets is based upon the human desire the world over for more, rather than less freedom of choice," and is "fueled by the idea that markets are supportive of enhanced freedom of individual and collective choice."[36]

- Voices from the Christian Right: "Civil and religious freedom, progress, and the preservation of human rights are inextricably linked with economic freedom, with the right to own property, and with a minimum of state interference in economic affairs."[37] "If this freedom and flexibility [of the business corporation] are not protected, the entire society will suffer."[38]

- Milton Friedman: "As liberals, we take freedom of the individual, or perhaps the family, as the ultimate goal in judging social arrangements"; "Economic freedom is . . . an indispensable means toward the achievement of political freedom"; "The kind of economic organization that provides economic freedom directly, namely competitive capitalism, also promotes political freedom."[39]

- Francis Fukuyama: "liberal principles in economics—the 'free market' —have . . . sometimes preceded, sometimes followed, the move toward political freedom around the globe."[40]

Deception and Distraction

This notion of freedom disregards the impact of globalization on the freedom of many people and deceptively portrays the supposed "freedom" of market exchange in the global economy. "Freedom as market freedom" distracts from alternative notions of freedom that could serve the goal of sustainable and just socio-ecological communities. We consider these three paths of duplicity, focusing primarily on the first.

The claim that deregulated trade and investment nurtures human freedom erases the countless human beings whose freedom to survive is threatened by free trade and investment. Those lives either are ignored or are considered insignificant relative to the value of free markets. Note a few illustrations of the impact that market freedom, achieved through the North American Free Trade Agreement (NAFTA) and the World Trade Organization (WTO), have had on particular people's freedom to maintain a livelihood. These people represent not exceptional cases, but patterns repeating themselves the world over. Consider the "freedom" of:

- the small subsistence farmer in India when the WTO agreement on Trade-Related Intellectual Property (TRIPS) is fully effective as of 2005.[41] TRIPS agreements—considered a crucial component of liberalization—grant global corporations the right to patent seeds developed by this farmer's ancestors over generations. Under TRIPS agreements, subsistence farmers in India—and other nations already threatened by hunger—may not save that patented seed from one year to the next but must pay annual fees to use it. According to the United Nations Development Programme's *Human Development Report 1999*, one likely use of TRIPS is to create seeds that will germinate only when used with agrochemicals sold by the particular company that owns the seed, further endangering the "1.4 billion rural people who rely on farm-saved seed."[42] One influential leader of the International Seed Trade Federation states that: "Even though it has been a tradition in most countries that a farmer can save seed from his own crop, it is under the changing circumstances not equitable that farmers can use this seed . . . without paying a royalty."[43] Export income is also threatened by TRIPS. "Basmati rice," an important Indian export, was patented by the Texas-based company Rice-Tec after it slightly altered the Indian rice. Indian farmers no longer may export the rice without paying Rice-Tec for the right to do so. A coalition of prominent Indian civil society groups claims that TRIPS agreements "pirate the intellectual property of the farmers, healers, tribals, fisherfolk of India and other developing countries."[44] Vandana Shiva refers to this aspect of free trade and investment as "biopiracy."[45] Advocates of TRIPS refer to them as "market freedom."

- the United States worker who spent her working life at a good job in a General Electric (GE) aircraft engines plant that is to be closed and moved to Mexico as a result of the free trade inscribed by NAFTA. Countless jobs have been lost in similar plant closings. "At a meeting in Monterey, Mexico, earlier this year, GE told assembled vendors (over 70 companies) that they would move to Mexico or get cut off from all GE business," reports Jeff Crosby, president of the IUE Local 201 in Lynn, Maine. He cites GE CEO Jack Welch's infamous quote: "Ideally, you'd have every plant you own on a barge."[46]

- the Mexican peasant woman who, before NAFTA and the neo-liberal economic policy that paved the way for it, had managed a subsistence living by producing and selling corn. "Corn is the Mexican food staple and [was] produced by 2.5 million small farmers, mostly of indigenous descent. Half of the land of Mexico was dedicated to corn, which is as important culturally as it is economically."[47] Corn production was an anti-poverty program. Before neo-liberal economic policy took hold, Mexico had protected its corn producers from artificially cheap United States corn with tariffs and had maintained a centuries-old system of protecting cooperatively owned peasant lands called *ejidos*. In accord with NAFTA, Mexico signed away its rights to both the tariffs and the *ejido* system. The door was opened for large agribusiness to acquire the former *ejidos* and to import cheap corn. Corn subsidies were dismantled. No longer able to sell her corn, the *campesina* was unable to feed her family. Under threat of hunger, she sold land to transnational agribusiness. Forced off the land, she and her family migrated to the northern border, found employment in *maquiladoras* in the "free trade zone," and faced that hard destiny. Free trade offered them the freedom either to accept life in a *maquiladora*—which may include seventy-hour work weeks in dangerously toxic conditions, repression of employees who organize for workers' rights, sexual harassment for women, and wages inadequate to provide for the most basic needs of a family—or to flee to the United States.

- the Caribbean banana producer whose livelihood and culture are threatened by the WTO ruling that the European Union's long-standing policy of favoring Caribbean banana imports was WTO-illegal because the policy "discriminated" against U.S.-based companies growing bananas in Central America. Caribbean banana production is not owned by global fruit companies notorious for violating human rights in Central America. According to a spokesperson for a Caribbean women's coalition, banana production in the islands has afforded thousands of families a self-reliant livelihood with dignity, which will be devastated by the WTO decision.

- the middle-class Euro-American. She is free to use electronic goods assembled in a "free trade zone" on the U.S.-Mexico border by a Mexican sister whose baby may have been born with anencephaly, a fatal birth defect of the brain, due to toxins emitted by U.S. based corporate assembly plants.[48] This mother in the United States is free to buy fruit that may have been grown on land where children starve because the land produces not food for its own children but for hers. She is free to bank with a company holding African nations in a debt that "is full of the blood of African children."[49]

To claim that deregulated trade and investment enhances human freedom, without acknowledging the cost, seduces the hearer into forgetting the lives and bodies whose freedom is lost. The first means of deception, then, is by erasing from reality human beings whose freedom and lives are threatened by free trade and investment.

A second path of deception is theoretical. The claim that market freedom grounds human freedom is theoretically based in the work of Milton Friedman. A crucial fault line running through his theory, when it is applied in the context of global capitalism, invalidates the claim. The fault line is this: According to Friedman, the "free private exchange enterprise economy" benefits people and promotes freedom *only if* economic transactions are "bilaterally voluntary and informed."[50] This necessary condition does not pertain in the context of the globalizing economy.

The control granted to global corporations by free trade and investment agreements renders the "voluntary and informed" nature of economic transactions absurd. The displaced Mexican *campesinos*, the Indian farmers, the laid-off United States workers, and the Caribbean banana growers are not entering *voluntarily* into economic transactions that threaten their survival. The "free choice" between starvation or destitution on the one hand, and toxic working conditions in a *maquiladora* on the other, is not a *voluntary* transaction. The purchase of goods produced in oppressive or ecologically dangerous conditions is not necessarily an *informed* economic transaction. The claim that "free trade and investment" is a friend of freedom is constructed not on sound theory, but on deceptive use of theory.

Finally, the elevation of market freedom as freedom itself distracts from other notions of freedom more consistent with the moral norm of active embodied love for creation. Other notions of freedom, while varied and multidimensional, may center around freedom as the opportunity to flourish as whole beings-in-community, using one's gifts not only toward the well-being of self and loved ones, but also toward the well-being of the larger human communities and yet larger community of life. The implications of these "non-market" notions of freedom are beyond the scope of this project. The point here is that equating freedom with market freedom distracts us from considering freedom as the freedom of all to flourish.[51]

Sociologist Orlando Patterson theorizes that "freedom" as constructed in the West is a "tripartite value" composed of "personal freedom," "sovereign freedom," and "civic freedom." The first refers to the capacity to do as one pleases in so far as one can within the limits imposed by the wishes and needs of others. (I would amend his definition by adding " . . . and the limits imposed by the bio-sphere.") The second sense of freedom is the capacity to do as one pleases regardless of those limits. The third is the capacity of adults to participate in the life and governance of a community. Free market ideology elevates "sovereign freedom" over "personal freedom" and "civic freedom" and truncates the latter two forms of freedom for many people.[52]

Whenever "free" or "freedom" is invoked, we ought ask, "Freedom from what, for whom or what, toward what end, and with what public accountability?" The freedom to deploy at the global level economic theories, policies, and practices that have served to concentrate wealth, pauperize millions, and jeopardize Earth's regenerative capacity might not qualify as freedom.

Healing a Broken World

Market Myth #3: We Are Homo Economicus, Consumens, et Dominans

The Claim

According to neo-classical economic theory, the human being is, above all, *homo economicus*. That is, human beings are essentially autonomous rational subjects rather than beings-in-community, competitive rather than cooperative, and consumeristic rather than spiritual. Humans act primarily to optimize self-interest. In economic life, people are motivated almost entirely by self-interest measured by personal financial gain and have the inalienable and divinely ordained right to pursue that self-interest. Individual autonomy is expressed most fully through acquisition and protection of private property. Rational thought is the highest form of humanness, and self-interested economic activity is the highest form of rationality, implying that other motives for economic behavior (such as other-directed activity) represent a lower level of activity. Those who own and consume the most are the most valued human beings.[53]

The validity of *homo economicus* as a descriptive account of humanity raises complex questions not addressed here.[54] The relevant point, for my purposes, is this: The *homo economicus* of neo-classical economic theory, far from being neutrally descriptive, became normative and morally formative. With it, Western culture "accepted and encouraged both the social choice of the modern era for economic growth and the choice to focus on and cultivate the wealth-maximizing motive as the most efficient means for achieving the goal of growth." "'Wealth maximizing' behavior became a powerful dimension not only of Western economics, but of Western culture, and is being exported around the world."[55]

In the late twentieth century, at least in the United States, *homo economicus* had assumed a hybrid form, *homo consumens*. The goal of economic globalization, economic growth, requires ever-increasing consumption. President George H. W. Bush blessed this hybrid by declaring an annual "national day of the consumer." Noted theorists argue that the driving force of advanced capitalism is not production but consumption.[56] The *Human Development Report 1998* reports that "world consumption has expanded at an unprecedented pace over the 20th century," although this figure "masks enormous disparities . . . that have widened inequalities."[57] According to this report, the money spent annually on pet food in North America and Europe would more than pay for basic education and installation of water and sanitation for all, worldwide, who now go without. The amount spent annually on perfume by North Americans and Europeans would nearly cover basic health care and adequate nutrition for all who lack. "As

[some] Americans grow more and more wealthy," asserts biblical scholar Walter Brueggemann, "money is becoming a kind of narcotic for us. We hardly notice our own prosperity or that of others. . . . Though many of us are well intentioned we have invested our lives in consumerism. . . . Consumerism is not simply a market strategy. It has become a demonic spiritual force among us."[58]

Critics of mainstream economic theory are quick to criticize *homo economicus*, but less quick to link "him" inextricably to *homo dominans*, whose home in Western culture is Christian theologies of human dominion over nature. In this theological perspective, the human being is the pinnacle of God's creation and by divine mandate has dominion over the rest of creation. The Earth exists for human use. Translated into political philosophy, one who uses the Earth's resources for private gain contributes to humanity.[59] Called into question in the latter part of this century by feminist, ecofeminist, and Earth-centered theologies, "theology of dominion remains the reigning one where it counts most, in *practice*. Social arrangements, especially, and the busy structures of economic life, in particular, still assume the tenets of mastery and live by them: earth exists for us."[60]

Deception and Distraction

To define the human as *homo economicus, consumens, et dominans* is to veil the social and ecological costs of that definition and to erase alternative moral anthropologies more likely to cultivate sustainable and just communities. Human worth is placed in relationship to buying power. Euro-Americans, controlling vastly more wealth and having more successfully dominated Earth's resources than people of color, are inherently more valuable and more fully human and therefore have more human rights—including the right to make decisions regarding the shape of economic and cultural life for all people. Euro-American men have even more rights and worth. Earth's other-than-human resources are commodities to be used for wealth creation and therefore belong to whoever can buy them.

Since people are defined by their economic transactions, and some people have only their bodies to sell (for labor or for sex), some people are commodities. Their bodies, like that of Rosa Galvez, are to be purchased at the lowest price the market will bear. (A pre-NAFTA ad encouraging corporations to locate plants in Mexico and Central America featured Rosa Galvez, who could be hired for fifty-four cents an hour. A year after NAFTA was enacted, the same ad featured Rosa at thirty-seven cents an hour.) Human life is a tool for expanding wealth in the global market, rather than the market a tool for sustaining life. This moral anthropology undergirds globalization and is exported around the globe. Unacknowledged in public discourse, the implications of this "way of perceiving" are obscured.

Healing a Broken World

Homo economicus et dominans, boldly harnessing nature's resources for wealth creation and optimizing utility before all else, is today a dangerous dehumanized agent. No less so is "his" hybrid, *homo consumens*, contributing to growth the world over by measuring quality of life by the power to waste. To normalize, naturalize, and universalize this moral anthropology is to reproduce human beings according to it. (Increasingly, advertising agencies are targeting the preschool population, reproducing *homo consumens* at a morally formative stage of life.) Where having the means to promote and engage in exorbitant consumption constitutes identity, there human passion, knowledge, wisdom, imagination, hope, and memory are dedicated to gaining those means. These integral ingredients of moral agency (as defined in chapter 2) are siphoned away from ways of being that seek the "pluralistic socio-ecological widespread good."

Market Myth #4: Corporate- and Finance-Driven Globalization Is Inevitable

The Claim

According to this presupposition, corporate- and finance-driven globalization is evolutionary, a contemporary form of manifest destiny, a step in modernity's march of progress. This form of global political economy is historically inevitable. It coheres with the laws of nature. As a natural and irresistible phenomenon, globalization is universally "normative." The prevailing model of globalization, then, is not seen as a historically contingent social construct but rather is presupposed in the same way that physical laws are presupposed. Globalization is humanity's beneficial and inevitable destiny. Societies must adjust to it or face the consequences.

The global "free" market economy operates according to economics as a positivist science, which presumes a positivist epistemology (way of knowing). Economic life is governed by laws of nature, as is the physical world. In David Ricardo's words, "the principle of gravitation is not more certain" than specific economic laws and their consequences.[61] Mathematically informed economic laws rationalizing globalization are presumed to be structures of reality and as such pertain universally. They are irrefutable and value-free, rather than morally laden human constructs. They explain and predict outcomes according to theories detached from actual historical contexts but do not interrogate the underlying premises of those theories. For example, the right to protect and increase private property without counting the social and ecological costs is presupposed as fundamentally human.

This presupposition of inevitability is evident in nineteenth- and twentieth-century discourse rationalizing the rise of corporate power in the United States; in late-twentieth-century century discourse hailing a triumph of capitalism over socialism; and in the claims of globalization's advocates.[62] As expressed by Francis Fukuyama, "the logic of modern natural science would seem to dictate a universal evolution in the direction of capitalism." Modern liberal democracy and capitalism are "the end point of mankind's [sic] ideological evolution, and the final form of human government, and as such . . . the end of history."[63]

This presupposition extends beyond the inevitability of the global free market economy to the inevitability and evolutionary nature of *society as free market*. In line with *homo economicus*, capitalism is not just an economic form but a way of being. Larry Rasmussen "maps the core logic" of the transition from capitalism as an economic form to capitalism as a way of life. Key for this transition is "that the moral order and culture are organized on the same principles as the economy and share its ethos. . . . All society and its decisions can be fashioned and executed in the manner economic actors do. . . . Rational self-interest is the one language everyone understands and ought to apply to decision and actions in every domain."[64] Rasmussen also cites Gary Becker: "Market principles are 'applicable to all human behavior.'"[65]

Deception and Distraction

Note first the theoretical deception. The move to understand the free market as a "way of life" appeals to Adam Smith. Yet Smith distrusted the morality of the market as a morality for society at large. He neither envisioned nor prescribed a capitalist *society*, but rather a "capitalist economy within society, a society held together by communities of noncapitalist and nonmarket morality."[66] That morality, for Smith, included—among other things—mutual neighborly love; an obligation to practice justice; a norm of financial support for the government "in proportion to [one's] revenue"; and a tendency in human nature to derive pleasure from the good fortune and happiness of other people.[67]

The assumed inevitability of globalization—understood either as economy or as a way of structuring society—undermines a condition necessary for moral agency to resist and seek change. That condition is the perception that a given social structure—in this case the global free market—is the product of human decisions, a historically contingent construct not necessarily normative universally. As a historical phenomenon, this form of globalization is not inevitable and irresistible but rather is responsive to human agency. That is, in principle, globalization can be resisted, subverted, or changed.

If globalization is inevitable and natural, the possibility of legitimate and viable alternatives is undermined. As described by McMurtry, when the prescriptions of the global free market are conceived "as natural necessity . . . any opposition or attempted alternative to this necessary truth is . . . attacked." To confuse social norms and power structures with inevitable laws of nature is to "absolutize a social structure as the proper order of the cosmos . . . [and] claim its universal authority for all peoples and societies on the planet."[68] This dynamic is as old as history. New, with the globalizing economy, is the power to enforce it. The global free market is "declared inevitable. . . . Societies that dare to evade its stern requirements are threatened with 'harsh punishments' and 'shock treatments.' Ordinary people everywhere are required to make 'necessary sacrifices' to its demands."[69]

Classical Liberalism:
Roots of Global Free Market Ideology

These four theoretical and ideological underpinnings of globalization did not appear out of nowhere. They are key elements of classical liberalism carried to the extreme.[70] Classical liberalism, developing out of the Enlightenment, became dominant in the Anglo-American world by the late eighteenth and nineteenth centuries and has evolved since that time. It has shaped modern Western culture. Elements of classical liberalism include an anthropology, a political philosophy, an economic philosophy, and an epistemology. These elements revolve around concepts of a Newtonian mechanistic universe, a Cartesian rational man, the inevitable progress of human history, the perfectibility of the human, and individual autonomy as freedom.

The epistemology, not fully addressed in this chapter, warrants brief summary here. Liberalism upholds a positivist notion of knowing: empirical disinterested methods of inquiry assure universal truth, and human reason may be free from bias. Reason, according to mathematical principles, is the only path to valid knowing. All systems—including economic systems—correspond to the notion of a universe functioning according to discoverable rules.

I am not, in this project, joining the ubiquitous postmodern critique of the Enlightenment project per se. Rather, I am examining specific assumptions of classical liberalism that underlie globalization and disable agency. To the extent that those assumptions are rooted in Enlightenment anthropology, political and economic philosophy, and epistemology, this project critiques them. My critique, however, presupposes a resounding affirmation that classical liberalism also has produced concepts and presuppositions that undergird the very subversive agency for which I am calling. Most notable is the premise that—at least theoretically—all human beings have rights based upon their humanity.[71]

The following brief effort to historicize neo-liberal ideology in classical liberalism is a broad stroke. It is neither possible nor necessary here to do justice to the diverse trajectories and changing forms of classical liberalism as it has developed over nearly three centuries. The grounding of human freedom in private property is attributed to political philosopher John Locke, who wrote *Second Treatise of Government* in 1690. In the West, it is the founding rationale for the God-given right to private property and to its protection by law and public force. In *The Wealth of Nations,* Adam Smith (1723–1790) wed Locke's principle of the sacred and absolute right of private property to Smith's own two central ideas that (1) increase in wealth—through growth in the production of goods and their free market exchange—is the purpose of economic activity, and (2) the self-interested pursuit of profit, channeled by the free market mechanism, promotes the widespread good. Smith's treatise became the economic creed of classical liberalism and is claimed as the theoretical basis of neo-liberalism's presupposition that "growth benefits all" in today's globalizing economy.

Nineteenth-century philosopher John Stuart Mill theorized "'man' as the self-interested wealth maximizer." Mill's work built on Adam Smith's two cardinal ideas and on John Locke's sacred right of private property. According to Mill, political economy is concerned with "man . . . solely as a being who desires to possess wealth, and who is capable of judging the comparative efficacy of means for obtaining that end."[72] Moral considerations fall outside the model. The anthropology of classical liberalism, in general terms, held the human being to be an autonomous rational actor with divinely ordained freedom to pursue self-interest. Anything that obstructed this freedom was suspect.

The marginalists (a group of European economists whose work began to take hold in the 1870s) "set out to make economics as much like a science as possible—particularly like Newtonian physics," which posited "nature composed not of inherently related entities but of independent entities . . . related through such external 'laws of nature' as gravity."[73] The laws governing economic life were considered as mechanistic, rational, universal, and irrefutable as those governing mathematics and physics. Economics became an explicitly neutral or value-free science, predicting outcomes, but not rendering moral judgments. With the marginalists, economic theory moved from being concerned, in the work of Adam Smith, with how the wealth of nations is increased, to focusing on "maximizing individual pleasure in consumer goods."[74] (Mill's "wealth-maximizer" became "utility-maximizer." "On the production side . . . utility-maximization . . . is, in a word, profit-making; on the consumption side, it is 'getting the most for one's money.'")[75]

Marginalist analysis "makes individual choice the center of economic theory."[76] Individual freedom—the freedom of a person to maximize pleasure in consumption and to maximize profit—became the focal point of mainstream contemporary economic theory, known as neo-classical economics.

In the twentieth century and continuing into the twenty-first, two versions of freedom operating within the same neo-classical economic framework have structured the political-economic debate in the United States. Laissez-faire liberalism, as represented by the Chicago school of economics and its most historically visible player, Milton Friedman (born 1912), understands freedom of the individual (or possibly of the household) to be the ultimate goal. Freedom is autonomy to pursue economic self-interest. Anything obstructing that freedom, especially governmental intervention, is suspect. Social equity liberalism, represented in the work of economist John Maynard Keynes (1883–1946), maintains a tension between unmitigated freedom of economic choice and political equality. Both versions uncritically uphold a framework in which freedom is defined by individual autonomy to pursue self-interest and the goal of the economy is unrestrained growth.

Disabling Moral Agency

Moral agency, as defined in this project, is understood as the power to embody active love for creation including self, others, and non-human creation. Moral agency suggests the power to orient life around the ongoing well-being of communities and of the Earth community, prioritizing the needs of the most vulnerable. Moral agency is the power to live toward social structures, relationships, policies, and lifestyles that build communities characterized by ecological sustainability and social justice.

As I pointed out in the previous chapter, feminist, womanist, and eco-feminist thought contributes to this working concept of moral agency in at least the following four ways. Practices of daily life shape moral agency. The power to "embody love for creation" is not the purview of isolated individuals but rather is formed and sustained in relationship. Human agents are part of a larger-than-human community of life. Vision, memory, imagination, and hope are integral to moral agency. In other words, our practices of daily life; whether or not we know ourselves to be beings-in-relationship; whether or not we locate ourselves in communities that extend beyond the human; and what we see, remember, imagine as possible, and hope are strong determinants of moral agency.

We have examined powerful and inextricably linked "market myths" that rationalize the prevailing paradigm of globalization. It remains, then, to consider how the identified deceptions and distractions of each myth, working in concert, sustain a worldview that undermines the moral agency required to resist globalization and imagine and realize alternatives to it.

Free market ideology naturalizes, normalizes, and universalizes the human being as autonomous individual wealth maximizer and consumer, whose worth depends upon control of capital. Human beings possess divinely sanctioned freedom to choose between products, to consume, and to accumulate wealth, all relatively free from limit or constraint. Earth's resources, including people who have nothing but their bodies to exchange on the market, are commodities to be purchased by those with buying power in order to increase wealth. Humans are not accountable to earthly community beyond human community.

The construction of the human as *homo consumens*, of freedom as market freedom, of economic growth as the key to economic well-being for all, and of globalization as inevitable implies a *telos* (ultimate end) of human activity: economic growth fueled by consumption. The social good to be promoted by human activity is economic growth fueled by ever-increasing consumption. Rather than directing economic activity toward other social goods (for example, sustainable communities and social justice), we are directed to keep the economy growing by consuming. The social and ecological costs of that consumption are relatively irrelevant. The "constant and unshakeable ideological message conveyed is 'Consume!'"[77] The capacity to perceive consequences of globalization, the nature of human being and freedom, alternative economic models, and the purpose of economic life in terms that contradict free market ideology is diminished. Questions fundamental to the Christian moral-spiritual life—who are we and how are we to live in relationship with other people and the broader Earth community?—are answered.

What social dynamics grant an ideology this power? In *Unequal Freedoms,* John McMurtry exposes two defining features of a society in which an ideology gains power to shape social life according to its mores, even when that entails ongoing sacrifice and subjugation of life by destruction, minimalization, or commodification. I interpret these features as social dynamics by which a particular humanly constructed ideology—global free market ideology—with devastating consequences (including the corrosion of democracy) has become accepted as natural, normal, and universal, and thus unresponsive to moral agency. In other words, these social dynamics illumine how ideology may undercut moral agency. I add a third dynamic.

One defining feature of a society in which an ideology has become sovereign is "blind[ness] to the harm [it] causes" (23). Society refuses to recognize destructive consequences or anything that calls into question the norms and practices mandated by the ideology. Destructive consequences are ignored or considered inconsequential, unavoidable, or the fault of those who are harmed. Thus, for example, according to neo-liberal ideology, the increasing poverty of the very poor is inevitable because of their failings, or is necessary for the greater good. People of relative economic privilege are conditioned "into not seeing what is there—for example, not seeing the suffering of the jobless or of families who do not have enough food to eat, even if they number in the millions of our fellow citizens" (41). McMurtry points out a result of this blindness: "This tendency not to see seems to increase the more what is not seen contradicts the accepted view that no alternative exists to the status quo" (41). Perhaps this is the most dramatic impact of market ideology. It seeks to erase the boundless suffering of those whose lives or dignity are sacrificed—historically, today, or tomorrow—to the demands of the globalizing economy. The role of vision and memory in moral agency is called to the fore.

Secondly, McMurtry argues, where an ideology is sovereign, it is sustained by uncritical "identification of its demands with the public good" (22) and with the laws of nature. People "enact its prescriptions and functions as presupposed norms," (6) seen as more basic than values or ethical standards, as irrefutable as physical laws.[78] The ideology and the ways of life it mandates are not understood to be human constructs but rather are "presupposed as the structure of being" (15). People internalize the "structure of thinking by habitual repetition, allowing for no question, alternative, or critical exposure" (6). Alternatives are deemed inappropriate, unrealistic, unworkable, or contrary to the public good, and critics are stigmatized. The practices of daily life, uncritically accepted as "the way things are," reinscribe the ideology, and "deviant imagination" is subdued. The feminist insistence that practice and imagination shape moral agency is called to the fore. Worldview shapes practice; practice shapes what we become and what we imagine; who we are and what we imagine shapes worldview; and so on.

To McMurtry's two social dynamics, I add a fateful third.[79] Transgressive choice becomes impossible, either perceived of as impossible or actually impossible. That is, it becomes impossible to choose lifestyles and political-economic policies and structures that transgress the dictates of the global free market ideology. Market freedom allows us to choose between multiple kinds of breakfast cereal that provide no nourishment for the body, but does not allow us to choose ways of living that do no serious damage to the Earth or to the people producing the food, clothing, and other products we consume. The extent to which that powerlessness is perceived or actual is not the point here. It is assumed and hence effectively undermines moral agency.

Walter Brueggemann illumines the role of ideology in suppressing vision, imagination, and deviant choice, and the consequences for moral agency. He suggests that the ideology of global capitalism maintains hegemony in much the same way that centers of power critiqued in the Hebrew Bible did, by maintaining "a monopoly on imagination," and "a vision of reality." In his paper, "The Scandal and Liberty of Particularity," he points to the prophetic critique of Tyre as "the epicenter of a world economy that features opulence, self-indulgence and general social disregard."[80] "On the whole these concentrations of power tolerated little deviation in matters of importance to them. To ensure compliance, moreover, the political-economic-military power of hegemony is matched, characteristically, with imperial myths . . . which legitimated power realities . . . [and] maintained . . . a monopoly of imagination" (2). "I submit that in our time and place the hegemonic power of international corporate capitalism . . . creates a totalizing environment that imposes its values, its field of images, its limits of vision on all comers" (4). Brueggemann goes on to assert that our dearth of moral agency in the context of this totalizing environment is not unlike that of ancient Israel, which was "deeply perplexed about how to sustain any vision or practice of life that is not swept away by the force of hegemony" (5). "The ideology devoted to encouraging consumption wants to shrivel our imaginations so that we cannot conceive of living in ways that would be less profitable for the dominant corporate structures."[81]

What happens to moral agency when we nurture blindness, contort our vision and memories, stifle our imagination and hope, and ignore portions of our identity, including Christian identity? We acquiesce, rather than resist. To the extent that our memory, vision, imagination, practice, and identity adjust to reality as constructed by neo-liberal ideology, the structures of our economic life conform to the mandates of this reality. Not only is globalization taken for granted, but the practices of daily life mandated by it are taken for granted, are accepted as largely untranscendable. It seems not strange, then, that people of relative economic privilege in the United States—though they be compassionate and caring—agree to play soccer with balls made by child laborers; wear clothes made in sweatshops; eat strawberries grown on land that should grow beans and corn for its hungry children; buy stock in companies that dump toxic wastes in communities of color, devastate Philippine communities by deforesting their lands, and force subsistence farmers in India to buy seeds that will not reseed; and perpetuate an orgy of consumption that endangers Earth's capacity to sustain life.

Market myths orient crucial determinants of moral agency (noted above) around serving the global free market. These myths function as blinders, erasing or minimizing the dangers globalization presents, historical resistance struggles, and just and sustainable alternatives. The capacity to see "what could be" is crippled by inability to see "what is" and "what has been," and the passion for justice is squelched before it is born. Exposing the illusions is a step toward gaining moral agency. As Rosa Luxemburg, quoting

       Healing a Broken World

Lassalle, declared, "The most revolutionary act is and continues to be, always to say out loud, what is."[82]

The deepest spiritual-moral crisis of globalization is the disabling of our ability to know and to practice who we are called and empowered by God to be: beings-in-community-of-life, crafting ways of life that enable the Earth and its inhabitants to flourish. The God-given, grace-filled moral agency to live this way is obscured from our vision and memory and is lost from our practice.

Tenaciously pursuing powerful dynamics that seduce people of economic privilege into complicity with economic brutality is dangerous. Subtly and insidiously, that pursuit can breed despair, denial, and retreat into privatized morality, unless accompanied by hope. Hope, that is, for the agency to live otherwise.

To that hope we now turn. Faith stories that provide a "home" for people of Christian traditions offer stunning and startling promises. They are the ingredients of hope. God's gracious and mysterious love for the world and for each of us cannot be extinguished. So speaks the resurrection. That love assumes bodily form. So speaks the incarnation. God's power and presence, seeking the healing and liberation of all, is breathed into us. We are empowered to be body of Christ on Earth, to move toward living as we are called to live: loving "neighbor as self," seeking healing and liberation for self, others, and other kind.

How then are we to know and claim this power? Grappling with this question has been the work of countless people over millennia. In the remainder of this book, I do so in a contemporary context, asking, "How may this God-power be realized by economically privileged North American Christians to move us from complicity to faithful resistance and revisioning?" For insight, we journey into the theo-ethical terrain of Martin Luther in dialogue with contemporary feminist theologians and ethicists.

Part Two

The Indwelling God:
Enabling Subversive Moral Agency

4

Martin Luther:
Earth's Creatures "Filled to the Utmost with God"

∾

Those who eat my flesh and drink my blood abide in me and I in them.
— John 6:56

In Hebrew the word 'abide' denotes 'to remain' or 'to dwell' in a person. . . .
Now this is a precious dwelling place and something to glory in, that through
faith in Christ and through our eating, we . . . have Christ abiding in us with
[Her] might, power, strength, righteousness, and wisdom.
— Martin Luther

The Word of God, whenever it comes, comes to change and renew the world.
— Martin Luther

HERE WE EXPLORE the interplay between subversive moral agency and relationship with the indwelling God as seen in selected writings of Martin Luther.[1] I respond to two questions, emphasizing primarily the former. First, "In what ways did relationship with the immanent God, for Luther, issue in ways of being and doing that unmasked and undermined structures and ideologies of domination?" Asked differently, "In his context, in what ways did that relationship generate faithful moral agency in the face of systemic domination?" Secondly, "In the case of Luther, what ideological factors limited this subversive moral agency?" Before engaging these questions, I establish my premise that, for Luther, Christ indwelling communities of the faithful is a foundation of Christian moral life.

The working concepts of "moral agency" and of "subversive" previously established are central here. Bear them in mind, as well as the earlier discussion of "we" and "us." Recall also why, among many possible historical figures who could have resourced this inquiry, I turned to Luther. Those reasons are discussed in the introduction and the appendix.[2] Finally, hold in mind the purpose of this engagement with him: to seek insight for the enlivening of subversive moral agency in the contemporary context of globalization.[3]

Indwelling Christ: A Center of Luther's Ethics

Luther's ethics may be seen as revolving around any of three different centerpieces. For Luther, one of these is the "indwelling Christ." Two others are "the holy orders of society" and "the freedom of a Christian." All are built upon Luther's conviction that justification is by grace alone through faith alone on account of Christ.[4] My purpose here is neither to weigh the relative significance of these three, nor to tease out the interplay between them, but rather to establish my premise that "Christ indwelling" is a viable centerpiece of Luther's ethics.

Luther appeals to the indwelling Christ as wellspring of Christian moral life. Christ indwelling is the locus of moral identity, purpose, vision, norms, and agency. The centerpiece of Christian moral agency is the crucified and living Christ dwelling in and gradually transforming the community of believers, the form of Jesus Christ taking form in and among those with faith. Christians as objects of Christ's love become subjects of that love. Faith is both "faith *in* Christ" and "faith *of* Christ." The indwelling Christ, mediated by practices of the Christian community, transforms the faithful toward a manner of life that actively loves neighbor. The moral life is simultaneously gift and imperative, a mystical as well as physical reality, ontologically (fundamentally) communal while also individual, a necessary outflow of the sacraments, and a dimension of Christian life without which salvation is not present.[5] Union with Christ renders justification inseparable from the moral life.

I locate "moral agency as indwelling Christ" within Luther's doctrine of salvation for reasons that should become evident. Thus, my understanding of Luther's ethics presupposes my interpretation of his soteriology (theology of salvation). While space limitations disallow a thorough account of that interpretation, my premise requires a glance at three dimensions of Luther's soteriology most integral to his ethics. They are a role of Christ, what happens to people when they are made righteous, and the relationship of works to salvation. We consider each in turn, and then move to consider the implications for moral agency.

A Role of Christ

Four roles of Christ in salvation are evident in Luther's teachings:[6]

- *Christ the redeemer/ liberator,* who gave his life on the cross as gracious gift to save us from sin, death, the devil, hell, and all evil.[7] As such Christ crucified and risen is both *Christus* victor over the devil, liberating us from the devil's dominion unto Christ's dominion, and *Christus* victim or lamb of God, who paid for our sins with his blood.

- *Christ the mediator, intercessor.*[8]

- *Christ the exemplar* especially of self-giving servant who seeks the welfare of others.[9] For Luther, Christ serves as example only after one has received him as one's own, that is, after one has come to faith in him.[10]

- *Christ who dwells in us, in whom we dwell, with whom we are united, and who transforms us.*[11]

It must be understood that "Christian moral life as indwelling Christ" presupposes all and contradicts none of the aforementioned roles, yet it draws primarily from the fourth, in which Christ is not only object of faith but also active agent of faith.

Nuanced differently in various works, this role is evident both in theological treatises and in sermons.[12] Luther indicates four related aspects of what I refer to as "the indwelling Christ." They are Christ dwelling in the faithful, Christ transforming the faithful into servant of all, Christ rendering union and communion among the faithful, and Christ rendering the faithful "divine" or "partaker in the divine." All involve the Holy Spirit.

The following excerpts from sermons and treatises, read together, reveal these aspects of the indwelling Christ. "[T]his is . . . one of the exceedingly great promises granted to us poor miserable sinners, that we should become partakers of the divine nature, and should be so highly honored as not only to be loved by God through Jesus Christ . . . but should even have the Lord Himself dwelling completely in us."[13] Regarding one in whom God dwells, Luther says: He "makes daily progress in life and good works . . . is useful to God and man; through him . . . men and countries benefit . . . such a man's words, life and doings are God's."[14] Likewise, "'Filled unto all the fullness of God means . . . full of God . . . adorned with his grace and the gifts of his Spirit . . . who illuminates us with his light, lives within us, saves us with his salvation, and enkindles love within us . . . having God and all his blessings dwelling in us in fullness and being effective to make us wholly divine."[15] "For through faith Christ is in us, indeed, one with us."[16] Through Christ's love, "we are to be changed and to make the infirmities of all other Christians our own; we are to take upon ourselves their form and their necessity, and all the good that is within our power we are to make theirs, that they may profit from it. . . . We are changed into one another and are made into a community by love."[17] "Christians are indeed called and made the habitation of God, and in them God speaks, and rules, and works."[18]

Isolating a single term or concept by which to signify this multidimensional notion in Luther's theology is difficult. "Indwelling Christ," "union with Christ," "Christ mysticism," and a nuanced understanding of *theosis* (participation in God) all capture a portion of the significance for Luther. Some Luther scholars at the University of Helsinki use the term *union with Christ*.[19] My reading of Luther leads me to lean on *indwelling Christ* as the term best conveying the implications of Luther's conviction that Godself in the form of Christ is given by God to indwell and transform the faithful, and to create communion and union of love and service among them. In order to remind the reader of the notion's multidimensional nature, I occasionally use *union with Christ* interchangeably with *indwelling Christ*.[20]

It is crucial to note that—without exception in Luther's writing—union with Christ is on the level not of *similitude* but of *dissimilitude* and is realized not by human effort but only by God's gift. Herein lies Luther's radical departure from medieval theology. As Reformation historian Stephen Ozment explains, Luther assailed the fundamental axiom of medieval theology: the conviction that "likeness" to God is the sine qua non for union with God, and hence for salvation.[21] Likeness was achievable by human effort and was the indispensable condition for salvation. This principle underlaid monastic practice, mysticism, and the sacramental system of the church. Saving faith was formed by sacramentally infused grace in concert with human effort toward godliness or perfection.[22] Luther absolutely rejected this move toward similitude between creature and creator on the basis of creaturely effort as the basis of salvation.

However, I disagree with a commonly assumed assessment of the crucial point at which Luther departs from this axiom of medieval theology. That assumption holds that Luther's departure point was in his belief that "God became human so that humans need not become divine." To the contrary, I find Luther, in some writings, indicating that—by the work of the indwelling Christ and the Holy Spirit—Christians *are* becoming divine or partakers in the divine. He writes: "God becomes man so that man may become God."[23] Luther does not oppose the notion that "God becomes human so that humans may become God." Rather, he diametrically opposes five assumptions, integral to medieval theology, regarding human beings "becoming divine." They are as follows.

1. Regarding cause and effect: We become partakers in the divine not as *cause* of salvation but as *effect* inherent in salvation.

2. Regarding how we become divine: A number of points are crucial. First, it is not achieved through our effort or perfection, but rather through God's gracious gift of Godself to dwell in the Christian through faith and to transform the Christian by love into love in Christ's form. Secondly, the believer is united with God through dissimilitude; the union of the holy and

the unholy renders the *unholy* holy. Christ unites with sinners. "This is the love of the cross, born of the cross, which turns in the direction where it does not find good which it may enjoy but where it may confer good upon the bad and needy person."[24] Next, moral transformation as "union with Christ" is gift, as opposed either to obligation or to reward. Though Luther occasionally employs language of obligation with reference to the moral life, far more often he speaks the language of gift, and never does he speak of the Christian moral life as reward. Fourthly, Christ may be received only after the person has utterly despaired of his or her own ability to justify self.[25] The next key point is that divinization does not occur by *ascent* toward heaven. Luther preaches, "Much has been written about the way we are to become godlike. Some have constructed ladders whereby we are to ascend to heaven, and others similar things. But this is all patchwork. . . . The truest way to attain godlikeness . . . is to become filled to the utmost with God, lacking no particular; to be completely permeated with him until every word, thought and deed, the whole life in fact, be utterly godly."[26] As Larry Rasmussen, a Lutheran ethicist, points out, Luther "emphatically turns back Augustine's contention that Christ descended to help us ascend. . . . The prevalent view that 'the intellectual journey to truth and the moral journey to goodness is one with the journey from bodily beings to disembodied Being' simply goes by the boards" in Luther.[27] Finally, Luther insists that becoming divine never is fully completed in this lifetime. "Christians are indeed called and made the habitation of God, and in them God speaks, and rules, and works. But the work is not yet complete; it is an edifice on which God yet works daily and makes arrangements."[28] This is key and brings us full circle to the first point. Christ does not make the faithful Christ's abode *because* they have been transformed or otherwise have earned Christ's presence. Quite the opposite. The faithful are gradually transformed *by God's grace alone,* which includes the gift of Christ making habitation in and with them. About this Luther is explicit and vehement.

3. Regarding what it means to become divine: It does not mean to strive after the invisible things of God ("virtue, godliness, wisdom, justice, goodness")[29] by our own power and as our own. This would be wrong both because it usurps for oneself what is God's alone, and because it is not Christlike; as Christ relinquished that form to God the "Father," becoming among us simply servant of all, so are we to do.[30] To become divine is to become bearer of Christ, the power of redemptive love; it is to become "habitation" of the one who seeks the well-being of others in love.[31]

4. Regarding what happens to our humanity: In conforming to the form of Christ, we do not leave behind our humanity, our earthliness, our creaturehood. Divinization as understood by Luther did not entail freedom *from* creatureliness, but freedom *for* it. We do not cast aside earthly fetters. As

Lutheran theologian Kristen Kvam notes, Luther's doctrine of creation teaches that "God's original intention for human persons was neither that we flee from our bodies nor that we rise above them. Instead, God intended for human persons to honor—even enjoy—their embodied lives. . . . Luther incorporates embodiment of physical capacities into his understanding of the *imago dei*."[32] It is as finite creatures that we bear the infinite. For Luther, as for Irenaeus before him and Bonhoeffer after, we are Earth creatures bound to the gift of God's good Earth. Ceasing to strive for godlikeness and instead receiving the transformation inherent in justification, we are saved unto what we were intended to be: fully *human* and finite beings on Earth, humans in communion through union with Christ, humans as Earth creatures assuming the form of Christ, the servant of all. That Christ has come to dwell in, to be, and to serve humanity elevates the faithful as *human* beings to lord and servant of all.

5. Regarding our goal: Union with Christ, as a goal, would be a manifestation of sin. We are not to seek our divinity, own goodness, servanthood, Christlikeness. We are rather to seek right relationships and by so doing we become Christlike.

People Made Righteous

When made righteous, people are first given a radically different relationship with God, and then a radically different relationship with other people. These two gifts correspond to the two inseparable "principles of Christian doctrine."[33] What is entailed in these two gifts? We look to two of Luther's essays, "Two Kinds of Righteousness" and "The Disputation concerning Justification."

The "first kind of righteousness" places us in a radically different relationship with God; we are totally forgiven and become righteous in God's sight. This occurs by the grace of God alone through faith alone on account of Christ.[34] Luther insists in "Two Kinds of Righteousness" that we receive—*not earn*—two kinds of righteousness. "The first is alien righteousness," the righteousness of God in the righteousness of Christ. "Instilled from without . . . [it is] given to men in baptism and whenever they are repentant."[35]

After this first gift, we are placed in radically different relationship with other people by the "second kind of righteousness . . . our proper righteousness" (157) which is the "product . . . fruit and consequence" of the first (158). The second kind of righteousness is in essence "that manner of life spent profitably in good works." (157). Luther goes on to define the moral life in terms of relationality in three spheres: "living soberly with self, justly with neighbor, and devoutly toward God" (158). Our proper right-eousness "does not seek its own good, but that of another, and in this its whole way of living consists. . . . This righteousness follows the example of Christ in this respect (1 Pet. 2:21) and is transformed into his likeness (2 Cor. 3:18). It is precisely this that Christ requires" (158). Luther's "Disputation concerning Justification" reiterates the two kinds of righteous-ness, their cause-effect relationship, and love as the essence of the second kind.[36]

Luther's understanding of justification is, thus, transformative.[37] Justified sinners gradually are changed—individually but only in community—by the gratuitous righteousness of Christ. They are transformed into people who increasingly seek the well-being of others. They are in fact "made one with all others" by union with Christ.[38] The radical implications for economic life will become evident shortly.

Luther's notion of justification as transformation does not contradict the centrality of sin in his theology. The terrible and condemning reality of sin as constituent of human being is key in Luther's theology, including his the-ology of the indwelling Christ.[39] Luther understands sin as *se incurvatus in se* (self turned in upon self), the human proclivity to do everything for the promotion of self, out of concern for self, and using resources claimed as one's own rather than as gifts of God. "Man is so self-centered that he uses not only the physical but also spiritual gifts for his own advantage and seeks his own advantage at every opportunity."[40] Sin is thus fundamentally unfaith—failing to trust God for all and to attribute all to God. Sin as unfaith is rooted in the "inmost heart" and is in the nature of fallen human-ity.[41] "Our weakness lies not in our works but in our nature; our person, nature and entire being are corrupted through Adam's fall."[42] Luther argues (against the Aristotelian theological tradition, which held discipline as a morally significant counteractive to the condition of sin) that this condition is absolutely inescapable by human effort. Human beings are bound to this condition of sin, cannot make their way out of it. Humans can be freed from this condition only by God, as undeserved gift from God. God can grasp and turn the sinner. Thus the terrible pervasiveness and inescapability of sin is linked to the incredible beauty and power of grace. Luther claims that fail-ure to acknowledge the gravity of sin is failure to know the truth about Christ.[43] Luther's doctrine of sin is consistent with his notion of moral life as indwelling Christ. I will argue that, in Luther's theology, it is the power of the indwelling Christ and Spirit that "turns" sinners from *se incurvatus in se,* empowering them gradually, although never perfectly, to love with the actual love of Christ within.

Justification as transformation is *not* justification as moral perfection, now or ever in earthly life. Luther's notion of immense and increasing human moral agency grounded in the indwelling Christ is accompanied by no illusions of human perfectibility. Christians remain simultaneously sinners and righteous. They are "rusty tools" being polished by God for as long as they live.[44] Luther teaches and preaches that the "polishing," to a significant extent, is the indwelling Christ and Spirit building human creatures into earthy and earthly "habitation of God," with the moral power that identity implies.

The Relationship of Works to Salvation

Luther's understanding of what happens to people when they are made righteous by God coheres with his central convictions regarding the relationship of works to salvation: works do not cause salvation, but they necessarily follow from salvation. This claim refutes medieval morality; human works become meaningless in the sense in which they had been known, as meritorious for salvation. Luther's claim regarding the relationship between works and salvation, which does not lend itself to systematic formulation, is seen in the following excerpts from sermons and treatises.

In his essay "Disputation concerning Justification," Luther writes:

> Works are necessary to salvation, but they do not cause salvation, because faith alone gives life. . . . Works save outwardly, that is they show evidence that we are righteous;
>
> Works only reveal faith . . . show that we have been justified . . . indicate whether I have faith. . . . Those who . . . do not show this faith by such works . . . are not Christians at all;
>
> I believe in Christ and afterward I do truly good works in Christ.[45]

Concerning thesis 25 of the "Heidelberg Disputation," he argues:

> Not that the righteous person does nothing, but that his works do not make him righteous, rather that his righteousness creates works. For grace and faith are infused without works. After they have been imparted the works follow. . . . In other words, works contribute nothing to justification. . . . The works which he does by faith are not his but God's. . . . Christ is his wisdom, righteousness, . . . that he himself may be Christ's action and instrument.[46]

Luther expresses in a lecture on Genesis that "Faith is followed by works as a body is followed by its shadow."[47] In "The Freedom of a Christian" he clarifies that "faith in Christ does not free us from works but from false opinions concerning works, that is from the foolish presumption that justification is acquired by works."[48] Luther writes in his "Sermon on the 4th Sunday after Epiphany:" "God makes love to our neighbor an obligation equal to love to himself."[49] In "The Sacrament of the Body and Blood of Christ—Against Fanatics" Luther identifies "two principles of Christian doctrine." The first principle is that Christ gave himself that we may be saved, and we are saved by no effort of our own. The second "is love . . . as he gives himself for us . . . so we too are to give ourselves with might and main for our neighbor." Luther insists on the inseparability of the two: they are "inscribed together as on a tablet which is always before our eyes and which we use daily."[50]

His identification of these as the "two principles of Christian doctrine" and his characterization of them as inseparable sum up Luther's construction of the relationship between salvation and works. Justification by God is inseparable from a "manner of life spent . . . in good works," seeking the well-being of the neighbor without "distinguish[ing] between friends and enemies."[51] Shortly, we will see that, according to Luther, this "way of living" entails not only loving service, but also denouncing economic injustice and the autonomy of capital from political constraints; ensuring education for poor children; creating jobs for the unemployed; refusing to charge what the market will bear when selling products, if so doing jeopardizes others' well-being; and other radical economic proposals.

These references to the necessity of works *in* salvation (not *for* salvation) do not contradict Luther's bottom line and consistent polemic against the scholastics and the Church of Rome: one is not justified by one's love or by any form of work either before or after justification. Grace, including Christ's indwelling presence, is not given as reward for human effort; it is a free gift given to sinners. Human beings can, in no way, contribute to their salvation.

Three Dimensions of Luther's Soteriology

We have viewed three dimensions of Luther's soteriology in light of—and as required by—an inquiry into the indwelling Christ as wellspring of Christian moral life. This brief glance reveals a rich weave of multiple strands. Luther's understanding of salvation cannot be reduced to a single phrase or concept. Justification by grace through faith is central. However, an exclusively forensic view of God's saving relationship to humanity obscures other aspects of that relationship such as union with Christ, its fruit of moral change, and Luther's "second principle of Christian faith." To obscure these is to miss crucial moral agency consequences of justification and is to sever key links between justification and justice.

Occasionally, internal contradictions appear in Luther's soteriology, although the various strands are usually complementary. The multiplicity of strands and the presence of some internal contradictions are two different matters. Both, however, are due to the same factors. They include theological complexity in Luther's understanding of what it means to be saved; the fact that his teachings were addressed to varied audiences in response to varied issues and opponents; development of his theology and theological task over a span of decades; and the fact that he wrote in both German and Latin. Luther neither renders his soteriological claims in systematic form nor claims to do so.

The complexity of Luther's soteriology does not detract from the main findings of this inquiry into three related dimensions of it. According to Luther, in making people righteous, Christ as gift comes to dwell in them. Union with Christ puts believers on a path of transformation, never completed and not always forward-moving. The shape of that transformed and transforming life is the shape of Christian moral life and the shape of Christ's love. Believers—as Earth creatures—are first objects and then also agents of that love. Agency to live toward the well-being of self and others indwells believers as Christself. The centerpiece of Christian moral life is the crucified and living Christ dwelling in and gradually changing the community of believers.

Indwelling Christ as Source of Subversive Moral Agency

In what sense did relationship with the indwelling Christ, as known and theologized by Luther, issue in ways of being and doing that unmasked and undermined structures and ideologies of domination? In what ways did that relationship generate moral agency and, in particular, subversive moral agency in the face of systemic domination in Luther's context?[52]

We unravel this inquiry step-by-step, keeping in the background the two sets of dynamics, uncovered in the first three chapters, whereby neo-liberal globalization disables the moral agency required to resist it and to forge alternatives. The process here is structured by the following questions:

- As seen in selected treatises and sermons, and in Luther's "practice," what moral anthropology, notion of freedom, and *telos* (end) of human activity issue from the indwelling Christ, and what are the implications for moral agency?

- What processes and powers gradually transform the faithful into a dwelling place of Christ and empower them to become ever more fully agents of Christ's love? How do these processes and powers shape moral agency?

- How does the "indwelling Christ as source of moral agency" play out in actual practices of everyday life, and particularly in economic life?

- In what sense is this moral agency "subversive"?

- How are the gifts of Christ's indwelling and transforming presence, and of the resulting radical neighbor-love, mediated? That is, how are these gifts received and realized? What are the implications for moral agency?

We consider each question in turn.

What moral anthropology, and telos *of human activity, and notion of freedom, issue from the indwelling Christ, and what are the implications for moral agency?*

Luther's sense of the indwelling Christ as locus of the moral life issued in a particular sense of who Christians are in relationship to God and to other human beings. Who Christ is—according to the incarnation and the cross—determines who we are. First, we are a dwelling place of a God who has taken the form of the human body. We are filled with a Christ of flesh and blood, an incarnate God. The finite bears the infinite. We are saved by a God who was and is body. Luther's doctrines of creation and of vocation in themselves challenge medieval morality's negative valuation of bodily earthly life. That Christ dwells in flesh and blood and in the stones, fire, water, seeds, bread, and wine of this Earth[53] utterly overturns that negative valuation. As Lutheran theologian Walter Altmann points out, in the medieval context to be holy was to be dissociated from the world, and especially from bodily aspects of the world.[54] For Luther the holy is intimately associated with Earth and body, for they bear the divine. Thus are established his norms against medieval morality's dissociation of the earthly material dimensions of life from the religious, and against elevating the latter as morally more significant than the former.[55] The practical implications in Luther's day were vast. For example: asexual life was dethroned from its position of moral superiority over sexual life, and mundane physical tasks done in faith (for example, farming, cleaning diapers, nourishing one's body) were rendered as morally significant as the "spiritual" activities considered by medieval theology to be of higher moral worth.[56] Luther's doctrines of creation and vocation suggest that to negate embodied earthly life by trying to rise above it is sin for three reasons. First, so doing negates the goodness of creation. Second, it leads to self-glorification. And third, it denies our "earthly purpose for being."[57] The indwelling Christ adds two further reasons: negation of embodied life denies who Christ is today and who we are, and it negates a locus of moral doing, material bodily activity. It is in earthly, earthy, bodily life that the faithful become agents of Christ's love, lovers of neighbor and doers of good.

Secondly, we are habitation of a God who also inhabits all created things. For Luther, the creatures of God are not only human beings. God's creatures include "water, air, the earth and all its products."[58] Likewise, the creatures *indwelled by God* are not limited to the human. Luther insists that God and Christ (as both humanity and divinity) are actually present not only in human beings but in all created things. "Nothing can be more truly present and within all creatures than God himself with his power."[59] "God . . . . exists at the same time in every little seed, whole and entire, and yet also in all and above all and outside all created things."[60] "Everything is full of Christ through and through."[61] "All creatures are . . . permeable and present to [Christ]."[62] "Christ . . . fills all things. . . . Christ is around us and in us in all places. . . . he is present in all creatures, and I might find [Christ] in stone, in fire, in water, or even in a rope, for [Christ] certainly is there."[63] While for Luther, the scope of redemption and of the theo-ethical universe is the human—and these are fault-lines with grave consequences[64]—the scope of God's created dwelling place and of revelation[65] is cosmic.

Furthermore, we are a dwelling place of Christ crucified, who lived and died for the sake of abundant life for all, and whose love for human beings could be stopped by nothing. As abode of that Christ, Christians become Christs to neighbor. They grow ever more able to seek the well-being of neighbor, as well as of self, and do not flee the suffering that may be wrought by neighbor-love. Thus is established not only the norm of receiving and giving neighbor-love, which for Luther has two dimensions, but also the power to live that love. Those two dimensions are: (1) love manifest in loving service to neighbor, and (2) love manifest in renouncing, condemning, and counteracting the oppression—especially the economic oppression—of those who are vulnerable.[66]

Feminist and womanist critiques of self-giving love as the apex of Christian love demand a critical look at this understanding of who Christ is and who we are because of it. Giving self in service to others is not a moral good if that giving is antithetical to self-love and self-care or is necessarily morally superior to them, glorifies suffering, or *imposes* servanthood.[67] An apparent theological opposition between neighbor-love and self-love permeates Luther's writing.[68] Yet, on closer look, moral power as indwelling Christ mitigates against Luther's apparent inattention to the needs of self. The immanent Christ renders *communio* in which one not only serves but *is served*. Not only does one bear others' burdens, but one's burdens *are born by others*. One receives the love of Christ and of others before being called upon to give that love. For Luther, being *for* others becomes a reality only in the context of being *with* others who are also for and with us.[69] This important issue, and Luther's notion of neighbor-love in relationship to it, is addressed more fully in the subsequent chapter's discussion of neighbor-love as solidarity.

With that perspective in mind, we consider further implications, for Luther, of being dwelling place of a humiliated and broken God revealed in compassion and suffering. If Christians are to *be who they are*, they will not run from suffering at the cost of failing to serve neighbors in need.[70] Christian moral life entails not escape from worldly life and the suffering entailed in seeking the well-being of all, but living fully in that life. The implications regarding moral identity and agency are rooted firmly in Luther's insistence on the "indwelling Christ" at the center of the moral life in two senses. First, for Christians to shun the suffering that may result from neighbor-love is to flee from being who they are. Second, the power to remain with and on behalf of the other in her suffering abides in those who love *with the actual love of Christ*. Luther insists that Christians *are* "Christ's action and instrument," for Christ dwells in them.[71]

New identity as "habitation" of Christ establishes the purpose of human activity, which is this: "The Christian . . . does not live for himself alone . . . but he lives also for all men on earth." The Christian should be "guided in all his works by this thought and contemplate this one thing alone, that he may serve and benefit others in all that he does, considering nothing except the need and the advantage of his neighbor . . . each caring for and working for the other. . . . This is a truly Christian life." "I will . . . give myself as a Christ to my neighbor."[72]

Neighbor-love raises another problem in drawing upon Luther. Perhaps the most morally freighted category in Luther's ethics is that of "neighbor," or "other." As we will see, his most dangerous inconsistencies regard the boundaries around that category, and the treatment of people excluded from it. Nevertheless, the point made here stands: for Luther, the power to embody the moral purpose and vision established in Christ flows out of a new identity. Moral identity is a necessary ingredient of moral formation and moral agency.[73]

According to Luther, who we are because of Christ—first objects and then both objects and agents of God's love—determines also what freedom is. Freedom is, in the first place, *from* "the foolish presumption that justification is acquired by works." That is, freedom is "from all works" as a means of purging away sins and attaining salvation. Freedom is, in the second place, *for* "trusting God" and for "giving myself as a Christ to my neighbor, just as Christ offered himself to me; I will do nothing in this life except what I see is necessary, profitable, and salutary to my neighbor."[74] Said differently, freedom is from *se incurvatus in se*. The self turned in on self, Luther's definition of sin, stands in contrast to both self turned toward God in trust and toward neighbor in active love. Freedom perishes when works are done to attain salvation, or when works to benefit neighbor are not done.

What processes and powers gradually transform the faithful into a dwelling place of Christ and empower them to become ever more fully agents of Christ's love?

Luther, in his consistent inconsistency, describes the process of empowerment differently in different writings. But upon a close look, the varied explanations are complementary rather than contradictory. I see four principle versions of Luther's response, all inextricably linked to one another and to the indwelling Christ. They are Christ enkindling our love in grateful response to his, Christ as example empowering our love, Christ indwelling us, and the Holy Spirit filling us.

The first version, evident in "The Blessed Sacrament of the Holy and True Body and Blood of Christ, and the Brotherhoods," teaches that the love of Christ transforms us by enkindling a response of love within us. "[L]ove engenders love in return." Christ loving us and taking our form engenders in us such love that we take on his form.

Another version holds that Christ, as exemplar, empowers us morally. "If we look at [Christ's works], we are moved to imitate them. . . . 'Every act of Christ is instruction for us, indeed a stimulant.'"[75] "Each individual Christian shall become the servant of another in accordance with the example of Christ"; "Our proper righteousness . . . does God's will, living soberly with self, justly with neighbor, devoutly toward God. This righteousness follows the example of Christ in this respect . . . and is transformed into his likeness . . . It is precisely this that Christ requires."[76] The powers by which we adhere to Christ's example—the indwelling Christ and the Spirit—point to the remaining two versions.

"Christ who lives in me" is the love that loves one's neighbor.[77] Christ's love has two dimensions: "The love Christ bears toward us, and the love we owe our neighbor."[78] The indwelling Christ transforms us in a seemingly two-step process of cause and effect. Recall that in "Two Kinds of Righteousness," "actual righteousness" entails a manner of life spent in good works. That actual righteousness and manner of life are given as consequence or fruit of God's alien righteousness *first* being given.[79] Likewise, in "Disputation concerning Justification," our justified relationship with neighbor is an *effect* of our justification in relationship to God. In a sermon written five years after

"The Freedom of a Christian," Luther explains again the sequential process whereby we become both "lords of all" and "servants of all." First, through faith, we become "pious, free from sin, alive, saved, and children of God." "After [that] . . . we do good and exercise love to our neighbor . . . become servants of all." Luther explains more fully: "You see how love makes him a servant, so that he helps the poor man freely and for nothing. . . . This is what I often have said, that faith makes of us lord and love makes of us servants. Indeed, by faith we become gods and partakers of the divine nature . . . but through love we become equal to the poorest . . . servants of all. By faith we receive blessings from above, from God; through love we give them out below, to our neighbor."[80] The change is rendered possible by the love of God not only *manifest* in Christ but also *formed in us* as the indwelling Christ and by the Spirit's power.

Finally, the Holy Spirit is agent of the believer's transformation into an agent of Christ's love. Luther employs varied imagery in portraying the Holy Spirit's role. In a sermon he declares: "The Holy Spirit streams into the heart and makes a new man, one who loves God and gladly does his will. . . . He writes a fiery flame on the heart and makes it alive. . . . A new man is made who is conscious of a reason, heart, and mind unlike he formerly had. Everything is now alive. . . . He has . . . a heart which burns with love and delights in whatever pleases God." This is the Holy Spirit's office: to rule inwardly in the heart, making "it burn and create new courage so that a man grows happy before God . . . and with a happy heart serves the people." "The Holy Spirit inspires new thoughts and creates a new mind and heart. . . . In addition to the grace by which a man begins to believe and hold fast to the Word, God rules in a man through his divine power and agency, so that he . . . makes daily progress in life and good works . . . essentially becomes more able to serve men and countries in that his life and doings become God's."[81] In "The Freedom of a Christian," Luther writes: "If we recognize these great gifts, then our hearts will be filled by the Holy Spirit with the love which makes us free, joyful, almighty . . . servants of our neighbors, and yet lords of all."[82] And the "Disputation against Scholastic Theology" teaches that the Spirit spreads the love of God in our hearts.[83]

All four of these responses are dependent upon or assume the indwelling Christ. All four address two dimensions of moral agency: becoming moral agents and continuing to act as those agents. For Luther, both dimensions transpire by divine act. Yet, as I now argue, he understands that divine action to be mediated necessarily by the practices of human communities.

How does the "indwelling Christ as source of moral agency" play out in actual practices of everyday life, and particularly in economic life?

Luther was specific about moral norms and practices of everyday life grounded in God's gracious gift of indwelling presence. Reforms in everyday "moral" practices issuing out of Luther's theology were deep and broad— impacting family life, economic life, social welfare, and more. These reforms presuppose significant moral power, or more specifically, power to live toward the well-being of the neighbor in need. To illustrate, we turn to an ethical issue about which Luther was vehement, explicit, and prolific; which he related to a eucharistic understanding of human relationship with God and neighbor; and about which he spoke on multiple levels of ethical discourse.[84] It is the social-ethical issue central to the concerns that animate this study: economic life.[85]

Using economic life to examine the moral agency inherent in Luther's indwelling Christ is valid only if "human as habitation of Christ" is essential to Luther's economic ethics. We must inquire, "Do the principles, norms, and judgments that he formulates regarding economic life pertain without a notion of union with Christ, Spirit, and neighbor?" I think not. Both in terms of theological rationale and in terms of moral agency, the indwelling Christ is essential to Luther's economic ethics. In the following, we look at economic life in light of one question only: "What is the interplay between Luther's teachings on economic life, his sense of the indwelling Christ, and moral agency?"

"Luther's great concern was for justice and equity in the economic sphere." Luther's was a time of "economic revolution gradually transforming Germany from a nation of peasant agriculturalists into a society with at least the beginnings of a capitalist economy."[86] Consequences included high prices, growing disparity of wealth, and increasing poverty, especially of those with low or fixed income. The poor "were a cheap labor pool for an expanding profit economy"; "Poverty was a growing social problem that the medieval tradition of almsgiving and personal charity was incapable of addressing."[87] Increasing "large" scale international trade required capital, which sought profitable investment, feeding the emerging capitalist economy. In this context, the ethics of capital transactions were in public discussion.

The church's ancient endorsement of poverty as a path to salvation and of almsgiving as a salvific virtue theologically legitimated poverty. "The imitation of Christ in poverty was the sure way to heaven."[88] Almsgiving enabled vicarious participation in the poor's poverty and closeness to God. In Reformation historian Carter Lindberg's terms, God had ordered there to be poor that the rich might gain eternal life through them. Almsgiving, in line with the piety of achievement, atoned for sin.[89] Salvation had become big business. Devotional practices and charity were "price of passage."

In this context, Luther theologically dismantled the medieval piety of achievement and notion of union with God through similitude. He vehemently denounced economic exploitation, arguing "that the source of contemporary impoverishment was not the feudal system but the new profit economy."[90] Luther condemned the emerging trade economy, and beseeched German political leaders to do the same, to "put the bit in the mouth of the Fuggers and similar companies."[91] He articulated norms for economic life that subverted standard economic practices, and inaugurated and theologically legitimized local systems of social welfare as outgrowths and components of worship.[92]

Luther's notions of the indwelling Christ and justification had two central implications for social welfare reform. First, justification and union with Christ happen through grace rather than through human effort, and through dissimilitude with Christ rather than through similitude. These monumental theological changes undermined the medieval assumptions that poverty was a spiritual virtue that could help with salvation. Luther's notions of justification and Christ indwelling opened the door for him to reconstruct poverty as a social problem to which the "true" Christian responded. Thus he altered the framework in which enormous social problems of poverty and economic oppression were conceptualized; he shifted the discourse. Lindberg says this shift "enabled the Wittenberg reformers to envision a new social ethic in relation to poverty."[93]

The other implication for social welfare is more salient for grasping what Luther's theology of the immanent Christ implies for moral agency. "Moral life as indwelling Christ" theologically created both the obligation and the moral power for Christians to develop social welfare systems and to oppose economic oppression. This theologically grounded duty and power has a number of dimensions, only one of which is noted here: For Luther, in the Eucharist, the union between believer and Christ renders union between believer and neighbor. Those unions engender community ontologically oriented around addressing people's needs—including material needs. "The sacrament has no blessing and significance unless love grows daily and so changes a person that he is made one with all others."[94] Lindberg asserts that worship was the principle resource from which Luther's notion of social welfare was constructed. "Social welfare for Luther was . . . the liturgy after the liturgy, a work of the people flowing from worship. . . . Poor relief expressed this community solidarity. . . . It was, in fact, an act of worship, of divine service."[95] The Eucharistic community is a community of moral agency.

Viewing a specific treatise may illustrate norms for the economic life of Christians issuing from "moral life as indwelling Christ." We turn to Luther's 1524 treatise, "Trade and Usury."[96] Luther's stated purposes in this treatise are primarily to save individuals from participation in "the abuses and sins of trade" (247), and secondarily to admonish civil authorities to forbid exploitative economic practices. His analysis of the political economy—grounded in what he sees happening around him—includes the convictions that buying and selling (trade and commerce) as commonly practiced are "financial evils" (245); and yet that they are necessary and can be practiced in a Christian way by adhering to "strict rules and principles" that contradict common trade practices.

In this treatise, Luther clarifies his moral norms for economic life. All are argued in theological terms. We consider a few, beginning with those that pertain to society as a whole and ending with those pertaining only to Christians.

1. Because selling is an act toward neighbor, its goal should not be profit but rather "an adequate living" and serving the needs of the other (250).
2. Economic activity ought be subject to political constraints. For example, "Selling ought not be an act that is entirely within your own power and discretion, without law or limit." Civil authorities ought establish "rules and regulations," including "ceilings" on prices (249–50).
3. Trade in ostentatious items rather than useful items ought not be permitted (246).

Four additional norms guide the economic life of Christians (255).[97]

4. In buying and selling, adhere to firm rules, one of which is: no selling at a price as high as the market will bear (261).[98]
5. Lend willingly and gladly without interest and without asking to be repaid if the borrower is unable to do so. Lend without regard for personal gain. Lend even "to those who are unwilling or unable to repay us, such as the needy and our enemies" (257, 291).[99]
6. "Let them rob or steal our property" (256, 273–80).
7. "Give freely to anyone who needs it" (256, 280–89).

In addition, Luther admonishes pastors regarding their roles and obligations in the face of economic practices that exploit the vulnerable. Pastors are to "unmask *hidden* injustice, thus saving the souls of duped Christians and opening the eyes of the secular authorities for their mandate to establish civil justice."[100] Luther goes so far as to admonish clergy to preach (for Luther, that is to speak the living Christ) against usury and to withhold the sacrament from a usurer unless he repents, for he is "damned like a thief, robber and murderer."[101]

Healing a Broken World

Out of these norms, Luther renders specific judgments. He condemns particular "tricks and evil practices" including charging a higher price for goods sold on credit, raising prices when supply is low, buying out the entire supply of a commodity and then raising the price, and buying at a low price from one who needs money so badly that he or she sells low. He denounces trading companies' monopolistic practices. The two most recent diets, or legislatures (Diets of Nuremburg in 1522 and 1524), had failed to curtail these. Trading companies are "a bottomless pit of avarice and wrong-doing. . . . They control all commodities . . . raise or lower prices at their pleasure. They oppress and ruin all the small businessmen. . . ." Through their practices "all the world must be sucked dry and all the money sink and swim in their gullets."[102]

Luther's economic norms and judgments are based on the following theological principles: God alone is to be trusted for everything; God wishes human life to be orderly and peaceful; Christians are to love their neighbors as themselves. The first two of these principles stand without "moral life as indwelling with Christ." The third does not. For Luther, Christian neighbor-love and the economic norms pertaining to Christians are realizable only in light of the moral identity, purpose, vision, and agency established by the indwelling Christ.

Luther's distinction between norms for Christians and norms pertaining to the broader society supports my claim that the indwelling Christ is crucial. The last set of norms (which Luther refers to as "four righteous ways of exchanging goods") are for Christians only. In Luther's thought, non-Christians are normed and bound only by natural law and civil law, in part because they would be unable to adhere to the norms established by the gospel and God's law. Said differently, Luther assumes that, because of moral agency established by the indwelling Christ, Christians are morally obligated and able in ways that non-Christians are not.

In what sense is this moral agency "subversive"?

In the next chapter, I will explore the subversive implications of moral agency rooted in the immanent Christ, as that agency played out in Luther's economic ethics. In short preview: all activity in relationship to neighbor is normed and empowered by one theological principle—true Christians actively embody Christ for neighbor by serving the neighbor's well-being in all that they do. Economic activity is ontologically activity in relationship to neighbor, and therefore is to serve the neighbor's well-being. Economic practices that undermine the well-being of neighbor (and especially of the vulnerable) are to be rejected and replaced with alternatives. That is, those practices are to be subverted. On these grounds, Luther vehemently denounced aspects of the emerging capitalist economy that he considered harmful to economically vulnerable people. The norm was neighbor-love, and the agency to live it was Christself making habitation in the faithful.

Here we consider the subversive quality of "moral agency as indwelling Christ" in a more all-encompassing sense. Luther held the fundamental conviction that we are saved by a living and present God, a Word that must be proclaimed and heard in order to save, and which can be obscured when sacramental practice is ignored or distorted, or when institutions, power structures, or ideologies deceive or distract people from remembering who they are *coram deo* (before the face of God) and *coram mundo* (before the world).[103] "Luther was convinced that the greatest abuse of the church in his day was that 'God's Word has been silenced.'"[104] More important than all else was that the living Christ be proclaimed, heard, believed, and remembered. His intense hermeneutic (method of interpretation) of suspicion was aimed at whoever or whatever—including institutions, worldviews, or hegemonic powers—he thought distracted or deceived people from hearing the Word and remembering who they were as objects and agents of Christ's love. What obscured or silenced the Word must be demystified and resisted.[105] For Luther, this moral obligation issued a subversive challenge to "the basic institution for the coordination, hegemony, and reproduction of the existing system," the ecclesiastical power structure.[106]

The primacy of resistance to what distracted or deceived people from hearing the Word is evident in Luther's exception to his norm of obedience to temporal authority. Luther's convictions regarding the hierarchical ordering of society—fruit of his theology wed to social theory—gave rise to powerful moral norms. The most evident and vociferously expounded is the divine mandate to obey temporal authority—in the form of civil authorities, masters (for servants), and parents—which shaped, among other things, Luther's response to the peasant rebellion.[107] According to this norm, rebellion against civil authority is the most evil deed on Earth, more evil than murder, for rebellion against civil authority attacks the divinely established head and interferes with the divinely ordained function of rulers.[108] Rebellion against civil authority is, in fact, demonic.[109]

The point here, however, is not Luther's norm, but his exception to it and the genesis of that exception. As a public theologian and a theological political figure uncritically committed to and theologically justifying a norm of obedience to civil authority, Luther demanded, on soteriological grounds, one exception to that norm. Where obedience to civil rulers contradicted obedience to God or to conscience, or where the demands of civil rulers "tends toward the suppression of the Christian faith, the denying of the divine word," Christians were "to resist them at least with words," and to "obey God . . . rather than men."[110] According to Luther in 1523, that resistance could take the form of words, and of refusal to hold certain beliefs or to obey the proclamation that certain books could not be read or possessed.[111] Yet by 1531, in "Dr. Martin Luther's Warning to His Dear German People," the mandate to resist became stronger.[112] To *not* disobey civil authorities was to jeopardize one's salvation, and resistance could take even armed form, because civil authorities were jeopardizing the proclamation of the gospel and demanding that people disobey God. Where rebellion against rulers was for any other reason, it was wrong. In essence, where Luther finds the proclamation, hearing, and remembering of the gospel to be at stake on a large scale, and the souls of the German people at risk, he calls for resistance to civil authorities.

At first glance, it may appear that this "subversive" impulse in Luther pertains regardless of his conviction that God lives within the believing community. A deeper look makes clear the contrary; this impulse is closely linked to Luther's belief in God's indwelling presence and power. While other aspects of his theology supply the obligation to resist, the indwelling Christ and indwelling Spirit supply the courage. Resistance to hegemonic authority, where that resistance is life-threatening, requires courage. Courage is an ingredient of subversive moral agency. For Luther, the most powerful courage known in humankind is generated by the Spirit and Christ living in the faithful. We turn to Luther's "Sermon for the Sixteenth Sunday after Trinity," in which he speaks of the power, strength, and courage that may be imparted to the faithful by the immanent presence of Christ and Spirit. Christ is brought into the faithful by the Holy Spirit; Christ and Spirit indwell together. The Spirit may bring into its human abode "true courage—boldness of heart." "The Hebrew word for spirit," Luther preaches, "might well be rendered 'bold, undaunted courage.'" That "bold, dauntless courage . . . will not be terrified by poverty, shame, sin, the devil, or death, but is confident that nothing can harm us and we will never be in need." This empowering courage is, according to Luther, greater and more powerful than any other force on Earth.[113]

How are the gifts of Christ's indwelling and transforming presence, and of the resulting radical neighbor-love, mediated? That is, how are these gifts received and realized? What are the implications for moral agency?

Luther usually speaks of the moral transformation inherent in "union with Christ" in descriptive rather than prescriptive terms; he believes that we gradually *are changed* toward beings who "live justly with neighbor," even when that means radically countercultural economic practices, suffering, or risk of death. This lofty notion of moral agency contrasts startlingly with the contemporary dearth of it in the face of neo-liberal globalization. What accounts for the stark contrast?

Luther's response is explicit: where moral agency is missing, the community has not properly maintained certain practices. For Luther, the mediator of union with Christ is the *practice* of Christian communities. In the communities' practice, the living Christ is received and, with the Spirit at work, is gradually transforming the faithful into beings who love the actual indwelling love of Christ.

This statement does not negate or contradict the profound Lutheran and "Luther-an" truth claim that faith alone saves. Nor does it counter the claim that the Creator indwells the creatures only as gracious gift and in no way as a reward or as earned consequence of good works. Here we seek neither to systematize nor to resolve the apparent paradox that what is pure gift is dependent also upon the communities' practices. Rather we highlight and live into that paradox in order to uncover clues to moral agency. It is perhaps in sermons that Luther best expresses this paradox: While "faith is the one essential thing," "it is not enough merely to accept the gospel, or even to preach it. There must be a motive force consisting of the inner belief of the heart and the outward proofs of faith: not mere speaking but doing: not mere talking but living." "We pray for the strength and for the power of the Spirit," yet we know also that "wherever the Word is proclaimed . . . the Spirit of God must be with us." The relevant point is this: While the faithful are indwelled and gradually transformed by God as gracious gift alone, God gives that gift through the practices of communities of which God is a part through God's gift of faith. Where human communities fail in the practices through which God comes to and into them, they do not know the Word and "taste the Word;" they do not receive the gift of presence and power, of "bold, undaunted courage."[114]

What, then, are the practices through which the living Christ indwells and empowers communities of the faithful? Luther refers to six. One is the practice of being with and for those who suffer. As the abode of a broken and suffering God, we know God most fully by being with and for those who are suffering and in places of brokenness. To avoid those people or places is to avoid being who we are as people who love with the actual love of Christ.

Another is hearing the Word preached and believing it. The Word must be proclaimed, heard, remembered, even "tasted" in order to indwell and transform.[115] Based upon Paul, Luther "contrasts a knowledge of the Word with the power of the Word. Many have the knowledge, but few the impelling and productive power that the results may be as we teach. . . . What is the blessing for which Paul's prayer entreats? Something more than continuance of the Word with his followers, though it is a great and good gift even to have the Word thoroughly taught: [Paul] prays that the heart may *taste* the Word and that it may be effectual in the life."[116]

Healing a Broken World

Prayer, according to Luther, is a third practice whereby the living Christ indwells and empowers the faithful. The moral power of God's love, received by faith and actively serving the world through the faithful, is found through earnest prayer:

> It is not enough merely to accept the Gospel or even to preach it. Acceptance must be followed by that spiritual power . . . a motive force consisting of the inner belief of the heart and the outward proofs of faith: not mere speaking but doing: not mere talking but living. . . . Note how Paul devotes himself to the welfare of the Christian community. . . . But we do not rightly heed his example. . . . We do not avail ourselves to the Gospel's power in the struggles of life. *Unquestionably the trouble is we do not earnestly pray.*[117]

> Paul desires Christ to be efficacious in the hearts of his followers. . . . But the heart which has not yet arrived at this point is here advised what course to take, namely, to pray to God for such faith and strength, and to avail himself to the prayers of others to the same end.[118]

> It is necessary for us continually to pray God to replace our weakness with courage, and to put into our hearts his Spirit to fill us with grace and strength and rule and work in us absolutely.[119]

Yet another practice is reading and interpreting the Bible, and grappling with the Word as it speaks through the Bible to the context of our particular realities—especially the struggles, bondage, and suffering of self and others. A fifth is daily reading, meditating on, and conversing about the Lord's Prayer, the Creed, and the Commandments.[120] Finally, Luther points to the Eucharist and the *communio* created by it.

In these practices, according to Luther, the living Christ is received and empowers the faithful as agents of Christ's love. The following chapter delves more deeply into the first and last of these practices.

Ideological Dimensions That Undermine Subversive Moral Agency in Luther

For Luther, "moral life as indwelling Christ" issued in profound moral agency in service of what he considered "the widespread good," and especially on behalf of people in need.[121] Yet that moral agency was truncated in key social relationships. The hermeneutic of "appreciation," thus far guiding this encounter with Luther, here is placed in dialectical relationship with a hermeneutic of suspicion. I argue that, in the case of Luther, transformative moral power was undercut, in certain social relationships, by his Constantinian, patriarchal, and anti-Semitic ideology.

The purpose here is neither a full elaboration of Luther's worldview vis-à-vis social structural relationships, nor a critique of Luther in light of that worldview. The purpose is to learn from Martin Luther and his context, both positive and negative aspects. Here, I expose dynamics by which positivist social theory may undercut the potential of religious experience and conviction (in this case, experience of and belief in the indwelling Christ) to generate liberative and subversive moral agency.

While the bases of Luther's ethics were theological, especially christological and soteriological,[122] also formative were his passionately held medieval convictions regarding the ordering of society; his allegiance to the social hierarchy of German society; and the fears and passions associated with those convictions and that allegiance. Those convictions, fears, and passions at crucial points undergirded Luther's theological justification of oppressive social structures and practices such as anti-Semitism, the hierarchal ordering of society, the patriarchal family, and the repression of peasants. Theological rationalization of these structures and practices as divinely approved or ordained worked against structural change toward justice.

My purpose here is to indicate, through two illustrations, ways in which Luther's social theory and accompanying theology severely undermined moral power to serve the well-being of one's neighbor.[123] The two illustrative cases are Luther's stand regarding the "peasant rebellion" of 1525 and his vitriolic condemnation of Jews.

Luther's descriptive and normative convictions regarding the ordering of society include the following. Christian life is structured and contained by three "holy orders and truly religious institutions established by God," all of which serve divinely ordained purposes with divinely given tools.[124] These basic social units are the office of priest, the estate of marriage (which encompasses the entire household including servants), and civil government. The latter two are arranged in hierarchies, the transgression of which is sin; people are to remain in the station to which they were born, there to serve God and neighbor. This hierarchical ordering of society contributes to the widespread good. Alteration of it would undo the widespread good. Violent resistance to this social structure would result in the destruction of German society. Social change is deviance and would lead to anarchy. In Luther's society, and for Luther reflective of it, "order and security hold priority over social equality."[125] Luther held that society could not be governed by the gospel, but that peace, order, and justice (as Luther understood them) would reign if temporal authorities exercised their divine mandate to protect the righteous and punish the wicked, and did not extend their authority too far. Finally, Luther's "conviction that history had come to an end and that the second coming of Christ was near at hand . . . made Luther see, in all attempts to reform society, merely efforts to repair a social order doomed to collapse very soon."[126]

Present in many of Luther's key writings, this ideology is imbedded in his descriptive and normative accounts of human life and is supported by his interpretations of scripture.[127] The convictions are expressed in theological terms, giving them the weight of divine mandate.[128] Although this worldview bends and is nuanced in Luther, it never gives.

Justice, as Luther understood it, and love were inseparable and sometimes the terms were used interchangeably by him.[129] Thus, since neighbor-love was a norm, so was "justice." Yet for Luther, "justice" did not entail "social equality." Human society was necessarily hierarchical and composed of social inequality. Freedom did not entail freedom from slavery or serfdom. His social theoretical assumptions render the norms of neighbor-love and justice ineffectual where they would call for structural reform. As seen explicitly in the first of his three tracts regarding the peasant rebellion, for serfs or slaves to claim freedom "because Christ has made us all free . . . absolutely contradicts the gospel."[130] Scripture proves that a slave is to remain a slave, and a serf to remain a serf. The body of slave or serf belongs to the master; to claim equality is to "rob" the master of his rightful "property."[131]

In the case of the 1525 peasant rebellion, Luther's ideological stance, as identified above, gave rise to judgments that—although levied against both nobility and peasants—ultimately weighed in against the peasants. For example, although Luther finds the nobility to blame for the rebellion—for they "rule tyranically and with rage, prohibit preaching of this gospel, and cheat and oppress the poor" so that they "may lead a life of luxury and extravagance"[132]—and although he finds many of the peasants' demands just, Luther judges the peasants wrong on three accounts, all of which warrant eternal condemnation: The peasants had broken the feudal oath of submission to rulers, had used force in rectifying injustice, and had claimed the gospel as justification for both.[133] In his second tract regarding the peasant rebellion, "Against the Robbing and Murdering Hordes of Peasants," Luther judges that Christian rulers who fail to punish peasants with force (that is, who fail to protect the social order), commit a sin as great as murder. Here, using deadly force against the peasants renders rulers God's faithful ministers and, if they die, martyrs.[134] Anyone, in fact, is morally obligated to slay rebels without mercy.

The powerful pull of Luther's socio-political ideology on his theology and ethics is seen in the fact that the *only* place in which Luther slips and claims that works may save is in writing against the peasant rebellion. "[A] prince may win heaven by bloodshed," Luther declares. Later, he acknowledges this slip, claiming to have "forgotten" himself in ascribing salvation not only to a work but even to "the heinous work of bloodshed!"[135]

Luther's condemnation of Jews comprises the second illustration. At play here are not convictions regarding the ordering of society but rather presuppositions regarding Jews and regarding the "neighbor." "Neighbor" is a morally freighted category in Luther's ethics. His most dangerous inconsistencies regard the boundaries around that category and the treatment of people excluded from it. Luther's notion of "neighbor" varies dramatically. The "neighbor" whose well-being the Christian serves (even at great cost) is variously "all men on earth . . . not distinguish[ing] between friends and enemies" (in "Freedom of a Christian"), "all other Christians" (in "Blessed Sacrament of the Holy and True Body and Blood of Christ and the Brotherhoods"), or co-residents of a locality (in "On Whether One May Flee from a Deadly Plague"). Furthermore, parts of humanity are excluded from all three versions of neighbor, the scope of life for whom the Christian lives. Jews, for instance, by 1543 were outside the boundaries not only of neighbor but of the human, in Luther's social theory and theology. They were not even the "enemy" that Christians were to love. Jews were demons about whom Luther spread life-threatening lies and against whom he advocated horribly cruel actions.[136]

The moral significance of "live toward the neighbor's good" as a fundamental moral norma depends upon "Who is my neighbor?" For Luther, relegation of some to non-neighbor status crippled and betrayed the liberative, subversive, and compassionate power of the indwelling Christ to shape Christians' life according to the well-being of neighbor. The compelling question is this: By what social and theological presuppositions did Luther determine who was neighbor and indeed who was fully human? By what criteria were some excluded from the circle of neighbor? The response was (and is) a matter of life and death. The question ought be directed toward any who seek to live faithfully in the globalizing political-economy of today.

Luther's moral judgments regarding the peasants and the Jews may have been different had the moral identity, vision, purpose, and power created by union with Christ not been undercut by an ideology that naturalized as divinely ordained a certain ordering of society and a limited parameter of the "neighbor" and of the fully human. We have noted ways in which that ideology altered the norms and judgments that might otherwise have flowed from "moral agency as indwelling Christ." The point is this: Uncritically assumed social theory and theology that justify a given social order as divinely ordained undercut the subversive moral agency that may be generated by faith experience and conviction—in this case experience of and belief in the indwelling Christ.

Perhaps most important in querying the interplay between Luther's worldview and his "moral agency as indwelling Christ" is the self-reflective task. The indwelling Christ was at the center of the moral life for Luther. In coming to know the ideological forces that interrupted, obscured, and betrayed the power of that indwelling presence for him, we may see more clearly those forces in our own lives and faith communities. Recognizing those limiting dynamics is a first step toward subverting them. Luther may mirror our own betrayals of the gospel and warn us. On the other hand, unearthing Luther's understanding of the indwelling Christ and the moral power flowing from that presence may lead to wellsprings of moral agency long ignored by most North Atlantic Lutheran traditions and by many other Christian traditions in modern and postmodern Western societies.

5

Subversive Moral Agency Today:
God "Flowing and Pouring into All Things"

◎

With Jesus, we are called to embody you, O God of life and justice, share you, celebrate your gift of life, and pass it on . . . all this by the transformative Power of your Presence! [emphasis added]

—Carter Heyward, March 1999

This is our hope against hope, that our efforts on behalf of our planet are not ours alone but that the source and power of life in the universe is working in and through us *for the well-being of all creation, including our tiny part in it.* [emphasis added]

—Sallie McFague, *Body of God*

A STRANGELY ANCIENT YET UNCHARTED JOURNEY is called for, if people of economic privilege are to wrest moral agency for resistance in the face of "the forces of stampeding globalization . . . destroying a beloved world."[1] This quest for moral-spiritual power is propelled by a disturbing paradox. Human beings are called to live justly with neighbor (both near and far) and to nurture and be nurtured by Earth's bounty. To that end, we are to shape lifestyles, public policies, and socio-ecological structures that enable social justice and life-sustaining Earth-human relations. Yet, as a society, we comply with a mode of globalization that structures exploitation into the fabric of our lives and threatens Earth's capacity to sustain life as we know it. Nearly every aspect of our lives is embedded in economic arrangements that degrade or destroy many human beings and Earth's life-systems.

The purpose of this chapter is twofold: (1) to contribute to North American Christian praxis in which relationship with God dwelling in creation, together with critical analyses of the globalizing economy, engenders subversive moral agency in the context of globalization; and (2) to lay groundwork for further inquiry into the moral power that may flow from God's indwelling presence and into methods for drawing upon the wisdom and mistakes of faith forbears for guidance toward that power.

Where We Have Been and Where We Are Going:
A Map

We first inquired: "How is the moral agency of relatively economically privileged people in the United States so disabled that we acquiesce to the prevailings paradigm of globalization? Why have we neither the power nor the vision to resist?" In partial response, my thesis has been this: Corporate- and finance-driven globalization structures and normalizes political-economic relationships that cripple human capacity to make decisions and take actions other than those that serve the utility of the market. Chapters 2 and 3 each explored a constellation of dynamics whereby globalization corrodes the moral agency required to resist it and to move toward economic structures, policies, and lifestyles that contribute to social justice and sustainable Earth-human relations.

We then asked: "Where, in Christian faith traditions, lie wellsprings of moral agency to fight the powers of death and destruction perpetuated in neo-liberal globalization?" While those wellsprings are many, this project explores one: relationship with God living in creation. The previous chapter probed the interplay between moral agency and relationality with the immanent God by examining that interplay in Luther.

This chapter brings that encounter with Luther to bear on the task at hand: enabling subversive moral agency in the face of current global economic systems that do not serve just and sustainable communities. Drawing upon Luther, in dialogue with selected contemporary voices, we ask: "By what pathways may relationship with the indwelling God give rise to faithful resistance, issue in alternative visions, and generate movement to realize them? How may relationship with God, present in all of creation counter the morally disabling dynamics of globalization?"

Sacramental Cosmic *Communio:*
A Broader Moral Framework

The following section contains theoretical discussions necessary to undergird the task at hand, but not necessary to engage it. Readers disinterested in these theoretical underpinnings may choose to pass over this section. In it I suggest that Western ethics, as commonly conceived, is inadequate in circumstances calling for moral power that seems beyond what is humanly possible. I argue too that Luther's articulation of relationship with the indwelling Christ transgresses the boundaries of Western ethical frameworks and offers an alternative more adequate to the challenges of social transformation. In addition,

I point to fascinating continuities between Luther and contemporary streams of recent feminist relational theology.

&

Our inquiry seeks subversive moral agency in response to a particular moral crisis of neo-liberal globalization, as elaborated in the initial chapters. Indeed Luther's indwelling Christ responds to that crisis, offering radical alternatives to the neo-liberal myths and the curtailed political participation identified as intrinsic to contemporary globalization. We will examine those alternatives presently. Yet immersion in Luther's experience and theology of the indwelling Christ as a centerpiece of Christian moral life challenges also constructions of Western Christian Ethics that undermine moral power.[2] These constructions largely have been accepted until contested by varied feminist and other liberationist voices, and more recently by emerging "Earth ethics."[3] We consider challenges to two boundaries of received Western ethical frameworks: (1) the construction of ethics as cognitively and expertly determined beliefs and normative behavior derived from them, and (2) anthropocentric limits to the moral universe.

Christian Ethics, as an academic discipline stemming from the Social Gospel movement in the United States, the social revolutions in England, and the social encyclicals of the Roman Catholic Church, has tended to ground moral being and doing in broad, normative categories derived from what we are to believe cognitively about God, the world, and relationships between God and the world, according to "expert" opinion.[4] (Note that, for my purpose here, *belief* implies the overlapping worlds of theology, philosophy, and social theory.) Ethics determines *what we are to be and do* in accord with *what we believe* by means of specified norms and sources.[5] The norms usually are developed along deontological, classical teleological, consequentialist, character, or communitarian lines—or combinations of these. Sources are engaged cognitively, and ethical reflection is largely a process of rational deliberation regarding beliefs and their implications for the moral life. This general ethical framework, reflecting Enlightenment confidence in reason, is construed in endless variety according to the aforementioned ethical methods or theoretical schools.

A number of recent developments digress partially from this framework. The intellectual and cultural shifts associated with postmodernism, in general and as they play out in ethics, contest modernity's preoccupation with reason and expertise as locus of disinterested, ahistorical, universal truth. Yet the postmodern turn does not challenge reason itself as gatekeeper for truth.[6] Cognitively determined belief and behavior, though shaped by particular contexts and multiple perspectives, remain the foundation of ethics.

Healing a Broken World

Another important development emphasizes a dialectic between belief and behavior and the role of social structures in shaping both.[7] Diverse streams of liberationist ethics deviate significantly from belief and behavior, cognitively considered by "experts," as the centerpiece of ethics. These streams hold that belief and behavior arise out of a community's reflection on its experience and cannot stand apart from that experience. Liberationist ethics require that belief and behavior be informed by historical and structural social analysis, the privileged perspectives of marginalized peoples, and critical rather than positivist approaches to knowing. Yet, many liberationist variations, while deconstructing "expertise," still tend to center the categories of "right behavior" and "right belief" about the world and God. A strong exception is voices in feminist ethics that bring relationality to the center of ethics.

Christian moral life construed *primarily* as reasoned belief and behavior—asking what we are to be and do as shaped by and as shaping what we believe cognitively—has not enabled North Atlantic mainline Protestantism to fashion ways of economic life or economic ethics that counter the Earth-threatening and life-threatening economic paradigm imposed by neo-liberal globalization. In other words, ethics structured on the two legs of *normative behavior* based upon and informing *cognitively and expertly determined belief* are inadequate to the question of moral agency. That "traditional" moral frame is bereft in the face of moral situations that seem beyond human agency. Rationally determining "what we are to be and do" and what we "believe" will not alone birth moral agency adequate to swim upstream against the blindness and complicity in which, as a society, we march forward in globalization's death-dealing ways.[8]

I do not deny that belief and behavior are crucial and integral to Christian Ethical deliberation and moral life. Rather I disclaim the "traditional" construction of Western ethics where it holds the systematic exposition of "right" behavior based upon "right" belief to be (1) the foundation of moral life and deliberation, (2) sufficient for them, and (3) determined largely by cognitive reason and expertise. Rational ethical reflection is indispensable and may render crucial cognitive knowledge regarding normative economic practices that would serve sustainable and just communities of life. Yet, something more is needed.

Luther's articulation of relationality with the indwelling Christ challenges this construction of ethics and suggests—even requires—an alternative. Human moral power flows *primarily* from deep communion between God, human creatures, and the broader community of life.[9] God incarnate in the community of life and socio-ecological practices whereby human creatures *know* (not merely *know about*) Her indwelling presence, touch and are touched by it, drink it, and nourish others with it are the heart of moral power. Where the burden of moral action surpasses what seems humanly possible, where crucial processes of rational ethical reflection offer inadequate courage, fortitude, and other resources for resistance, moral agency may flow from communion with God living in the creatures and elements of this Earth. That communion is intimately "personal," fundamentally "political" and "public," and sacramental. The sacramental *communio*—God incarnate in us and among us as human communities and as a planetary or even cosmic community of life—is a locus of moral power. Luther's experience of the indwelling Christ finds moral agency in "cosmic *communio* as sacrament," where the *communio* includes God and creation. That broader moral frame is Luther's challenge to traditional constructions of ethics.[10] Below, I sketch four progressive building blocks of that challenge, each building on the others to outline a broader construction of Christian Ethics capable of responding to questions of moral agency in situations calling for resistance that seems beyond human capability. Along the way, I note a startling resonance between Luther's challenge and trends in contemporary Euro-American feminist theo-ethics.

First, the moral life with indwelling Christ as its centerpiece is grounded primarily not in cognitively acquired beliefs about God but in intimate, sensuous, transforming relationship. Luther railed against the scholastics of his day for teaching that living faith (or true theology for that matter) depended primarily upon intellectual knowledge about God. For Luther, intellectual knowledge about God teaches us *that* God is and *about* God's metaphysical and ethical attributes but is limited in two ways. It knows neither *who* God is nor *that God wants to help me,* and it does not establish the relationship that saves and transforms.[11] This knowledge and saving, transforming relationship are given by grace through faith, which, in Luther's theology, is in itself a *relationship* of trust in God. The knowledge of God that issues in moral power is relational and is disclosed through God's grace by the Incarnate Word and the Holy Spirit who streams into the heart and "creates a new mind and heart. . . . so that . . . one makes daily progress in life and good works," becoming more able to serve people and countries.[12] Paul, Luther preaches, "contrasts a knowledge of the Word, with the power of the Word. Many have the knowledge . . . but few the impelling and productive power."[13] According to Luther, the life of faith and the moral agency inherent in it are given by God through relationships and are sustained by living daily life in those relationships, however imperfectly.

Second, the relationality at the heart of moral agency involves human beings, the rest of creation, and God. Agency rooted in human-human relationality alone, in the long run, will not suffice. *Human* relationality, however ideally it is constructed, as sole ground of moral power, implies an enduring presence of mutual love that is rendered impossible by the human proclivity to do everything for benefit of self. Brokenness as *se incurvatus en se* (self turned in on self) inhabits the realm of human love, even at its best. Morally empowering mutual love—love that both receives loving care from others and serves others' well-being—is a gracious gift of a God who *is* that love and who, as the Holy Spirit, spreads the love of God in our hearts and as Christ comes to dwell within us.[14]

Third, the relationality at the heart of moral agency is not abstract, otherworldly, or impersonal but rather is concrete, utterly earthly, and intimately "personal." The relationship is so earthy and personal as to be sensual. Luther preached that for the Word to become effective power, bearing fruit in human lives, we are to "taste the Word."

Fourth, the "personal" relationship at the heart of moral agency is incompatible with an apolitical or a privatized "personal relationship with God." The morally empowering relationality described by Luther is intrinsically political in the sense of "political," as I have defined it. That is, relationality grounded in the immanent God directly effects, and is effected by, the processes through which groups of people—be they households, institutions, localities, nations, international bodies, or other groups—determine the governing terms of their life in relationship to one another, other groups, and the rest of creation. The implications for economic life, according to Luther, are profound.[15] In contrast to being privatized, this personal relationality with God is ontologically communal.

The juxtaposition of the third and fourth points is crucial. The notion of "personal relationship with God" has been discredited for many people for its association with the politically conservative Religious Right and its unsavory cultural, economic, and political agendas. Yet the concept is rich and replete with subversive potential. The loss of this notion by Christian communities with liberationist commitments is to the detriment of all. Luther's articulation of the indwelling Christ, and the subversive moral power inherent in that Presence, invites reclaiming and redeeming "personal relationship with God" as communal and political. That reclamation is begged by the glaring need for public moral agency in the face of threats posed by globalization. To deconstruct the privatized, internalized, depoliticized, and domesticated notion of personal relationship with God and reconstitute it as a communal and political reality is beyond the scope of this project. Here I simply state the need based on my analysis of globalization, open the theological door grounded in Luther's articulation of the indwelling Christ, suggest the liberative potential, and offer this starting point: in considering intimate relationality between God and human creatures, the "personal" must be rethought in contrast to the autonomous individual subject of Western morality. I point neither backward to premodern notions of personhood, nor sideways to the prevailing postmodern disintegration of the moral subject, but forward to a notion of "personal" embedded in an incredibly complex community of beings of which humankind is but one kind.

Thus, the indwelling Christ, as known and theologized by Luther, constitutes a great rebuttal to two opposing claims, both common in the practice of liberal Euro-American Christianity and both undercutting the subversive moral potential inherent in relationality with the indwelling God. First is the claim that "personal relationship with God," while the centerpiece of faith, is private. As a private affair, this relationship does *not* bear directly on and is not influenced by political life, public life, or systemic injustice and exploitation. While this relationship forms personal character, and that character may shape public life, the relationship with God is not directly determinative of or influenced by public political being or needs. The social construction of human-divine intimacy as private has served the interests of established power structures, for singularly private relationship with God cannot issue in public challenge.[16]

The second claim refutes the first and is more characteristic of the "social Christianity" stream of liberal Christianity. Christian life is inherently political, and intimate "personal relationship with God" is *not* a centerpiece of that life. People of faith are called to focus on justice-making, on right relationships, on social change, but not necessarily to focus on intimate, compelling, personal relationality with God. The cosmic *communio* implied by Luther's notion of the indwelling Christ refutes both claims regarding "personal relationship with God."

Both claims reflect the theological anthropology of liberalism's legacy (the ideological site of modern Euro-American theological ethics). That anthropology is viewed clearly in the work of Reinhold Niebuhr, who held that the individual is the primary human unit in relationship with God; the self—although a social being—stands before God as an individual. The result is a private-public dichotomy in which the moral knowledge and norms that faith offers are understood and enacted by individuals, rather than by social groups. The dominant norm for Christian private life (for Niebuhr, *agape* love) is not the effective norm for public life, the realm of conflict and compromise between contending self-interest groups and of morally ambiguous decisions made in contrast to the pure norm of *agape* love. Relationships of intimacy are the purview of private life, and there shape moral character; they are not the important energies of public life. Thus while relationship with God may be central to personal morality, it bears on history only through the morality of private individuals influenced by it, not in a communal sense.

This theological anthropology is implicated also in a second aspect of Western ethical frames challenged by Luther's expression of God indwelling creation. Ethics has constructed the moral universe within anthropological boundaries. Not only is the individual the primary *human* unit in relationship to God (as noted above), but the human individual is the primary unit of all creation in relationship to God. Moral obligation extends only to the human species (with a few exceptions, such as animal rights). As Christian ethicist Larry Rasmussen notes, for instance, many moral dimensions of ecological destruction are not only ignored, they are not even perceived.[17] "Our ethical traditions," says priest and cultural historian Thomas Berry, "know how to deal with suicide, homicide, and even genocide; but these traditions collapse when confronted with biocide, the extinction of the vulnerable life systems of the Earth."[18] Moral agency, even more than moral obligation, is a non-category outside the human orbit. The limitation of the moral to the human is enforced by many disciplines contributing to moral theory, including philosophy, political theory, legal theory, and theology.

Anthropocentric boundaries to the scope of morality are rendered obsolete by the reality emergent in the last half of the twentieth century: human actions are degrading and destroying the ecosystems upon which life depends. The actual destructive impact of our species' presence on Earth expands the moral universe beyond human boundaries to biophysical and geoplanetary scope. Luther's insistence that the God of boundless love is in "all creatures" and that "everything is full of Christ through and through" challenges those boundaries theologically and opens a door to the provocative notion that moral agency to serve creation's well-being may indwell creation itself.

Fascinating continuities appear between Luther and varied streams of feminist relational theology that elaborate "relationality as a basic category of existence," if not the primary category.[19] First, the primacy of relationship "where the key concepts are mutuality, reciprocity, interdependence, a passion for right relationship, and the just interconnectedness of all things" is at the "heart of feminist reconstructions of ethics" and of moral agency.[20] The revaluation of relationships, asserts theologian Elizabeth Johnson, "has within it the beginnings of a moral revolution."[21] Seminal arguments for the primacy of mutual relation in contemporary feminist theo-ethics are by Beverly Harrison in "The Power of Anger in the Work of Love"[22] and Carter Heyward in *The Redemption of God: A Theology of Mutual Relation.* Others have built upon their work or have developed relationship as central to ethics from other angles.[23]

A second continuity is the shared acknowledgment of Divine presence in morally empowering relationality.[24] Third, varied streams of feminist theological and theo-ethical discourse share with Luther the affirmation of God's incarnation in and among human beings and other parts of creation.[25] A fourth point of continuity is the claim that God indwelling may empower human efforts at resistance and transformation.[26] (Neither Luther nor much feminist work adequately deals explicitly with the implications for moral agency, excepting that of Mary Grey in both *Prophecy and Mysticism* and *Redeeming the Dream*.) Luther's insistence that God indwelling humans also indwells all created things finds resonance in eco-feminist and relational feminist theologians' moves to deconstruct the nature/culture split by locating humanity *in* a cosmic web of life.[27] Sixth, they share a sensibility that relationship between God and creatures is deeply sensuous. Hear the similarity in expression between Luther and feminist theologian Carter Heyward. According to Luther, we "taste the Word," touch God, and see God marvelously revealed in a grain of wheat. For Heyward, "We want to see, to touch, to taste this power, this source of justice and compassion in our life together . . . this God."[28] Finally, both Luther and feminist relational theology challenge the modern dissociation of moral from spiritual life and the privatization of "personal relationship with God."

Clarification is in order regarding my use of the terms *sacrament* and *sacramental*. My intent is neither to engage the doctrinal history of the concepts and Luther's positions (plural) in that history, nor to enter the interpretive debates regarding Luther's sacramental theology (which developed over time in response to contextual factors). Rather, I use the terms constructively for the purpose of hearing and proclaiming the gospel in today's context of economic globalization. My use is grounded in Luther, goes beyond the "strictly speaking," enumeration of two (or three) sacraments that he wrote "has seemed proper" and is consistent with his sense of incarnation and gospel.[29] With Luther, I understand a sacrament to be a gift from God in which God promises and offers grace as both forgiveness of sin and Christ's actual presence and provides a material sign of that grace. While some interpreters of Luther equate the "gift" singularly with the "forgiveness of sins," Luther does not make this limited equation. The bread, he wrote, is given "for you *and* for the forgiveness of sins."[30] The gift of the sacrament is, according to Luther, vaster than the forgiveness of sins but always includes it. The gift is Jesus Christ incarnate: flesh and blood, born in this world, crucified, risen, and living with/among/in/above/below creatures. Reformation historian Heiko Oberman states it this way: according to Luther, "The manger and the altar confront the Devil with the unattainable. . . . as powerful as the devil is, he cannot become flesh and blood. . . . The demonic . . . adversary of God . . . [is] present in the world, but only Christ the Son is *corporally* present."[31] My interpretation that the gift given in the sacrament includes Christ in bodily form today is supported by Luther's claim that "we go to the sacrament because we receive there a great treasure, through and in which we obtain the forgiveness of sins."[32] The "great treasure" is the living, incarnate Christ. Sacrament, then, refers to God's gift—promised, offered, and experienced as a sensual,[33] earthly, embodied sign—of God's creating, saving, sustaining love for the world and corporal presence within it.

My use of "sacrament" to describe the *communio* of God incarnate in and among us as human communities and as a cosmic community of life coheres with these "Luther-an" notions. The cosmic scope of sacramental *communio* is an ancient tradition with strong and varied theological roots. The tradition is reflected today in Lutheran Eucharistic liturgy calling upon human beings in the *communio* to "sing with all the creatures of God and join in the hymn of all creation."

I do not claim that Luther went the way I am going with his theology of the indwelling God. Rather, Luther's expressions of God immanent—held in light of my theological sensibilities and the moral crises inherent in globalization—open doors in the directions I suggest and point a way. Luther—as a contextual, experiential, critical, and constructive theologian—did not uproot the theological formulations of past teachers and deposit them into his context but worked critically and constructively with them to reveal the gospel in his time and place. Luther's theological heirs, drawing upon him, ought do no less.

Cosmic *Communio* as Subversive Moral Agency

The "subversive" claim, drawn from Luther's articulation of the indwelling Christ, is this: The power of God's compassionate, justice-making, unquenchable love for creation may live within/among human beings and the rest of nature. Moral agency for living toward the flourishing of creation—which includes subverting economic systems that render death and destruction—may flow from embodied *communio* in which God incarnate is received and given. The more fully people receive Her love and become it, the more able they are, as *communio*, to resist economic structures and ideologies that thwart the gift of abundant life for all. Practices and beliefs that deepen communion among the incarnate God and the creatures deepen moral power.

This assertion, considered in the context of globalization, provokes countless questions. Some questions concern the claim's *normative* implications for economic life. According to Luther, Christ indwelling theologically names an invitation and obligation to "neighbor-love"—qualified by self-care and by prioritizing the vulnerable—as the guiding norm of economic life. This chapter finds a second implied economic norm: regenerative Earth-human relations. Where Earth, "neighbor," or self is subject to economic exploitation, these two norms call for denouncing and resisting that exploitation and working toward economic policies and structures that serve social justice and Earth's ongoing flourishing.

While we will consider those economic norms and the economic practices to which they point, normative considerations are not the focal point of this inquiry. Rather, we continue to center on questions of agency for living toward the norms of neighbor-love and sustainable Earth-human relations in the context of globalization. These norms would be utterly daunting were they not accompanied by a source of power for living into them.

At issue, then, is *how* the indwelling Christ may be realized in our time and place as moral-spiritual power for resistance to unjust economic structures. Luther, read through the lenses of liberationist sensibilities and of contemporary feminist theologies of the immanent divine, suggests many possibilities—more than can be followed in one book. We consider just two interdependent lines of inquiry, both in relationship to morally disabling dynamics identified in previous chapters.

- In the context of globalization, what *moral anthropological framework* —specifically pertaining to moral identity and freedom and the *telos* (end) of economic activity—*flowing from* communion with the indwelling God might counter the "market myths" and curtailed democratic political participation undergirding globalization?

- In the context of globalization, what *practices flowing from* communion with the indwelling God might counter the "market myths" and curtailed democratic political participation undergirding globalization?

In the remainder of this chapter, we consider in turn: (1) a moral anthropological framework issuing *from* the indwelling Christ and issuing *in* moral agency, (2) two sacramental practices issuing from and in the same, and (3) the convergence of this framework and these practices as subversive moral power in the context of globalization. Finally, we glean crucial warnings by examining the morally disempowering impact of Luther's socio-theological ideology and his exclusive constructions of neighbor.

Moral Identity, Freedom, and Purpose

Chapter 4 examined the moral identity, the freedom, and the *telos* of economic activity implied by Luther's expressions of the indwelling Christ. Here I argue that this framework theologically counters the market myths of (1) human being as *homo economicus, consumens, dominans*; (2) freedom as freedom for endless acquisition and consumption; and (3) the *telos* of economic activity as economic growth alone. This framework points to economic ways that serve justice, compassion, and sustainability. Consider two salient dimensions (among many) of the moral anthropological framework inherent in Luther's notion of human as habitation of God: first, freedom is from *homo economicus, consumens, et dominans;* and second, together with other-than-human creation, human beings are co-bearers of God.

The notion of self inscribed by neo-liberal globalization, *homo economicus, consumens, et dominans*—the autonomous individual wisely optimizing utility above all else, boldly harnessing resources (intelligence, time, possessions, Earth's bounty, etc.) for wealth creation, and whose worth depends upon power to control capital and to consume—is, in Luther's terms, a "self turned in on oneself." For the "self turned in on oneself," freedom is the freedom to consume and to accumulate wealth without limits and to do as one pleases in the marketplace with one's property. Freedom is *from* the demands of the "pluralistic common good" and from public accountability, scrutiny, regulation, and responsibility. The purpose of economic activity, for *se incurvatus in se,* is consumption and wealth accumulation. As Lutheran theologian Elizabeth Bettenhausen notes, Luther's *"se incurvatus in se*—self turned in on oneself—is one of the best categories for critical analysis of . . . the dominant culture. . . . To live turned in on oneself is synonymous with the autonomous individualism running rampant in this culture dominated by consumer capitalism."[34]

Luther's sense of the indwelling Christ fundamentally agrees with this moral anthropology but, in contrast to neo-liberal ideology, offers a notion of freedom *from* it, not *for* it; a *telos* of economic life that contradicts this moral identity, rather than coheres with it; and a radically alternative identity received by faith through grace alone. Left on our own, and seeking salvation by human power, human beings are "selves turned in on self." As such, we also are beloved ones of God. Receiving God's love by grace alone through faith alone, trusting God's love, and experiencing it in the *communio,* we are changed—over time—in two interdependent senses: We are changed by God's love into a *communio,* and we become not only objects but also agents of God's unquenchable love for creation—lovers as well as beloved. Both changes imply moral-spiritual power to seek a well-being beyond that of self. As lovers who, in *communio,* love with God's love, our lives—and specifically our economic lives—serve the neighbor's well-being and an "adequate livelihood" for ourselves. Christ provides not only the norms for economic life, but also, by Christ's indwelling presence, the identity and agency to live ever more closely to those norms. Human beings, in sacramental *communio,* become both Christ-bearers to others and the Earth community, and recipients of Christ from them. Freedom is *from* life according to *se incurvatus in se.* Freedom from *se incurvatus en se* is freedom from *homo economicus, consumens, et dominans,* and *for* "that which seeks the common good of all."[35] Self is no longer an autonomous individual, but a being-in-*communio.* As economic life is fundamentally an act in relationship to neighbor, community, and Earth, its *telos* is to serve their well-being, as well as one's own. As argued in chapter 4, these theological notions of the human, freedom, and purpose of economic activity—inherent in Luther's articulation of the indwelling Christ—issued in standards for economic life that theologically denounced and contradicted the emerging capitalism of Luther's day.

A feminist lens reveals problems in this notion of moral agency. As a premodern man, Luther mastered a postmodern task: decentering the autonomous moral agent. The western ethical tradition has been trapped for at least three hundred years in the assumption that moral agency is a function primarily of autonomous individuals. Luther springs that trap by insisting that moral agency is a function of the *communio*; no community, no moral agents. Yet he presents another problem. The agent of moral being and doing is not the person; the moral agent is the indwelling Christ received only after being and doing, grounded in our own agency, has ceased and we have become totally dependent upon God. The moral actor, for Luther, is less the person than the indwelling Christ.[36] Feminists have long fought against the negation of women's moral agency. Moral agents only in community sits well; but moral agents whose moral power depends upon an apparent form of self-negation could undermine the reclaiming of moral power by women and others long denied full agency. Feminist relational theology and process theology offer, as a constructive theological route through the dilemma, their insistence on mutually creative interaction between human and God. The same path is suggested by Luther himself in his claim that God works not only "through us" but "with us." While the problem is not resolved here, for now, this is clear: Moral agency as the indwelling Christ offering freedom from *homo economicus, consumens, et dominans* radically empowers the moral agent. To do so in a context in which moral agency is disabled by the structures and ideologies of economic globalization offers possibility and hope worth pursuing.

Luther's panentheism (sense of God's presence everywhere, in all things) beckons toward the second dimension of potentially subversive moral identity extending from the immanent God: human creatures, *together with other-than-human creation,* are habitation of God.[37] Recall that, for Luther, God's indwelling presence is given not only to human beings, but to all creatures and elements. They are dwelling place and revelation of God (and source of marvelous wonder[38]). "The power of God . . . must be essentially present in all places even in the tiniest leaf."[39] God is "present in every single creature in its innermost and outermost being. . . ."[40] Earth bears and reveals the infinite.

God "is in and through all creatures, in all their parts and places, so that the world is full of God and He fills all. . . ."[41] The presence of God taking bodily form in "our" many forms suggests a web of connectedness pregnant with implications for moral identity and agency. We consider one: God as boundless justice-seeking love, living and loving not only in human beings but also in the rest of creation implies that other-than-human creatures and elements may offer moral power toward creation's flourishing.

To think theologically about the moral agency that flows from God indwelling an intrinsically intra-related creation, God inhabiting "every little seed" and "all creatures," is to struggle for and with "a concept that does not exist" in western Protestant ethics.[42] The most fruitful intimations are by Irenaeus, the "Great Cappadocians," and other pre-Augustinian theologians; some (other) mystical theologians throughout the ages; contemporary feminist theologians of mutual relationship and of divine immanence; and nascent notions of "ecological ethics *as* method in ethics."[43] From the latter two categories, I draw both inspiration and insight in order to "think with" Luther's theology of the indwelling God toward subversive moral agency in the globalizing economy.

Elizabeth Bettenhausen describes Luther's panentheism as a "theological feast." She inquires how it might help "bump us out of cultural captivity" and enable the church to "subvert" preferential treatment of the privileged and exclusionary norms regarding sexual orientation.[44] Mary Grey draws upon Carter Heyward's model of God as empowering, liberating, life-giving mutual relation and expands that relationality to include all creation. She refers to relationality between all things as the "a dynamic flow of passionate energy . . . the fundamental creative and healing energy of existence . . . [that] flows from the being of God." Her ethical aim is to connect this cosmic relationality with the Christian redemptive mystery in a way that may be "transformative of society as a whole."[45] Grace Jantzen argues, from historical theology and philosophy, that God has a body and it is the universe, including human beings. Her ethical point is not her main point, but it is clear: "Those who have seen themselves and the world about them as embodiment and self-manifestation of God are unlikely to continue to treat it in a vulgar way or feel it utterly alien or devoid of intrinsic significance and worth."[46] Sallie McFague constructs a theo-ethical "model" of the universe as God's body, rooted in the common creation story and qualified by a "cosmic Christic paradigm . . . of inclusive love for all, especially the oppressed, the outcast, the vulnerable." God is "in the bodies of all creatures and things." Her ethical agenda resonates with mine: to help "first-world, privileged, mainstream Christians think and act differently, . . . [according to a] new shape for humanity, a way of being in the world [that will] help the Earth survive and prosper. . . . It is a Christic shape for humanity, the body of God qualified by the liberating, healing, and inclusive love of Christ."[47] Nancie Erhard breaks new ground, probing the moral power that may inhere in more-than-human dimensions of creation.[48]

My work builds on these contributions. Heyward's theology of mutual relation is foundational. Bettenhausen's insistence on subversive and trans-formative ethical implications of Luther's panentheism en-courage my impulse to "mine" Luther for clues to subversive moral agency. Grey's triple moves—"to enthrone community as mystic," to widen Heyward's relational theology explicitly to "embrace the natural world,"[49] and to find in those steps transformative power on the macro level—affirm my insistence on cosmic *communio* as wellspring of subversive moral agency for public life. Jantzen provides invaluable theological and philosophical grounding for "world as God's body." McFague's constructive proposal ends with the ques-tions and conditions of agency with which I begin. "At the end of the day," she says, "one can easily lose heart. . . . planetary responsibility is too much for us. . . . How [does one] get up in the morning and keep going?" "This is our hope against hope, that our efforts on behalf of our planet are not ours alone but that the source and power of life in the universe is working *in and through us* for the well-being of all creation, including our tiny part in it."[50]

Sacramental Practices: Eucharist and Solidarity

Where theological reconstruction offers oppositional identity cutting against the myths and mandates of neo-liberal globalization, what empowers people to practice that identity? What enables us to embody it in economic life? How does a claim that God lives in us and in the rest of creation play out as moral power to forge economic ways that counter exploitation and ecological destruction?

We turn to Luther for clues. His impassioned descriptions of the moral power flowing from God's indwelling presence contrast glaringly with the moral inertia of our contemporary North American context. Luther claimed that Christ indwelling would gradually lead and enable Christians to shape economic practices that "love" (that is, serve the well-being of) vulnerable neighbors. In contrast, we buy from, invest in, and work for transnational corporations that destroy ecosystems and extract the lifeblood from many global neighbors. We live subject to an economy that requires us to exploit rather than to serve both Earth and neighbor. We do not define oppositional economic norms and practices that serve the neighbors' good. Why this enor-mous contrast? If indeed the compassionate, justice-seeking love of Christ dwells and works in us, why are we passive in the face of our neighbors' need?

Luther's response is explicit: where moral agency is missing in a faith community, it has not properly maintained certain *practices*. The previous chapter argued that, according to Luther, in the communities' practices, the living Christ is received. People in Christian communities come to *be* the neighbor and to live in ways that love the neighbor when Christ indwells and transforms. Christ indwells and transforms when Christ is known.[51] Christ is known through certain practices. It is, thus, in certain practices that the living Christ becomes known, builds in the faithful her abode, and transforms them into beings who love with the actual active love of Christ. While the indwelling Presence and its transforming power are *gift alone*, God gives that gift through the practices of sacramental communities. When human communities ignore the practices through which God comes to and into them, they do not know the Word and "taste the Word"; they do not receive the gift of presence and power, of "bold, dauntless courage."[52]

The previous chapter identified six practices through which, according to Luther, the living Christ indwells and empowers communities of the faithful. Here we consider two of them in more depth: (1) the sacramental practice of the Eucharist, and (2) the sacramental practice of "being with and for" those who are in need, by becoming Christ's love for them and receiving Christ's love from them. I refer to the latter as the practice of accompaniment (being with) and solidarity (being for); henceforth, I use the term *solidarity* to signify this practice. In the end, these two sacramental practices—Eucharist and solidarity—converge as inextricably interdependent, and as subversive *communio* in the contemporary context of economic globalization.

Eucharist: "So Changes a Person . . ."

As Elizabeth Bettenhausen suggests, for Luther the motive and agency for love manifest in just relationships and service is eucharistic.[53] The reality of Christian community is eucharistic. The Eucharist is a "communion [of] love," says Luther.[54] Ethical implications of the Eucharist—especially in terms of moral agency—are immense and concrete, as seen in "The Blessed Sacrament of the Holy and True Body and Blood of Christ, and the Brotherhoods." Luther writes:

> Christ has given his body for this purpose, that the one thing signified by the sacrament—the fellowship, *the change wrought by love—may be put into practice.*
>
> The sacrament has no blessing and significance unless love grows daily and *so changes a person* that he is made one with the others.
>
> Thus by means of this sacrament, all self-seeking love is rooted out and gives place to that which *seeks the common good of all.*
>
> When you have partaken of this sacrament, therefore, or desire to partake of it, you must in turn share the misfortunes of the fellowship. . . . Here your heart

must go out in love and learn that this is a sacrament of love. As love and support are given you, you in turn must render love and support to Christ's in his needy ones. . . . See as you uphold all of them, so they all in turn uphold you; and all things are in common, both good and evil.

In times past this sacrament was so properly used, and the people were taught to understand this fellowship so well, that they even gathered food and material goods in the church, and then . . . distributed among those who were in need. . . . This has all disappeared, and now there remain only the many masses and the many who receive this sacrament without in the least understanding or practicing what it signifies. . . . They will not help the poor, put up with sinners, care for the sorrowing, suffer with the suffering, intercede for others, defend the truth.[55]

The fruit of the Eucharist, "properly" practiced, is a community of moral agency that attends to human needs, including material needs, and privileges the needs of the "vulnerable." (We will see presently the surprising extent to which, for Luther, "helping the poor" refers not merely to charity but to vehement, theologically grounded—even confessional—denunciation of economic exploitation, and to economic principles and practices diametrically opposed to the emerging capitalist economic order. Thus, for contemporary purposes, I "translate" Luther's language—"helping the poor"—into less patronizing terms actually more consistent with this broader referent in his economic ethics.)

Implicit in Luther's work is the notion, found also in Dietrich Bonhoeffer and in Carter Heyward, that we can be "for" others only as we are "with" others and they are with and for us.[56] "Walking the walk" is not the purview of isolated moral individuals. On December 2, 1518, after having refused in Augsburg to recant, and realizing that his very life was in danger, Luther wrote to his friend Spalatin, "Pray for me, I am in the hands of God and my friends." According to Luther, people do not become moral agents outside of the mystical and practical, earthly reality of sacramental community. Christian moral life is ontologically sacramental and communal. In fact, according to Luther's almost quaint yet theo-ethically complex and loaded explanation, God "wants" to be in community of moral agency with us: "[God] is able to help everyone. . . . He does not want to do it alone. He wants us to work with him . . . wants to work *with us and through us*."[57]

Eucharist with Solidarity: "Re-membering the Body of Christ . . ."

North American Christian communities, in sites of relative economic privilege, regularly and sincerely celebrate the Eucharist, yet economic life rarely is transformed toward justice and sustainability. We do not love neighbor (human and other) by resisting economic brutality and injustice. "The one thing signified by the sacrament," according to Luther, "the fellowship, the change wrought by love is" not "put into practice" in economic life. "By means of this sacrament, all self-seeking love is" not "rooted out, giving place to that which seeks the common good of all." Often, the Eucharist does not issue in communities of moral power. Why? What is missing or distorted in our practice of the Eucharist? How might this absence or distortion be undone?[58]

Luther's response, grounded in the indwelling presence of Christ, is the *inextricable connectedness* of the two sacramental practices identified above: the practice of the Eucharist and the practice of solidarity (being with and for others). If it is to cohere with its meaning and bear fruit in moral agency, the Eucharist is inseparable from solidarity with people who are exploited or suffering, economically or otherwise. Luther insists that when the Eucharist was properly understood and practiced, the people also were meeting the material needs of the poor, but "this has all disappeared, and now there remain only the many masses and the many who receive this sacrament *without in the least understanding or practicing what it signifies*. . . . They will not help the poor" (italics mine). Where Christian communities do not seek to live out the Eucharist in the active love that it promises, moral power to conform economic practice to who we are, the communal *body* of Christ, is not born.

Luther's response is echoed, theologically and practically, in William Cavanaugh's *Torture and the Eucharist*, an account of resistance to the torture systematically imposed by the Chilean regime of dictator Augusto Pinochet.[59] Cavanaugh argues that moral power for resistance was born of Eucharist wed to solidarity. He writes, "Eucharist is the key to Christian resistance to torture." "The effect [of torture is to] atomize the citizenry through fear, thereby dismantling other *social* bodies that would rival the state's authority over *individual* bodies" (italics added). "If this is the case, then true resistance to torture depends upon the reappearance of social bodies capable of countering the atomizing performance of the state." Under Pinochet's regime, parts of the church were able to "draw on the resources of the Eucharist" to become those social bodies by "practicing the body of Christ," a social body of mutual solidarity, despite the risk involved. The theology and practice of "Eucharistic solidarity" was the "church's eventual reappearance as the body of Christ in opposition to the social strategy of torture." That body developed networks of mutual assistance (called "The Vicariate of Solidarity") in all aspects of life threatened by the regime. Where the regime isolated people from one another, solidarity "knit people back together, connecting them as members of one another . . . reknitting the social fabric torn by the regime's strategy of atomization, . . . enacting the body of Christ." Eucharist with solidarity became a "literal re-membering of Christ's body, a knitting together of the body of Christ . . .

conform[ing] the followers of Christ to the true body of Christ. . . . Jesus commanded his followers, 'Do this in re-memberance of me' (Luke 22:19)."[60]

In a sense that goes beyond full understanding into "mystery," the sacramental practices of Eucharist and solidarity are inseparable.[61] Eucharist, bound to solidarity, disallows complicity with a model of globalization that mandates the antithesis of solidarity—exploitation. Where we eschew the sacrament of solidarity, the "sacrament [of the Lord's Supper] has no blessing and significance"; the *communio* of moral agency given in the Eucharist is not born.[62]

Solidarity: "A Sacrament of Love . . ."

The term *solidarity* is overused and misused. In naming solidarity as normative—especially when that move is derived partially from Luther's theology—the ground gets murky, the terrain strewn with dangerous pits invisible to the eyes of privilege, pits of good intentions blindly held, that may spell ongoing violation of those on the flip side of privilege. So complex is the path that the urge is to turn away. Yet, the insistent pull of this incarnational notion—that the God of compassionate justice-making love breathes in us—pushes us to explore solidarity as the practice of that indwelling presence. While the problems with solidarity as a norm warrant book-length treatment, the most dangerous responses would be to desert the normativity of solidarity, or to perpetuate its uncritical use. These responses I reject. In order, then, is a sketch of three key difficulties with solidarity as normative, and responses to them.[63]

The first problem pertains to solidarity when it occurs across power differentials and lines of difference that are historically configured by domination. Womanist ethicist Emilie Townes paints the problem in stunning terms.

> to talk about standing with one another
> to conjure solidarity across differences . . .
>   is . . . to tempt the agony of the absurd . . .
>   to work in solidarity with those who are like me
>   unlike me
>   or resemble me
> does not demand or require that I save those who would see others dead
>   or annihilated
>   either through neglect
>   indifference
>   calculation
>   or theo-ethical musings

I will not rescue the killers . . .
in other words
> *for me and my house*
> *standing with others across differences*
does not require that I be run over in a mad teleological drive toward a
misbegotten notion of solidarity. . . .[64]

Solidarity, from positions of relative economic privilege, is solidarity with people brutalized by the very ideologies and structures providing that privilege. What kind of hypocrisy is implied when "those who would see others dead or annihilated either through neglect [or] indifference" claim solidarity with the victims?

Yet, despite this contradiction, Townes refuses to relinquish solidarity and its centrality to faith:

> *to speak of solidarity*
> > *to conjure standing anywhere together*
> *is, then, to tempt the agony of the absurd*
> *but frankly, I simply don't know what else to do*
> > *and remain faithful*

Neither can I relinquish solidarity as integral to faith life. Having experienced the daily life of people for whom poverty is death, having found myself accountable to the mothers and fathers of youth killed for resistance to systems that impose that poverty, and having encountered Luther's theological appeal to solidarity as inherent in the Eucharist "properly practiced," I cannot relinquish solidarity, as a "form of Jesus Christ taking form in us."[65]

The question becomes, "By what norm does solidarity across historical lines of difference—where difference spells domination/subordination—serve the cause of justice and creation's healing?" Comprehensive response, not possible here, revolves around the norm of attending to differences for the purpose of dismantling structured domination. Theorizing solidarity requires theorizing difference and, as feminist ethicist Marilyn Legge writes, "discourse of difference requires attention to power in relationships that have been historically shaped by domination and subordination."[66] If "solidarity respectful of difference is the basic norm of theological praxis," then solidarity must be reclaimed from all theorizing and practice that suppress difference, and reclaimed for dismantling domination.[67] And solidarity must cross multiple categories of difference including but not limited to race, gender, class, and sexual preference.

A second problem: a feminist lens suspects "solidarity as neighbor-love," where neighbor-love is constructed as "servanthood," or as antithetical to self-love.[68] Luther's construction of neighbor-love as servanthood, and an *apparent* theological opposition between neighbor-love and self-love, permeates his writing.[69] Yet (as noted in chapter 4), a closer look reveals that his understanding of Christ indwelling believers cuts against that seeming disregard for self-love. The indwelling Christ builds *communio* in which one not only serves but *is served.* Not only does one bear others' burdens, but one's burdens are born by others.[70] That is, solidarity is normed by *mutuality*, a weave of being with, being for, and receiving from.[71]

In the context of globalization, mutuality as a norm for solidarity plays out concretely in the emerging acknowledgment that crucial knowledge for the long journey toward just economics and sustainable Earth-human relations will come from indigenous peoples and others on the margins whose ways of life are being extinguished by the mechanisms of liberalization. Mutuality in solidarity may also take shape in the growing realization that ultimately, if globalization is threatening the air, waters, and soil on which all human life depends, we all are "victims."

The indwelling Christ, held in the light of Luther's conviction that the living Word is known in the believer's particular life struggles, offers an additional resource for undoing the problem of neighbor-love as servanthood and as antithetical to self-love. Luther insists that the Christ who dwells in human beings is not Christ as interpreted by Luther, but rather Christ present in the realities, struggles, and crises of particular communities and people. Thus, for example, Christ indwelling a person brutalized by enforced servanthood might not be primarily the Christ of servant love, but the Christ of self-respect and self-love. Luther offers this: Christ, who lives and loves in human beings, lives and loves in different fashions depending upon the particular struggles of the believer or community of believers. Luther's "contextual" christology opens the door to contextually shaped forms of Christ's embodied love.[72]

A third problem with solidarity is its usually anthropocentric construction. As noted earlier, the lethal threats posed by neo-liberal globalization to other-than-human species and to Earth's life-support systems, the dawning realization (in theology, the physical sciences, and elsewhere) that life is an interconnected web, and Luther's panentheism repudiate boundaries limiting solidarity to the human sphere. The norm of a geoplanetary and biophysical, rather than anthropocentric, moral scope is added. This norm becomes richly suggestive when wed to the aforementioned norms of mutuality and of defying domination. Mutuality suggests, for instance that lifesaving guidance toward economic alternatives may come *from* Earth's ecosystems. Defying domination implies dismantling the structured (and theologically rationalized) relationship of exploitation between the human species and the Earth.

In sum, although solidarity may not be claimed uncritically, we must revive and rethink it in our contemporary economic context. "It could not be otherwise," writes womanist theologian Shawn Copeland, "for the incarnation is God's own radical act of solidarity, God's act of love, hope, life enfleshed in Jesus. And is this not the task of authentic Christians of different histories, cultures, times and places—to enflesh love and hope and life wherever love and hope and life are fragile?"[73] Solidarity as "embodying the compassionate, justice-seeking love of God" in the context of neo-liberal globalization is normed by planetary scope, mutuality, and attending to difference for the purpose of dismantling domination.

We return to the central task at hand: to unfold the implications of a challenge posed to economically privileged Christians today. The challenge is this: The Eucharist is inseparable from the sacramental practice of solidarity. Where solidarity is not practiced, the *communio* of moral agency given in the Eucharist does not come into being. Eucharist, thus, disallows complicity with a model of globalization that mandates the antithesis of solidarity: exploitation.

Solidarity in economic life takes different forms in different circumstances. Here I suggest a guidepost for the practice of solidarity by economically privileged North American Christian communities today. In response to globalization, solidarity should take one paramount form—that of "perceiving and remembering from the perspectives of people, peoples, and other parts of creation on the 'underside' of globalization, and heeding what is seen and heard there regarding past, present, and future consequences of globalization, and regarding sustainable and just alternatives." Solidarity entails seeing, hearing, and heeding what is obscured by privilege: people and other parts of creation destroyed, degraded, or impoverished by five centuries of globalization, culminating in its contemporary form.[74] Said differently, people of economic privilege will seek out and hear the stories of those who experience globalization as a threat to life and will respond to those voices.[75] Solidarity as "perceiving from the underside" is worthy of the name only if it issues in responsible, responsive action.

These claims, in light of our quest for moral power, raise many questions. For instance, in what sense is solidarity as "seeing and remembering from the 'underside'" *crucial* for enabling moral agency in the context of globalization? Asked differently, what necessary ingredients of subversive moral power does this form of solidarity offer?

Opening mind and heart to historical and current realities of people marginalized or exploited in "three waves of globalization," and to the ecological devastation it has wrought, begins to undo the blindness and amnesia enabling those waves to proceed relatively unchallenged by people who have benefited from them. Recall the role of blindness and amnesia in undercutting moral power, as noted in chapter 3. Drawing on the work of John McMurtry, I identified two "defining features" of a society in which an ideology gains power to shape social life according to its mores, even when they demand ongoing destruction or degradation. One defining feature was "blind[ness] to the harm [the ideology] causes." Society refuses to recognize destructive consequences or anything that questions the norms and practices mandated by the ideology. Destructive consequences are ignored or considered inconsequential, unavoidable, or the fault of those who are harmed. Socio-ecological blindness and historical amnesia, together with actual physical avoidance, allow economically privileged people to disregard the consequences of neo-liberal globalization and thus to deny the moral imperative for alternatives.[76] Moral power for resistance is a mute point where the need for change goes unrecognized.

That amnesia and blindness undergird the market myth of inevitability, according to which the prevailing form of globalization is a natural step in the irresistible march of progress under "democratic capitalism." Liberal Christianity's alignment with this myth, and the necessity of *not seeing* in sustaining it, are summarized well by theologian Douglas John Hall:

> [Western] Christianity in the modern epoch . . . gave itself over to a vision that promised the imminent emergence of a better world within history . . . manifest in daily demonstrations of progress. . . . The nonrecognition, minimization, and resolution of evil formed an integral part of this new world view from its inception. So long as the ideology of progress could seem to be sustained by experience it did not require so great an effort to *close ones eyes* to the evils that were present, always, even at the height of the age of progress. . . . In these decades [the vision of progress] can be maintained only at the expense of *shutting ones eyes* to experience altogether. The nonrecognition and minimalization of evil, which was part of this enterprise from the outset, has assumed the proportions of a way of life. . . . To cling to this . . . today is to abandon the world of daily suffering and responsible stewardship.[77]

Modern Christianity, Hall asserts, has "shut [its] . . . eyes to the data of despair."[78] This is the blindness and amnesia that allow people of economic privilege to carry on with life as though the ways in which we eat, clothe and transport ourselves, recreate, and work (and the "free" trade and investment regimes sustaining those ways) are not jeopardizing our children's future, the ecosystems on which human life depends, and the lives and dignity of multitudes. The refusal to *see* globalization's current and future consequences and to remember five hundred years of impact on the indigenous peoples of Africa, the Americas, and Australia is a critical factor "disabling" our moral power to resist globalization in its dominant form. "Enabling" that

Healing a Broken World

moral agency requires seeing and remembering from perspectives of the brutalized. That Christian moral life requires learning to see, to see differently, and to be guided by a different vision of reality is argued frequently. This crucial claim is utterly insufficient in contexts of domination—economic or other—unless qualified. The missing qualifier is this: the indispensable lens for dismantling domination is the lens of the underside.

Awakened historical memory and critical vision are both a blessing and a curse. The curse is the pain of seeing infinite suffering and glimpsing one's complicity in it. From this kind of pain we naturally shrink. It is dangerous. It may debilitate, paralyze, breed self-hatred, or reinstate avoidance and denial unless the pain is tended carefully and respectfully, wed paradoxically to self-respect, and shared by knowing companionship. That companionship, as eucharistic *communio*, assures the presence of grace beyond the pain. A *communio* of solidarity and Eucharist may be the "place where people can speak the unspeakable"[79] and be heard and heeded, where people can hear the unhearable and respond.

The blessings offered by critical vision wed to historical memory are "vital" in both senses of that word: life-giving and necessary. They include: (1) rage, grief, and fear regarding the destruction and degradation of human and other life; (2) wisdom of subjugated communities, which may offer crucial knowledge for the long path toward economic reordering; (3) critical moral imagination; and (4) hope.[80] These are ingredients of subversive moral agency. That is, they move people to stand up and walk toward resistance and alternatives, where immobilization was the unacknowledged norm.[81] As taught by feminist ethicist Beverly Harrison regarding the first of these: "We should never make light of our power to rage. . . . It is the root of the power to love."[82]

Eucharist and Solidarity Inseparable: "The Change Wrought by Love . . ."

Luther indicates that where moral power is missing, the community is not maintaining certain practices through which the living Christ is known, received, builds abode in the faithful, and loves through and with them. Luther noted six such practices. We have explored two that are called for and flow from relationality with the indwelling Christ as articulated by Luther: the practice of Eucharist and the practice of solidarity. Both are gifts, not rewards or earnings. They merge in communion. The inseparability of these practices is glimpsed in Luther's descriptions of the Eucharist. "Christ has given his body for this purpose, that the one thing signified by the sacrament—the fellowship, the change wrought by love—may be put into practice." The sacrament of the Eucharist becomes communion, the actual presence of Christ "so changing a person that he [or she] is made one with the others," creating active love which "seeks the common good of all."[83] And the sacrament of solidarity becomes "communion," receiving Christ from others and being Christ for them. The one sacrament without the other does not bear fruit in a *communio* of moral power to seek the well-being of all.

Moral Anthropology and Sacramental Practices Converge in Subversive Moral Agency

We first explored moral anthropological constructions inherent in the conviction that God as compassionate justice-seeking love lives in human beings and the rest of creation. These constructions refute contemporary market myths and the diminished role of "the political" inherent in globalization, and open doors to alternatives. Theological constructs, however, do not issue in moral power for social transformation if not embodied in practice. Thus, we considered the practices of Eucharist and solidarity. The convergence of these practices with the aforementioned moral anthropology has stunning implications for moral agency in political-economic life, in Luther's context and in ours. Here, I suggest some of those implications, first for human-human relations and then for Earth-human relations. The focus throughout is on moral agency, although this focus requires also noting normative issues.

As argued in chapter 4, a primary locus of "being with and for" others, in Luther's sacramental theology and economic ethics, was economic life. Economic practices—aimed both at directly addressing the immediate needs of the poor and at denouncing economic exploitation—flowed from the Eucharist. Luther's economic ethics and his sacramental theology are inseparably intertwined. Not surprisingly "The Blessed Sacrament of the Holy and True Body of Christ, and the Brotherhoods," expressing Luther's theology of the Eucharist at the time it was written, also presents his "first suggestions of a communal use of resources for the poor, the common chest."[84]

Economic life as practice of neighbor-love transgressed the emerging capitalist economic order of Luther's day. His struggle against economic exploitation was, in part, a "struggle against . . . the developing money economy of early capitalism."[85] A defining characteristic of contemporary corporate- and finance-driven globalization is the "commodification of money," advanced capitalism taking the "money economy" to a new level. Some economic structures and practices denounced by Luther also undergird economic globalization in its dominant form today. So close is the coherence that, were the norms proposed by Luther adopted today as guiding principles of economic life, they would subvert the prevailing paradigm of economic globalization.

Luther's economic norms, identified in the previous chapter, challenge specific dynamics inherent in that paradigm. Those dynamics include: (1) the elevation of "profit," rather than "an adequate living" for self and household and serving the needs of others, as the goal of economic life, and specifically as the goal of selling products; (2) the severing of economic activity from political constraints; (3) high levels of trade in ostentatious items; and (4) pricing commodities as high as the market will bear, where so doing undermines the well-being of the poor. These dynamics are integral to economic globalization as described in this project's first chapters.

In more general terms, Luther's impassioned economic ethics denounced unregulated market activity that enabled a few to make a profit at the expense of the widespread good or the well-being of the poor. Many of his words speak directly to the global economy today, mirroring the claims of its critics. Both Luther and many contemporary voices protesting the World Trade Organization and various multilateral free trade and investment agreements insist that unregulated transnational "free market" activity endangers the poor and those with limited income. Concerning the "free public market," Luther declares: "Daily the poor are defrauded. New burdens and high prices are imposed. Everyone misuses the market in his own willful, conceited, arrogant way, as if it were his right and privilege to sell his goods as dearly as he pleases without a word of criticism."[86] Luther, as today's critics, insisted that the buying and selling of products ought be subject to "rules and regulations," including "ceilings" on prices, that protect economically vulnerable people. Thus, he writes, public officials "should be alert and resolute enough to establish and maintain order in all areas of trade and commerce *in order that the poor may not be burdened and oppressed.*"[87]

Recall, as noted in the previous chapter, that Luther is very specific. He denounces such economic activity as raising prices when supply is low, buying at a low price from one who needs money so badly that he or she sells low, and buying out the entire supply of a commodity and then raising the price. He condemns the monopolistic practices of large trading companies and calls them "a bottomless pit of avarice and wrong-doing. . . . They control all commodities . . . raise or lower prices at their pleasure. They oppress and ruin all the small businessmen." Through their practices "all the world must be sucked dry and all the money sink and swim in their gullets."[88]

In the words of Reformation historian Carter Lindberg, "in Luther's eyes the international cartels, the multinational corporations of his day, were continually burdening and defrauding the poor."[89]

Note that Luther was concerned not merely about an individual's use of money, but also about the structural social damage inherent in the idolatry of the 'laws' of the market. Ideas of an impersonal market and autonomous laws of economics were abhorrent to Luther because he saw them as both idolatrous and socially destructive. *He saw the entire community endangered by the financial power of a few great economic centers. . . . He saw an economic coercion immune to normal jurisdiction that would destroy the ethos of the community. . . . Luther believed that the church was called to reject publicly and unequivocally these economic developments and to develop a constructive social ethic that would include public accountability of large businesses through government regulation. Only through government regulation was justice possible for the poor.*[90]

"In the end, Luther considered early capitalism to constitute a status confessionis . . . for the church."[91] Many contemporary voices, in like manner, claim that complicity with economic globalization is contrary to Christian faith.

These connections between Luther's audacious norms for economic life and economic globalization today are striking in light of my earlier historical analysis, which situates contemporary globalization as the third wave in a historical trajectory that began in Luther's era. That analysis identifies the "first wave" of globalization as the colonization of three continents by the tribes of Europe, a development intimately and chronologically connected to the emerging capitalist economic practices against which Luther railed theologically.

My point is not to advocate a direct and uncritical application of Luther's economic analysis or norms to the contemporary situation. Given Luther's inflammatory denunciations of Jews, peasants, and Anabaptists, never are his social analyses or social ethics to be adopted uncritically as normative. Nor is my point to imply that Luther was a "progressive" early anti-capitalist. The implication would be false, failing to acknowledge that his condemnation of emerging capitalism and his crafting of alternative economic norms and practices were not rooted in a bent toward progressive social change. His critique was rooted, social-theoretically, in his "conservative" defense of feudal social arrangements and prohibitions on interest, and theologically in his conviction that economic life—as all dimensions of human life—must serve the proclamation and hearing of the gospel, and neighbor-love.[92]

Rather, the salient points are these: Luther's economic ethics had subversive implications in his context, which bore uncanny resemblance to the context of economic globalization today. The subversive nature of Luther's economic norms, and the moral power for heeding them, derives from their theological foundation. That foundation is neighbor-love, manifest in economic life and empowered by Christ's indwelling presence. Economic activity is, ontologically, an act in relationship to neighbor, and all activity in relationship to neighbor is normed and empowered by one principle: true Christians, having received God's love through grace alone, are "filled with" God and grow to actively embody God's love for themselves and others, and to receive it from others. For this reason, widely accepted economic practices that undermine the widespread good or the well-being of the poor are to be subverted—that is, theologically denounced, defied, and replaced with radical alternatives—by the power of Christ's indwelling love. Christians are called and empowered to be "lovers" in their everyday economic lives.

Thus far, our concept of "economic" has pertained to *human* relations. In the current context, however, the beliefs and practices under consideration converge in yet another sense challenging the anthropological boundaries of mainstream western ethical frames that truncate modern humanity's cognizance of the ecological threats posed by globalization. Recall that, for Luther, God who indwells and empowers the faithful, is "flowing and pouring into [all creatures], filling all things."[93] This pregnant theological claim extends the community, the "pluralistic common good," the sacramental *communio,* the neighbor beyond the human to the larger community of life, the Earth community, the "cosmic *communio.*" Luther did not make this extension per se. Yet his panentheist claim, held in light of his contextual theo-ethical method and his conviction that the Word is to be grappled with in places of brokenness and brings life to those places, compels his theological heirs in a time of ecological brokenness to do so.

Before moving in that direction, note that scientific underpinnings of "Earth community" and "cosmic community" are not hard to come by, given dramatically changed views of the physical universe inaugurated in the first three decades of the twentieth century. Physicists and cosmologists speak of a web of connectedness, a relational force or energy, within even the tiniest organism and between the units of the universe. As noted by physicist Fritjof Capra, "In contrast to the mechanistic Cartesian view of the world, the world view emerging from modern physics can be characterized by words like organic, holistic, and ecological. . . . The universe is no longer seen as a machine made up of a multitude of objects, but has to be pictured as one indivisible dynamic whole whose parts are essentially interrelated and can be understood only as patterns of a cosmic process."[94]

Theological foundations for communion between the immanent God and all of creation are readily available if one searches the theological landscape preceding Augustine; emerging again with process theology and eco-feminist theology; and present (but largely unrecognized by mainstream Western ethics) during the centuries between in Orthodox theology, Luther's panentheism, and some streams of Anglican theology. In fact, the intersection of the biophysical sciences with contemporary eco-theologies and relational theologies is precisely in the shared claim that "the fundamental energy of life is relational."[95] Some versions of emerging theological "Earth ethics" build on those long-standing theological foundations.[96] Far more evident, however, is the historical tendency in Western theology to exclude other-than-human parts of creation from community, God's immanence, and the communion between God and creation.[97]

Some descriptive and normative implications of Luther's "world as habitation of God," viewed in the context of economic globalization, are relatively obvious. First, the "pluralistic common good" served by economic life is biophysical and geoplanetary. Our economic lives are judged by whether or not they contribute to the ongoing—that is, regenerative—health of the broader planetary dwelling place of God. As expressed by Larry Rasmussen, in the context of globalization, which "affects all things, not least the Earth's life sources themselves," the moral universe expands beyond the human to encompass Earth and all of its bounty.[98] "The good of all things is more than their good for us, and our own interests are relative to the more inclusive life communities of which we are a part and upon which we utterly depend."[99] Human activities "must now be measured by one stringent criteria: their contributions to an Earth ethic and their advocacy of sustainable Earth community . . . fidelity to Earth."[100] While these norms do not depend upon a claim that God indwells creation, that claim adds to them a provocative and solid theological foundation.[101]

Second, irreconcilable contradictions—both descriptive and normative—appear between life according to "world as habitation of God" on the one hand, and according to the neo-liberal market myths on the other. Where the former sees creatures and elements "filled with God," *homo economicus, consumens, et dominans* sees commodities for acquisition by the highest bidder and resources to be exploited for profit. In contrast to an intradependent economy of life of which human economies are just one part, the neo-liberal model dissociates that "great economy" (the self-renewing economy of nature) from the "big economy" (the present globalizing human economy).[102] This model constructs human "economic activity" as a closed system independent of "the great economy" and "free" constantly to deplete it. An economic model aimed at growth that does not account—morally or economically—for ecological destruction and degradation, and market myths that construct Earth's life systems as exploitable commodities become suspect if the world is God's dwelling place. Collective complacency at the destruction of creation is fed by neo-liberal ideology and feeds it.

Our primary concern in this undertaking, however, is not the normative but the transformative implications of Luther's "creation as habitation of God." That is, how does creation as God's dwelling place create moral power for human beings? One point flows naturally from the discussion thus far: the presence of God within us *as* compassionate justice-seeking love may empower economic practices consistent with that love, even where they entail difficulty or risk. Yet Luther's insistence that God is present in every creature and element hints at another dimension of moral agency rarely considered in Western ethical discourse: by virtue of God's immanence, moral power—formative and transformative—is present in other-than-human dimensions of creation. If God dwells not only in human creatures but also in all of Earth's bounty, then in what sense does or might Her presence and power here nurture human agency to live toward the healing and sustaining of creation.

Contemporary theological forays into ecological ethics tend to be critical (calling attention to the role of Judeo-Christian traditions in the demise of the "environment") or constructive (calling for Earth-sustaining theo-ethical frameworks). I have encountered only two (the work of William Brown and Nancie Erhard) that explore explicitly the morally formative and transformative potential in non-human creation. They question not the impact of human agency on the other-than-human world, but rather its impact on human moral agency.[103] Luther's panentheism (re)opens that door theologically.

Exploring the expansive, fertile terrain on the other side may be a vital step in re-situating humankind in the moral universe in ways that open human capacity to receive and embody God's presence as moral power to forge more just and sustainable ways of living. Dominion theology's "human as master of the created world" with all else subject to "him" fed the market myth of *homo consumens et dominans.* "Human as caretaker of creation" (having largely replaced dominion theology) is riddled with falsehood. Descriptively speaking, the human species' primary role has been ecological destroyer rather than caretaker. Furthermore, "human as caretaker of creation" is challenged by our species' utter dependence on other species for our survival, while other life-forms (except those domesticated by human beings) do not depend for life upon us. Luther's panentheism offers alternatives to both human as master and human as caretaker.

Unfolding those alternatives awaits future work. Here we but raise possibilities and questions. If Christ is indeed present in all creatures, then undauntable, redemptive, liberating love lives in the creatures and elements of this good Earth. Earth *embodies* God not only as creative and revelatory presence, but also as teaching, saving, sustaining, empowering presence.[104] One species wields power to destroy life on Earth as we know and love it and—aided by the laws of economic globalization—is exercising that power. How might subversive moral agency be fed and watered in human beings by God's presence and power coursing through all creation?[105]

Luther's Limitations, Our Limitations, and Beyond

Ideological factors that interrupted, obscured, and betrayed, for Luther, the transformative moral power offered by the indwelling God also undercut that power today. In coming to know those dynamics in Luther's context, we may see them more clearly in our own lives and churches. Illuminating our mistakes by mirroring them, Luther may warn us. As elaborated in the previous chapter, two limiting factors in Luther were exclusive boundaries around "the neighbor" and a socio-theological ideology associating a rigid, hierarchical social order with the laws of nature, God's mandate, and the "common good." We point to both in turn to demonstrate the use of faith forebears to mirror contemporary dynamics that may undercut subversive faithful moral agency.

"Neighbor," as noted previously, is a morally freighted category in Luther's ethics. I noted dramatic inconsistencies in Luther's notion of "neighbor." Despite the inconsistencies, the term, overall, in Luther is a kind of code word for the scope of humanity—outside of self and family— that Christians are to serve "with might and main" the people for whom Christians embody Christ. The point here is not the inconsistencies, but the fact that, for Luther, parts of humanity were excluded from all versions of neighbor (and even, arguably, in the case of the Jews, from the category of fully human).[106] The moral significance of "embodying Christ for neighbors" as both moral norm and source of moral power depends upon the question, "Who is my neighbor?" The compelling question in our day is this: By what social and theological presuppositions do we determine who is "neighbor," and indeed who is fully human? By what criteria are some—human and other—excluded from the parameters of neighbor? The response may be a matter of life and death. The question pertains for any who seek to live faithfully in the globalizing political-economy.

Secondly, I observed in the previous chapter that the subversive moral agency engendered by relationality with the indwelling Christ was undercut, for Luther, by passionately held medieval convictions regarding the ordering of society. These convictions generated allegiance to the social hierarchy of German society and an assumption that the orders of society are the orders of creation. The social order was seen as divinely ordained and as necessary for the well-being of all. Luther's socio-political ideology, we observed, rendered *a norm against* social justice as social equality where it undercut the social order. Today, socially constructed orders of society undermine agency toward economic social justice where those orders are identified with the widespread good, the ways things naturally are, or the inevitable. Relevant here, of course, are social constructions suggesting that some people in the globalizing economy "naturally" have less need or right to education, health care, adequate nutrition and water, just working conditions, or aesthetic and intellectual fulfillment than others.

As with Luther, with us. The moral identity, freedom, purpose, and power created by relationship with the immanent God are undercut by ideology that limits the parameters of neighbor or that naturalizes the reigning socio-ecological order of privilege and exclusion. To see clearly those limiting dynamics is a first step toward subverting them.

In Sum

We have journeyed far. Our "journey between worlds" has been between the ideological and practical workings of neo-liberal globalization, and the mystery of God's boundless love indwelling creation. In the end, we held each in light of the other. We began in the lives of people—many of whom are compassionate, caring, and morally conscientious in many aspects of life—who march on as destroyers of a splendid world. We sought sources of agency for those same people to walk, albeit falteringly, step by step toward ways of economic life—from everyday habits to international structures—that engender social justice and sustainable Earth-human relations. The voice has been one of despair and hope, with hope prevailing, for hope is born of tenaciously pursuing the claim that compels this inquiry.

That subversive claim, explored in Luther's expressions of the indwelling God, is this: as gracious gift, God comes to dwell in the faithful, and in all of creation. Dwelling in the faithful, God transforms them, gradually and in communion with others, into lovers as Christ loves. First objects of Christ's love, they become agents of that love. They are empowered by the indwelling Presence to love beyond self. That love obligates and *enables* denouncing economic exploitation and crafting alternative economic practices, even where those practices are risky and oppositional. In short, moral agency for living toward the flourishing of creation may arise from God's presence within the faithful, and within all of creation. The more fully people receive Her indwelling love and become agents of it, the more able they are, as community, to resist structures of domination, including economic. This process of transformation happens slowly and is never completed in earthly life. Nor is it always evident, for the faithful remain simultaneously sinners and righteous. They are "rusty tools" being polished by God as long as they live.[107]

The claim *that* God indwells and empowers gave rise to the question probed in the current chapter. *How* may "the gracious, furious mystery of God" residing within the creatures and elements of this Earth, and working toward the flourishing of creation, be realized in this time and place as agency for resistance to economic structures that thwart the gift of life?[108]

That is, how may economically privileged North American Christians be empowered by the indwelling God to move from immobilization and complicity to faithful resistance and rebuilding on behalf of Earth and its communities? I argued, in response, that relationship with God inhabiting all of creation issues in an identity utterly contrary to the identity required and constructed by neo-liberal globalization. To *practice* human moral identity as "communal dwelling place of God who inhabits also this good Earth" is to defy and disarm neo-liberalism's "market myths." Identity as "communal dwelling place of God who inhabits also this good Earth" bears fruit in moral agency as that identity is *practiced* in the sacraments of Eucharist and of solidarity when the two are held together.

The mystery of God indwelling the faithful and all of creation, and "tasted" in the bread and wine, is the mystery of Her love incarnate in solidarity. The locus of moral agency is the indwelling presence of God whose love is boundless and unquenchable, will restore the community of life and liberate human beings from being its destroyers, and courses through all of creation. For "nothing can be more truly present and within all creatures than God [Her]self with [Her] power."[109]

6

Invitation

❧

"If the imagination is to transcend and transform experience it has to question, to challenge, to conceive of alternatives, perhaps to the very life you are living at that moment."

—Adrienne Rich

GOD MAKES HOME IN MATTER. The finite bears the infinite. As we awaken each morning, the great Lover and Liberator is alive in and among our bodies. The mystery of creation "is the indwelling of God within it."[1] Our agency to resist economic violence and to live differently is the living Christ, pouring and flowing through us and among us. We "mud creatures" are home to One who breathes through creation healing, making whole, undoing injustice, and restoring right relationships, so that all might have life and have it abundantly.[2] Having received God's subversive love, we are bearers of it.

The purpose of all that I have said is that we might live differently, that we might rise up and walk away from compliance with economic violence and toward resistance, new vision, and rebuilding. The point is that we, in our time and place, might "practice the economic implications"[3] of "the finite bears the infinite." The vision toward which I write is of ordinary people resisting economic brutality and crafting economic ways that enable the household of Earth to flourish. The hope is for everyday people empowered to live toward right relationships—however fallibly—because the "Word, having been made flesh . . . entered into communion with us . . . restoring to all communion with God."[4]

Imagine what this all means—practically—in everyday life, for in the end that is where discipleship takes place. Step back for a moment to where we began, in the concrete lives of economically privileged North Americans. Envision a hypothetical worshiping community composed largely of relatively well-to-do people in a particular place, the Pacific Northwest.

Begin with a day in the life of many in this congregation. They take their Christian faith seriously and seek to live in accord with it. Aware of their call to follow Jesus, they are mature in many ways of doing so. They worship God faithfully, pray, tend compassionately to one another's pain and brokenness, give generously to the church and to charities, serve children of the city as coaches and friends, bring consolation to others facing death or loss, are compassionate to animals, volunteer in soup kitchens and schools, are adept in the life-giving art of friendship. In very important and real senses, they are marvelously formed by faith.

They do not notice that their ways of life are fatally harmful to many people and other living things. That story is a harsh one. To simply tell it and stop there would sow denial or despair. I will not. Bear with that story, though, for a moment—in over-simplified form—for the purpose of seeing and then composing a different one.

The people of this congregation do not notice that with their SUVs and minivans, larger houses, and frequent travel, they contribute five hundred times more greenhouse gas per person than does the average Nepalese.[5] They do not see that oil sustaining their lifestyle comes from the Niger Delta in Africa where Chevron, Shell, and Mobil are cutting down forests, polluting water supplies and air, and "mowing down indigenous cultures and communities."[6] The people of this congregation do not hear the voices of African people demanding oil companies to leave the delta, or the Andean indigenous peoples threatening mass suicide if oil companies begin operations in their lands. Nor do they see the thousands of troops deployed to quell the protests in the Niger Delta.

The people prudently seek "good buys" in clothing, without knowing of young women in the Tianjin Garment Factory in China who sew that clothing for twenty-three cents an hour, sixty hours per week, are prevented from organizing, and will be laid off when Wal-Mart moves its contract to another factory in southern China with fewer regulations and far lower wages.[7] The good people of our congregation enjoy inexpensive bananas from Del Monte, Chiquita, and Dole. These companies, based in Central America, historically have been characterized by low wages and repression of people who organize for better conditions. The companies have pressured the United States to urge passage of World Trade Organization (WTO) policy that will devastate their competitors, the small independent banana farmers of seven Caribbean nations. Caribbean banana workers generally earn a living wage. Thousands will lose their livelihoods under the new WTO policy.

The people in our story have enjoyed high investment returns. Their investments fund a mining company that has displaced thousands of Dalits and other indigenous peoples of India from the land that enabled them to feed their children and sustain their health systems, values, familial structures, and identity. Investment returns too have come from General Dynamics, whose former CEO "made an estimated $9.35 million in salary, bonuses, and various stocks plans in 1991 while announcing that the company would be eliminating approximately thirty thousand jobs over the next few years."[8] People of the congregation bank with firms that have reaped profits from "debt" repayments by Two-Thirds World countries. In the words of former bishop Bernardino Mandlate of Mozambique, that debt is "covered with the blood of African children."[9] Many firms in which the people are involved as consumers, investors, and employees devote creative capacities and sophisticated psychological techniques to create desires worldwide for soft drinks, tobacco, violent electronic games, sugar-coated cereals, name-brand clothing, high-tech toys, and automobiles.

The congregation's children play with soccer balls made by an eleven-year-old boy from India whose back, fingers, and eyes are damaged by the labor.[10] He works so that his family may eat. They have been displaced to the city from their land by bauxite mines that provide aluminum for products in the homes of our congregation. The mining companies are based in Norway, United States, Canada, and elsewhere. Despite fierce and courageous resistance from people whose livelihoods and villages are destroyed by the mines, they continue to occupy more Indian lands.[11]

Church members' homes are lighted by General Electric bulbs. General Electric's CEO Jack Welsh personally took home more pay in 1999 than all the company's fifteen thousand factory workers in Mexico combined. The workers have left their home areas to work in plants in the toxic Free-Trade Zones of northern Mexico because the corn production and communally owned lands that formerly sustained their lives were undercut by Monsanto under the rules of the North America Free Trade Agreement (NAFTA). Monsanto provides our congregation with low-priced food and investment returns.

Under emerging WTO patent laws, Monsanto is gaining exclusive rights to seed strains developed over generations by indigenous farmers of India. The company has attempted to alter the seeds so that they will produce and reproduce only with chemical additives, jeopardizing the food supply and self-determination of many Indian agricultural communities. The chemical intensive mono-cropping pushed in many countries by Monsanto, Cargill, and other seed and agri-chemical corporations is, over a few decades, dangerously depleting the species diversity, aquifers, and humus levels needed by future generations for survival. These global companies and their investors in our congregation have profitted financially from the companies' growth.

For people in this faith community, the freedom to have and use things from all parts of Earth as they are accustomed seems desirable, good, a blessing for which to thank God. Their hearts and minds do not register the broader picture. In that picture, their way of life means that part of humankind "consumes in one year what it took the earth a million years to store up. . . . If all the countries followed 'successfully' the industrialized example, five or six planets would be needed to serve as mines and waste dumps."[12]

Among the congregation, some people are well aware of—or at least suspect—destructive consequences of economic globalization. Some are troubled, and deeply so. Yet these concerns are not addressed in their everyday lives, least of all in their church life. The issues seem too complex; the reality too overwhelming; the alternatives too few and feeble; and the concept of pushing toward alternatives too futile, lonely, and alienating. Serious consideration of countering the logic of global capitalism seems politically unfeasible. Furthermore, such notions run up against their very sense of who they must be to succeed and be happy in society, and against their assumption that "free" markets are integral to a free society. Gnawing concerns are quelled, too, by official reports that economies are growing, and that this growth will benefit people the world over. To challenge the apparently inevitable reality of economic globalization is not within their current range of vision.

This story, as told here, is vastly oversimplified. Simple cause-and-effect inferences cloud the moral and practical ambiguities and complexities of global economic interconnectedness. To illustrate, corporate investment adhering to certain guidelines may offer crucial economic opportunities for many people in some impoverished nations. Those guidelines vary, according to myriad factors, in each situation. Informed and sophisticated opponents of corporate- and finance-driven globalization in a given location hold diverse opinions regarding the conditions that render transnational trade and investment a curse or a benefit to their people.

Yet the complexity does not invalidate my point: the people of this congregation, who give tirelessly and generously to address the needs of friends, family, church members, and community, are "structured enemies" of Earth and of multitudes of people, enemies of their own children.[13] Their way of life is based on buying, taking, or degrading other people's life-sustaining resources; consuming them; and endangering Earth's life systems with the waste and by-products. The deadly cost—to others, to Earth, to themselves, and to future generations—of these lifeways is invisible to those who, in the short term, benefit materially from them.

A Different and Subversive Story

We are given a different and subversive story to live, a story of justice-making love incarnate in flesh and earth. We are charged with composing alternative ways of living and are offered moral-spiritual power to do so.

According to Luther's economic ethics discussed earlier, Christians are to denounce and reject economic practices that transgress the "second principle of Christian faith"—loving neighbor as self. Practices that concentrate wealth for some while compromising others' capacity to sustain sufficient livelihood for self and household are to be condemned and replaced with alternative economic practices. That ethic in today's context calls us to repudiate practices and policies orchestrated and rationalized by seductive, powerful, and apparently inevitable global political-economic arrangements, where those practices and policies thwart the possibility of life with dignity for many. We are called to craft ways of living never conceived of in the history of our species, to journey into uncharted territory.

The forces mitigating against substantive economic resistance and change are monumental. They include the ideological and the political-economic dynamics discussed in this project's early chapters. To swim upstream against these forces is almost beyond imagining. In many places it has been done at the cost of life itself.

Susan George says it well: "We can submit to the present global disorder or reject it. We can acquiesce to power, and to the ideology that undergirds it, or fight back. . . . Whether we live in the North or in the South, it is the shape of our own lives and those of our children that is at stake, like it or not. The old paradigm may entrench its control and win. But we are also present at the birth of a new one, and millions have chosen to protect, nurture, and sustain it. For such a revolution, many have already given their lives. My own choice is clear: the only honor is to make common cause with them."[14]

The moral agency required to counter the exploitation structured into economic life as we know it today, and to live in new ways, is given in relationship with God indwelling the web of life and working within us, among us, and with us toward life abundant for all. The previous chapter explored *how* that relationship may issue in moral power for faithful resistance, alternative visions, and movement toward them. The task here is to point toward practical implications of that work. To begin, I summarize two key clues developed thus far in the study.

First, this identity—habitation of God—contradicts neo-liberalism's life-shaping definitions of human being, freedom, and purpose. This alternative identity bears fruit of moral transformation only when it is practiced. In other words, *being* the communal dwelling place of God generates moral agency as that identity is *lived out*. Key then are practices of that identity. They are many. Two probed earlier in this inquiry are the sacraments of Eucharist and of solidarity, when the two are held together.

Second, if moral power is born in communal relationship with the indwelling God, and if that relationship is gift, then a task of those who seek moral power is to receive that relationship as gift and to nurture it.

The question becomes, "What practices enable us to do so? What practices enable human creatures intimately to receive and to *know* God's indwelling presence, touch and be touched by it, drink it, and nourish others with it?" Responses are infinite in scope and depth. This inquiry argued that we may receive and nurture that relationship in the sacraments of Eucharist and of solidarity, practiced in light of each other.

Hold these clues and this question in mind in asking what it would look like for the congregation in this story to journey toward the moral agency and the ways of economic justice that stem from God living in us. What would constitute the economic practices of people empowered by God's indwelling presence to seek ecologically sustainable and socially just communities for all? For everyday North Americans in the context of neo-liberal globalization, what, in practical terms, are the transformative implications of God living and loving in us today?

Full response to these questions awaits subsequent work. In the introduction, I identified a broad spectrum of tasks entailed in ethical treatment of economic globalization. All are necessary if we are to resist its dominant form and forge more just and sustainable ways of economic life. Yet, as clarified earlier, this book undertakes only a portion of those tasks. Among those awaiting further work is the two-fold task of exploring, in far more depth, alternatives to the dominant model of globalization and unfolding concrete ways of putting them into practice in the everyday lives of North Americans. The intent here is only to give indication of where that work might lead, paint a sense of the possibilities, glimpse that possibilities exist, and open doors toward further envisioning and embodying them. The invitation to engage that "life-savoring and life-saving work" (the words are Larry Rasmussen's) I place at the feet of all people whose hearts know even the faintest glimmer of a holy hunger to live toward the well-being of vulnerable neighbors far and near, and of this splendid and mysterious home we call Earth.

Dimensions of the Journey

To shed light on the "strangely ancient yet uncharted journey" toward ways of economic life that enable the household of Earth to flourish, I point out a few dimensions of the journey. They include: *phases of the struggle, sites of the struggle, theo-ethical questions* to ask about both, *guiding principles and public policies* to enact them, and *examples of practices*. They intersect. Together they are elements of systemic socio-ecological transformation and of solidarity. We consider each in turn.

Phases of the struggle include seeing and naming "what is going on" in neo-liberal globalization, resisting what cuts against the promise of abundant life for all, envisioning alternatives, and enacting them. These phases are not sequential in a linear fashion, but rather constantly re-occur and overlap, each phase informing and deepening the others. All involve both theological reflection and historical and structural social analysis.

Seeing and truth telling, resisting, revisioning, and rebuilding play out in multiple *"sites of struggle."*[15] They are lifestyle changes; public policy re-formation at local, state, national, and international levels; re-structuring of institutions at these levels; worship formation; and critical theological and ideological inquiry. None of these sites alone will bear the fruit of earth-friendly and justice-seeking economies. All are necessary.

Theo-ethical questions formed in the previous chapters illuminate the way. What are the practices of life and worship in each of these phases and sites of struggle when the purpose of economic life is not maximum growth or wealth accumulation, but enabling sufficient, sustainable livelihood for all and nourishing Earth's regenerative health? Practically speaking, what are the economic consequences of humans as God-bearers and as beings-in-community, rather than as the *homo economicus, consumens, et dominans* of neo-liberal globalization? What would happen in daily economic life if free-dom *to* acquire, consume, and promote unqualified economic growth in a global marketplace without counting the costs were challenged by freedom *from* that orientation? If other-than-human parts of nature are seen not as "natural resources" for sale to the highest bidder, but rather as habitation of God's power and presence, what are the practical implications for human economic activity? How and where will worshiping communities practice the Eucharist so that it bears the fruit of moral agency to reshape economic life toward the widespread good? What does the sacrament of Eucharist look like where it is inseparable from the sacrament of solidarity? What ways of "tasting the Word" in the Eucharist and solidarity will help us to remember that both are gift, and that these gifts may transform us by love into love in Christic form? What practices of Eucharist and solidarity will remind us that we are characters in a story told by the Prophets and by Jesus' early followers, a story of an intimate God who becomes flesh, a God who enters into union and communion with us that we might be fully alive? That we might live the gift of "love thy neighbor as thyself"? What Eucharistic rituals and practices of solidarity will recall that we are descendants of everyday people throughout the ages whose union and communion with God enabled resisting structures of domination, and that we too are indwelled by the One who lived and *lives* abundant life for all despite the risks? What forms of these sacraments will re-member who we are as undeserved gift—a cosmic *communio*, beloved dwelling place of the God embodied in Jesus Christ?

Answers to these questions do not come out of the blue. Some will develop as worshiping communities dare to let worship and economic life reflect and shape who they are as communal habitation of God. Some exist already in guiding principles being developed by people of both South and North in grassroots resistance movements, natural sciences, non-governmental organizations (NGOs), socially responsible business and governmental sectors, and other walks of life; in policy proposals being developed by the same; and in concrete practices of people the globe over. These *principles, policy proposals*, and *examples of practices* are hope-giving, life-loving, fumbling, courageous, broken and bleeding, unheralded alternatives. They require strength and vision, and offer the same. We consider three illustrative principles and examples of policies to enact them, and then move to view practices consistent with these principles and policies that are being lived by Christian communities or could be.

Just and sustainable communities and societies will need, in the words of Paul Hawken, *"a system of commerce and production* where each and every act is ecologically sustainable and restorative."[16] Ultimately, this will require transition from carbon-based economies to economies based on permanent sources of energy: solar, wind, water. Domestic policy proposals enacting this principle are vast in scope and are monumentally controversial. They include allocating research and development monies to the development of renewable energy sources; mandating that increasing percentages of public fleets run on non-fossil fuel; and taxing industry and consumers for activity that results in carbon emissions.[17] Obviously, such policy in the United States would not alter the practices of U.S.-based global corporations as long as "free-trade" agreements encourage them to shift production to sites of lowest environmental regulations. This points to the need to work toward global policies regulating commerce according to the principle of sustainable and regenerative economic activity. Here is woven the intimate connection between lifestyle change, public policy work, and structural change.

A second general principle is that *economic life is to serve the needs of people, communities, and the Earth rather than people and Earth serving the mandates of a global economy*. While serving the flourishing of the planetary household, economic life is to prioritize the needs of the vulnerable. According to this principle, economic policies and practices will be normed not primarily by economic growth, but by improvements in human and ecological well-being and the sustainability of communities and Earth's web of life.[18] According to this principle, the first priority in economic policy is "food security, health care, education, the right to participate in decision-making that affects every sphere of our lives, and work that is humanizing rather than dehumanizing."[19] Said differently, survival and dignity needs for all will take priority over profit for a few.[20] Existing policy proposals cohering with this principle span much territory. To illustrate: organizers in Seattle propose that the state minimum wage be changed to a "livable wage" based on local cost-of-living. United for a Fair Economy advocates a "maximum earnings level" which would curb the current practice of paying CEOs an average of 470 times the earnings of average workers. A broad-based coalition in India demands that international Trade Related Intellectual Property Rights (TRIPS) agreements be curtailed to protect the knowledge and resources of indigenous and subsistence farmers from corporate "biopiracy." The Jubilee 2000 coalition calls for cancellation of Two-Thirds World debt. European church networks organize on international levels for a currency transaction tax, such as the Tobin Tax, that would mitigate against excessive speculative investment. Environmental advocacy organizations call for laws that would prohibit large corporations from externalizing their social and environmental costs. Grassroots groups in Colombia demand laws that protect certain public goods, such as water, from commodification on the global market. Many networks advocate policies that prioritize agricultural production for domestic consumption followed by regional trade, rather than export-oriented agriculture.[21]

A third general principle is that *governance will safeguard equity in political processes and will protect people's capacity to make choices that may not coincide with market forces.* Thus the "freedom" of powerful economic players must be inseparable from accountability to a broad-based public. This principle pushes toward a serious contextual vision of democracy extending to the economic sphere. It implies policies that reduce, rather than increase, the role of large business coalitions in international trade agreements. International policies subordinating governments to transnational corporations would be replaced by policies that ensure "each state's right to regulate and exercise authority over foreign investment . . . and the activities of transnational corporations within its national jurisdiction."[22] Trade policies would be "regulated and guided by a framework of overarching global conventions" such as the International Declaration on Human Rights, and other international conventions including those protecting labor, environment, and indigenous peoples.[23]

Practicing the Transformative Consequences of God Indwelling Creation

These illustrative principles and policy proposals grow from and into the experience of people throughout the world seeking to counter destructive dimensions of economic globalization. We draw upon a few of those efforts now in returning concretely to the question at hand: in the lives of economically privileged United States citizens today, what might it mean in practice to be empowered through God's indwelling presence to forge alternative economic ways?[24] Consider first a specific existing community and then revisit imaginatively the congregation encountered at this chapter's outset.

The community is composed of about ten adults of varied ages, a child, frequent visitors, and a formerly stray dog. Long-term members are active in mainstream denominational congregations. They decided, years ago, to live together in two houses within short walking distance of each other in a low-income neighborhood of Washington, D.C. The community's founders were moved toward this decision in part by deep relationships with oppressed people struggling for survival and liberation in Latin America and in Washington, D.C.

The day opens with prayer in common. Remembered in this time are both the personal concerns of people in the community and the needs of specific people and peoples in the broader world. At times throughout the year, liturgy and Eucharist are practiced publicly, especially in conjunction with protest or other "public witness" actions. The community's spirituality is profoundly incarnate, grounded in knowing that the living Christ works in and among people toward liberation, healing, and restoration.

The value of the community's two houses increased significantly due to the construction of a public-transit station in the neighborhood. Recognizing this increase as "social mortgage," the community decided that when either house is sold, 100 percent of the increased value attributable to the new Metro station will go to Equity Trust.[25] The Trust is an innovative national project establishing a common fund for making affordable housing available to low-income people. The community banks through a local socially responsible bank, and investments are in a community investment fund that serves marginalized neighborhoods of the city.

Generally, vegetables are purchased from a Community Supported Agriculture (CSA) farm, bread from a worker-owned business, and coffee from a Nicaraguan fair trade cooperative. Clothing comes from hand-me-downs, second-hand stores, and fair trade businesses. Two small cars are shared and are repaired by a local woman-owned business. Public transportation is used extensively, as are bicycles and walking.

Solidarity with local and Two-Thirds World coalitions struggling for justice in the global economy is a central focus of the community's life, especially of vocation and celebration. The employable adults slowly have switched their work lives to jobs that support local or international justice efforts. As a result, income levels are low, relative to United States average incomes. The household frequently provides housing and hospitality for activists from Africa and Central America, including people on death lists in their own countries due to their leadership in justice movements. Members of the community have "accompanied" Salvadoran and Guatemalan activists returning to their homelands and have joined their efforts to regain lands lost to corporate powers.[26]

This practice of hospitality enriches the community's frequent celebrations. They are terrific. The abundant dancing, singing, stories, and potluck food are multicultural and multigenerational. Birthday gifts often include "good deeds" that the recipient is hungering to have done.

This community and others like it are far from perfect. As individuals and communities, they struggle with brokenness in multiple forms. Sin at all levels disrupts the effort to embody faithful alternatives to economic globalization. Yet faultiness and inadequacy do not derail the journey. The theo-ethical point is that sin's pervasive presence does not negate the faith claim that by grace, which includes the gift of Christ making habitation in and among us, the faithful gradually may be transformed into bearers of God's love, more able to seek the flourishing of all and to subvert what thwarts that flourishing.

The community described is not uncommon. It is, in fact, part of a "community of communities" seeking to live toward social and ecological justice. The examples of people practicing principles such as those discussed above, daring to swim upstream against the mandates of corporate- and finance-driven globalization, are myriad and diverse. Their efforts are vital food for others embarking on the journey toward regenerative Earth-human relations and economic justice.

∼

Return with me now to the congregation encountered at the outset of this chapter. Imagine that they have begun to suspect troubling contradictions between the calls of Christian faith and the ways of life mandated by globalization. Whatever the sequence of catalyzing experiences and reflections, they have been moved to a leap of faith. They have committed to journey toward living *as if* economic life were normed by the call to love neighbor as self and by sustainable Earth-human relations, and *as if* they were empowered to practice those norms by God living in them and in all of creation. They suspect that this commitment will lead down unforeseen paths. Uncertain what those paths will be, they have determined initially to accept that they do not know what church will look like, but that it will include prayer, reflection on Scripture, celebration of Eucharist and baptism, and solidarity with those endangered by globalization.

Imagine that the congregation's initial acts of solidarity are to seek out perspectives of people who claim to be endangered or impoverished by globalization; to take some small steps in response; and to engage Bible study on the immanent God, bearing those perspectives in mind. The congregation agrees also to hold these commitments in prayer. They pledge their "eyes to see and ears to hear" possible harm caused by the economic structures undergirding their material wealth, and to heed what they see and hear. This commitment moves them progressively outside the realm of the comfortable, crossing boundaries of economic privilege, race, gender, and geography into unfamiliar territory. They begin to see what has been obscured by privilege: people and other parts of creation destroyed, degraded, or impoverished by five centuries of globalization culminating in its contemporary form. What they are learning confronts them on every level of life and renders denial tempting but untenable. Slowly, they are compelled to "redefine their world."[27] They know grief, confusion, and anger.

As the extent of the ecological destruction, the intricate webs of economic brutality, and the magnitude of their complicity creep further into their consciousness, guilt and despair emerge. Adequate response as individuals or households seems impossible. Moral inertia born of overwhelming hopelessness and helplessness threatens to replace the moral inertia of blindness, denial, and historical amnesia.

Yet the congregation's initial commitments to take some small steps bear fruit. Bible study focused on the indwelling God nurtures hope in power beyond the human and convinces them to respond not as isolated individuals or households, but as a body, sharing the diverse passions and gifts of each. Different people contribute different efforts. They begin to experience hope and power in communal action and to see a vast array of actions possible and of networks with which they may join efforts. Their ongoing commitment to hear from the underside and to analyze their own economic lives in dialogue with those voices leads them toward unforeseen alliances, becoming part of a yet larger body. The moral power of solidarity begins to be glimpsed. Further energy and commitment is generated as people begin to suspect that they and their children are—in the long run—losers, not winners, in the enterprise of globalization.[28] What began as efforts to serve the well-being of other people—local and global—who are threatened by globalization soon comes to include the well-being of themselves.

Perhaps this congregation begins with consumer and investor action. One small group becomes boycott information specialists, making certain that all households have information about national and global boycotts, and writing letters on behalf of the congregation to the offending companies. Another serves as liaison with the Sweatshop Education and Mobilization Campaign, determined to enable members of the community to avoid companies that operate or subcontract with sweatshops or use child labor, and to purchase from companies that guarantee workers' rights to associate freely in their own and subcontractors' facilities and pay a living wage. For any household that desires it, the church subscribes to consumer guides enabling people to support "green businesses" and businesses that pay fair wages and honor labor, civil, and human rights, domestically and worldwide. Many avidly use the guides. One member with expertise in finance advises others who decide to shift their investments to socially responsible funds. A few members adopt a "graduated tithe," whereby when one's income increases, one gives away a higher percentage of it. Slowly these practices are noticed and emulated citywide through ecumenical and interfaith networks, and nationwide through denominational channels.

Land surrounding the church building is turned over to a garden program for homeless people. The congregation joins a Community Supported Agriculture enterprise, enabling them to support local small farmers and to purchase local organic produce. This is a step away from food produced on faraway lands that should be feeding their own children, and away from food transported long distances by fossil fuels.

With commitment, exposure, and hope, the people's creativity grows. Visions emerge of a bioregional economy structured to be a sustainable, integral part of the bioregion's ecosystem.[29] According to these visions, the bottom line of economic activity is the criteria of "renewability, recyclability, and nontoxicity."[30] Nothing is consumed or produced that cannot be "reclaimed, reused, or recycled."[31] The visionaries see a pedestrian- and bicycle-friendly city. They see co-housing in which households share common space and, together with schools and other buildings, depend heavily on the sun for energy. Industries "trade waste" for use in energy production. The local university pilots research and development in sustainable and restorative technology and agriculture. The people envision "community corporations," businesses anchored to the community through widespread local ownership and accountability.[32] These ideas are threatening to many and are complicated. Yet they move the congregation to engage with a regional movement toward sustainable bioregional economic activity.

The people come to see that social structures—including institutions, ideologies, systems, and policies—determine the extent to which economic life can be re-formed to serve justice and sustainablity. Finding the morality of their personal economic lives to be determined not only by personal commitments and decisions, but also by the structures of which they are a part, they are moved to work for policy and structural changes. After a time of discernment, a group assumes responsibility for managing advocacy on legislation related to multiple areas of economic justice and eco-justice. The task being enormous, they begin with specific efforts and alliances. On behalf of the congregation, they join United for a Fair Economy, a powerful movement seeking economic justice domestically, and Network, a national Catholic social justice lobby. On the level of international structures, their energies go to the Jubilee 2000 campaign for debt cancellation. At the urging of Jubilee South and other networks of the Global South, they encourage that campaign to see debt cancellation as just the first step on the way to international financial restructuring.

As the months and years go on, the people find their efforts to move the local business environment toward sustainability being curtailed by multilateral trade and investment agreements. This thwarting of their political participation seems inconsistent with living in a democratic society. They join networks seeking to undo and prevent multilateral trade and investment agreements that strip local and national governments of power to control corporate activities in their territories. Members of the congregation who see the importance of this work, but who have no time or interest for it, are grateful to those who are energized by it. Others find their abilities in this arena expanding with their awareness and engagement. They find their circles of friends expanding to include an ever more diverse array of people. People who were once strangers become trusted allies.

Slowly, seeing that economic solidarity calls for more than consumer, investor, legislative, and other policy action, the congregation determines to support farmers and others seeking to regain rights to land and seeds. To this end, alliances are forged with the protest movement in the Niger Delta, with a local group of homeless women, and with a faith-based coalition in India struggling against displacement by global mining companies. These alliances bring contact with networks around the globe. The congregation hears not only stories of oppression but also incredible stories of hope and fortitude. Options for resistance and alternatives begin to frequent their imaginations as they encounter the knowledge of subjugated people and peoples struggling to survive and to counter "free trade and investment" in Costa Rica, their own city, the Caribbean, Canada, the Philippines, and elsewhere. They see outrage, grief, and fear channeled into sustained, competent, courageous action. The alliances are controversial, difficult, and rich. They result in political stands unpopular with some people in the broader community.

One step leads to another. Eventually a "public witness coordinator" is organizing rides, food, speakers, banners, and networking for protests such as those against the WTO, and rallies like those supporting a local living wage law. The coordinator is careful to bring the requisite treats and hot cocoa for the kids. A group of older women form a chapter of "Raging Grannies," providing wild and salient political humor, even incorporating it into worship.

Individuals begin to question their vocational lives and to long for their work to reflect more truly who they are: bearers of a God who lives within creation, "compassionating" it toward restoration.[33] They call upon each other to discern vocational changes that will enable using their gifts of time and skill in service of justice and ecological sustainability. One highly successful businessperson leaves her position and devotes her business acumen to creating a viable local fair-trade coffee exchange. Another, the owner of a small corporation that produces restaurant furniture, is moved by encounters with struggling people in Central America and Mexico. He gradually transfers his company to a worker-owned status and becomes a leader in the worker-owned business movement in the United States. A relatively small-scale apple grower is moved to major changes in employment policies pertaining to migrant workers. The changes produce economic difficulties for him in relationship to the global apple industry, and other members of the congregation rally to his support.

Not only tremendous energy but also tremendous conflict is generated by these moves. Some are arduous and divisive. The moral, theoretical, and practical ambiguities and complexities of economic relationships move people to diverse stances on many issues. What to resist and what changes to seek are rarely clear.[34] Egos come into play as various individuals want to claim ownership or credit for certain developments. Analysis of power relations in the global economy spurs analysis of power relations in their church, homes, and work environs. Commitment to resist economic oppression ignites awareness of oppression in other forms. Hearing and respecting voices of people that history has not heard evokes questions about their church and places of work: "Who does the decisive speaking here and whose voices are silenced or unborn?" Conflict arises within families as partners and spouses differ on the extent to which they were willing to accept the personal financial losses that accompany these changes, and as youth are taking things to heart with an intensity unsettling to parents.

Yet, since numerous households share these experiences of conflict, the pain is shared, and many relationships deepen as a result. No one is alone in the strange process of swimming against the stream; they are doing so together. Discernment groups are formed to assist one another in difficult decisions and to enable moral deliberation within the congregation as a whole. Some people leave the congregation. Others learn the healing power of laughter and grow adept at using anger and conflict to build up the body. Worship life, biblical and theological reflection, and prayer are crucial in that process. Challenged by conflict and needing to ground themselves in moral-spiritual power for their unforeseen path, the people are thrown ever more toward resources of their faith.

Deepening "political" engagement spawns the need for a deeper contemplative dimension to it. Initial biblical reflection and theological refection on the indwelling God enriches that dimension and guides it. Listening to the voice of God *in* the Earth and its creatures, in trees and water, and in a "grain of wheat," the people hear songs of praise, pain, and power. Gradually, it seems that "mountains and all hills, fruit trees and all cedars" (Ps. 148:9) not only praise God, but also speak *as* body of God, being ripped apart and abused. The people find themselves seeing God in the homeless people near their church building, and in the lowest-paid workers in their business environs. For some, it becomes untenable to ignore inequitable pay scales and regressive taxation. When dismayed by their ongoing fears, the people are moved to pray for moral power and courage in the midst of their daily efforts and to depend on the prayers of others and of the "Spirit . . . interced[ing] with sighs too deep for words" (Rom. 8:26). New worlds open as they become more comfortable listening to God within themselves, others, and otherkind. Coming to trust the voice of God within, they also sense that to know God more fully, they need to hear God speaking within people very different from themselves, and especially within people on the underside of privilege. Their alliances of solidarity become stronger, more mutual, more compelling.

Theological reflection deepens with the commitment to "hear from the underside," and with the controversies facing the congregation. As people's perceptions of the global economy change, so does their vision of Christian discipleship and of God's action in the world. They grow hungry to search further theologically and in their political-economic analyses. Economic literacy becomes a mainstay of their adult education program. Patronizing overtones of their alliances begin to melt away as they seek out the analyses and theological insights of their partners in India, marginalized neighborhoods in their own city, Central America, Africa, and elsewhere. These insights lead the congregation to Bible study on wealth and poverty.

Bible study and theological refection on their situation evoke desire for encounter with historical faith communities for whom union and communion with Christ empowered resistance, material relinquishment, and countercultural lives of faith. Over time, the people come to know faith forebearers and to learn from them. Adults begin to teach children that they are descendants of strong and faithful resisters. These ancestors and their music, liturgical gifts, and stories begin to frequent the worship. The people see that their own path, while uncharted, is in line with an ancient journey travelled by their forebearers. Recognizing ideological and other forces that—in past contexts—impeded the moral power flowing from the indwelling God, the people see more clearly those forces in their own lives.

Over time, the congregation's understanding of the powers behind neoliberal globalization deepens. Hungering for moral courage, they take seriously claims (Luther's and others') about the transformative power of God's indwelling presence, and about communion—nurtured by Eucharist and solidarity—as locus of that presence and power. The indwelling God brings "bold, dauntless courage."[35] God's presence and power is in every creature and element. The fruit of the Eucharist is a communion of love, a community that addresses the needs of the marginalized and in which people bear one anothers' burdens. To deepen communion in which Christ incarnate is given and received, touched, tasted, and drunk is to deepen moral courage and power. Devoting themselves to these mysteries, the people seek practices that reveal them.

The church's visual iconography, music, and liturgy increasingly reflect sacramental communion and evoke it, becoming more multicultural and earthy. The Eucharist is celebrated with prayers exchanged with partner congregations among tribal people in India, homeless women in Seattle, and indigenous peoples of the Guatemalan highlands. "Readings from the book of creation . . . infuse Eucharist, the prayers, the sermon, the call to worship, the hymns."[36] New and diverse people frequent worship services and Bible studies and join in the church's work. The liturgical calls to "sing with all the people of God and join in the hymn of all creation," and "to dedicate our lives to the care and redemption of all that God has made" take on flesh and earth and mystery.[37] People begin to hunger for bread and wine, earth and water to be more present in the Eucharist, baptism, and other rituals. The walls of the building become too confining, and the congregation moves frequently to forests and waters for communion. The more the people hear the cries and songs of the Earth, the more empowered they are to resist what defiles it. Worship generates new visions of neighbor-love and Earth-tending manifest in economic life. The people dare to ask how Eucharist might, in their time and place, "re-member" the body of God.

This imaginative sketch responds to questions embedded in both mystery and concrete reality. What might it mean, in the North American context of economic globalization, to practice the morally transformative consequences of God indwelling creation? What might our *being* communal and communing body of God contribute to the transformation of economic structures that violate the body and its members—human and other? The vignette has been illustrative, imaginative, and suggestive; it points to a few existing possibilities in order to "invite into being . . . more than we can yet imagine."[38] It intends neither prediction or prescription, for the presence and power of God, living in and loving in creation, will lead those who dare to know that presence more intimately *and* to see the realities of globalization more clearly, along unknown paths.

Yet this story—drawn from the experience of many people—implies elements of faith life and ways of practicing them that may contribute to realizing the subversive moral power inherent in God's indwelling presence. The elements include ongoing theological and biblical reflection, economic and ideological literacy, solidarity in multiple phases and sites of struggle, Eucharist and other aspects of worship, the inclusion of the other-than-human in worship, and prayer.[39] All will be held in light of one another, and will be informed substantively by perspectives of people who claim that globalization endangers their lives or dignity or the regenerative health of Earth's life systems. Theological and biblical reflection will look not only for moral norms but also for memory, vision, hope, relationship with "subversive" faith forebearers, and intimate trusting relationship with God living in and among the creatures and elements of creation. Efforts both to know God and to know earthly political-economic reality more fully will hold together the ecological and the social, not only in terms of globalization's impact, but also in terms of God's presence. Finally, spirituality and public morality will not be disassociated or even fully distinguished from each other.

In Sum

These dimensions of faith life suggest ways whereby North American Christian communities may come to see more clearly the dynamics of neo-liberal globalization and may come to "taste"[40] the presence and power of God "fill[ing] all things."[41] Intimate, sensual, communal relationship with the Source, Lover, and Liberator of life indwelling creation may give rise to subversive moral power to resist the mandates and mores of corporate- and finance-driven globalization and to live toward alternatives. *Realizing* that moral power entails entry into the mystery of communion with others—human and not—and with God, whose love for this world is unquenchable, will restore the community of life, will liberate humanity from being its destroyers, and fills every cell of all being. Living ever more fully as bearers of God's justice-making love in the context of economic globalization is divine gift, and it is historical process. Said differently, realizing the indwelling God as subversive moral agency is gracious gift, and it involves seeing and naming ways in which globalization damages life, resisting those ways, and courageously acting toward alternatives.

The work of Christian Ethics, as I understand it, is to know ever more intimately and honestly the mystery that is God and the historical realities of which we are part, so that we may shape ways of life normed and empowered by God's radiant love for this world. It remains my hope that this book will contribute theologically, theoretically, and practically to the emergence of North American Christian praxis in which intimate relationship with the indwelling God—as a dimension of ordinary faith—and critical analysis of globalization engender subversive moral agency in the context of globalization. May this work contribute to an evolving and contextual morality-spirituality of resistance, revisioning, and rebuilding rooted in relationship with God "flowing and pouring into . . . all things."[42] I have only begun to explore the ancient and fecund claim that God as love, a "burning fire which . . . shall never, never cease in all the endless ages to come"[43] lives in our very bodies and in all of creation. That exploration will be the work of a lifetime.

Appendix

Methodological Guideposts

CHRISTIAN ETHICS IS THE DISCIPLINED ART of coming to know ever more fully the mystery that is God and the historical realities of life on Earth so that we may shape ways of life consistent with and empowered by God being with, in, among, and for creation. "Knowing" here refers not merely to "knowledge of," but to "being in relationship with." Where vision and knowledge of God and of life's realities are obscured, as they are by the dynamics of globalization, a task of Christian Ethics is *to know and see differently*, so that we might *live* differently. Where dominant forces distort historical realities by describing them falsely, ethics must "redescribe the world."[1] My method stems from this understanding of Christian Ethics and serves it.

Method derives from *meta* (meaning "inclusive of" or "that which gathers in the whole") and *hodos* (meaning "the way"). *Method*, then, refers to the way of gathering in the whole of the inquiry, both its architecture and the process of accomplishing that design. How the aims of an inquiry are pursued is the question of method. While method is said to determine questions asked, sources queried, and how knowledge is constructed and used, I hold rather that a dialectic pertains between these elements and method. That is, the method initially shaping an inquiry matures with it.

In particular, the working principles of theo-ethical inquiry identified in this appendix, while informed from the outset by feminist and critical theoretical sensibilities, grew out of the necessities of this project as it developed. It became necessary for me to understand more fully what methodological fault lines truncate the capacity of Christian Ethics to respond adequately to a moral issue of monumental import—the commonly accepted economic practices that contribute to economic brutality. Something, it seemed to me, was terribly wrong with the way of doing Christian Ethics, and—given the promises of Christian faith—something also was splendidly possible. As I probed, methodological principles developed.

I asked three broad questions pertaining to method in ethics: What methodological fault lines in the discipline itself contribute to moral inertia, and how might ethical method shift to mitigate against those inadequacies? What criteria would enable analyses of globalization to be accountable to those on the underside? In the context of today's globalizing economy and its corrosive impact on moral agency, *how* are we to draw upon faith forebearers in order to think critically about and recover the subversive moral power offered by the presence of God coursing through the creatures and elements of this Earth? While parts of method discussed herein pertain to the book as a whole, other parts pertain in particular to this last question. In response to it, I analyze issues entailed in exploring the interplay between God's indwelling presence and moral agency in historical and contemporary worlds. Taken together, these questions and issues constitute methodological guideposts for unmasking the morally corrosive effects of globalization and for drawing upon the wisdom of historical Christian communities for faithful response to those effects.

Factors shaping my method are many. They include the aims of this inquiry; perceived fault lines in the discipline of Christian Ethics; my communities of accountability and "location"; theological presuppositions; problems encountered in the inquiry and working resolutions to them; principles of critical social theory; and feminist theology and social theory. This appendix unfolds along lines reflecting these determinants.[2] As a whole, they present a necessary shift in ethical inquiry if ethics is to address adequately the moral crises posed by globalization. That shift entails a "new" ethical question and a path for responding to it.

Methodological Fault Lines

Humanity faces a crises never before known. The prevailing "way of life" rapidly being spread around the world by forces of globalization is "destroying a beloved world." In the North Atlantic world, Christian Ethics has not significantly enabled church or broader society to craft ways of life that counter the social and ecological brutality perpetrated by corporate- and finance-driven globalization.[3] The reasons for this failure are many. They include the location of the discipline's main voices (until recent womanist, feminist, and other liberationist ethics) on the "winning" side of white supremacy, male supremacy, colonialism, and capitalism's ascendance; the prevalence of theological constructs justifying those and other structured positions of dominance; and theological rationalization of the human species' obligation and right to dominate nature.

I suggest three other interdependent disciplinary fault lines thwarting Christian Ethics' capacity to address globalization adequately. First, the discipline, confined to the aims of moral deliberation assumed by traditional schools of ethics, has limited itself to the standard questions of "What are we to be and do?" (normative questions); "How is the moral subject formed?" (formative questions); and "What constitutes faithful and effective moral deliberation?" (deliberative questions).[4] Ethics largely has bypassed questions of "Wherein lies the moral agency to be and do what we ought, when that calls for highly oppositional practice?" (transformative questions). An economic paradigm that threatens Earth's life-systems and normalizes exploitation demands monumental structural changes in the systems, policies, and practices of economically privileged people and peoples. In societies such as the United States—which continue along the path of destruction in spite of the fact that normative principles and practices leading to sustainable alternatives *are* emerging on multiple fronts—normative, formative, and deliberative considerations are absolutely crucial but *insufficient*. They must be accompanied by inquiry into the moral-spiritual agency to live in dramatically new ways. In other words, the enormous social transformations required in the face of globalization, and the daunting powers lined up against those changes, call questions of moral spiritual agency to the fore.

The second fault line is modernity's unholy disassociation of spirituality from morality in constructions of faith life, and the accompanying disciplinary divorce within academia of Christian Ethics (in Protestant traditions) and Moral Theology (in Roman Catholic traditions) from the study of Christian spirituality. The dissociation, on the practical level, has many manifestations and expressions. They include, but are not limited to, the bifurcation of:

- contemplation, mysticism, and spirituality from faith-based activism or prophetic witness,
- interiority from exteriority,
- fleeing the world from changing the world,
- struggles toward personal holiness from struggles toward social justice,
- the person as justified individual from the person as historical social being,
- social righteousness from righteousness before God,
- Jesus Christ savior from Jesus Christ transformer of the moral life,
- personal salvation from cosmic restoration,
- integral spiritual wisdom from rational moral knowledge.

All revolve around the construction of spirituality as privatized, inner experience disassociated from public engagement in struggles against systemic evil. The problem is not that "spirituality" and "morality" are not held in light of each other. *Rather, the problem is that they are distinguished from each other in the first place.*[5]

The result has been catastrophic. Moral inquiry has not taken seriously the resources for agency inhering in aspects of faith life commonly referred to as spirituality, mysticism, contemplation, or piety. Differently said, a basic source of power to heed the call of Jesus Christ, the Spirit of God abiding in/with/among us, is not taken seriously in deliberations regarding the Christian moral life. Moral obligations, virtues, and values are debated and determined, but the power to embody them is not considered. This disassociation contradicts the persistent and pervasive biblical witness to lived faith, which draws no distinction between morality and spirituality.[6] Both Testaments, it may be argued, present the essence of moral life and of spiritual life as the same: to receive God's love, to love God, and to love neighbor as self.

This disconnect between spirituality and ethics is inseparable from the third disciplinary fault line considered here. It is epistemological. Ethics, firmly embedded in the Western analytical and anthropological intellectual tradition, has assumed the primacy of cognitive reason above all other ways of knowing. Cognitive inquiry not only is separated from, but is elevated above, all other forms of knowing, be they mystical, intuitive, artistic, or bodily. Cognitive knowledge—alone and supreme as source in crucial moral deliberation—erases the wisdom, vision, and agency to be drawn from knowing and seeing with faculties other than those of cognitive reason. These may be perceptive faculties of human being as mystic, lover, artist, poet, dancer, or "hearer" of the other-than-human. Lost or diminished is the capacity to see and perceive in ways that, held together with cognitive reason, might lead from moral quietude to moral agency in contexts of economic injustice.

This project responds to these three inadequacies in the discipline. Regarding the first, I bring the question of moral agency to the fore in Christian Ethics and propose and play out a method for pursing a particular line of inquiry regarding it. That line is defined both by source of moral agency (communion between the immanent God, human beings, and the rest of creation) and resource for learning to draw upon that source (faith forebearers). By locating "communion between the indwelling God and creation" as terrain of ethical inquiry, I challenge the second fault line: the dissociation of Ethics from studies of spirituality on a meta-theological level, and of morality from spirituality on a practical level. My thesis that moral wisdom and agency flow *primarily* from deep communion between and among God and creation begins to get at the third inadequacy.

Other ethicists and theologians endorse these interdependent assertions that: (1) Christian ethics must move beyond normative, formative, and deliberative moral constructs to questions of moral agency; (2) God indwelling creation is one locus of transformative moral agency; and (3) embracing ways of knowing beyond and before cognitive reason may bear the fruit of moral empowerment. Note three dialogue partners whose analyses of the moral crisis at hand, resonate with mine.[7]

In *Earth Community, Earth Ethics,* Larry Rasmussen's constructive theoethical agenda is to search Christian traditions not only for moral frames that underwrite sustainable and just Earth community but also for moral spiritual power to *become the people we need.*"[8] He writes, "the issue is the regular renewal of *moral-spiritual and sociopsychological energy* in a long season of forced society-nature experimentation . . . the issue is *sustaining power* itself for a long and traumatic journey."[9] The second point of affinity is that, for Rasmussen, too, the necessary moral-spiritual energy (which I refer to as moral-spiritual power or agency) is *immanent;* it "runs deep in life itself."[10] "Faith is the name of the strong power behind the renewal of moral-spiritual energy . . . a surprising force found amidst earth and its distress, creation carries its own hidden powers. . . . Said differently, the religious consciousness—and dream—that generates hope and a zest and energy *for* life is tapped *in* life itself. The finite bears the infinite, and the transcendent as 'the beyond in the midst of life' (citing Dietrich Bonhoeffer) is as close as the neighbor, soil, air, and sunshine. . . . The Spirit permeates all things (to remember the ancient Orthodox teaching)."[11]

Sallie McFague, in *The Body of God,* also ends by raising questions of moral-spiritual agency rooted in divine immanence. Although her focus is the "ecological crisis"—rather than a more inclusive socio-ecological crisis—her analysis of the profound threat to life posed by that crisis and of humanity's implication in it, her agenda for change, and her turn to God embodied in creation for moral agency parallel mine. The threat she examines is life's extinction by humanly caused ecological deterioration. McFague's agenda is to help first-world, privileged, mainstream Christians and other interested people think and act differently, according to a "new shape for humanity, a way of being in the world" that will "help the earth survive and prosper."[12]

Although I draw upon McFague's work, my project begins where hers leaves off, both by calling moral agency to the fore and by seeking it in divine immanence. "At the end of the day," she says, "one can easily lose heart. . . . planetary responsibility is too much for us."[13] She asks how we are to get up in the morning and go on with the agenda. "Throughout the centuries Christians have typically done so by being deeply rooted, personally and daily rooted, in God. Social responsibility and spirituality are not opposite tracks, rather, staying the course on any justice issue appears possible only by being grounded in a power and love beyond ourselves."[14] "Our hope against hope is that our efforts on behalf of our planet are not ours alone but that *the source and power of life in the universe is working in and through us for the well-being of all creation,* including our tiny part in it."[15] In other words, while she writes to construct a moral framework, she, like Rasmussen, ends by claiming that more is required and that it has to do with moral-spiritual energy grounded in divine power indwelling creation.

Carter Heyward, too, seeks moral agency for justice-making, and she locates that power in an understanding of God immanent. For Heyward, the locus of Divine immanence is mutual relationship. "I am looking for a way of speaking and writing of the power that brings us to life and keeps us going, the power that holds up when we can't imagine how we are managing not to collapse."[16] *"The divine presence is incarnate—embodied—in our relational selves."*[17] "I believe that God is our power in relation to each other, all humanity, and creation itself. God is the bond which connects us in such a way that each of us is empowered to grow, work, play, love and be loved."[18] Dorothee Soelle, commenting on Heyward's *Touching our Strength*, emphasizes that Heyward (like Rasmussen, McFague, and myself) focuses not only on moral frames adequate to the crises at hand but also on moral-spiritual agency: Heyward reminds us that "we have known a long time that God's power is love and nothing else, but we forget, often enough, that this power necessarily empowers the lovers of God."

These theologians are not alone in confirming my calls for ethics to grapple with the question of moral-spiritual agency, locate that agency in relationality with a God-power flowing through life itself, and embrace ways of knowing that extend beyond the faculties of cognitive reason.[19] These moves, foundational to this project, begin constructively to confront the three aforementioned fault-lines limiting the discipline's capacity to empower church and society for resistance to an unrelenting and life-threatening mode of economic globalization.

The Aims of the Project

This project is one relatively small—but indispensable—piece of a much broader and multilayered theo-ethical agenda with substantive and methodological dimensions. In the introduction I identified that broader purpose, sketched the tasks entailed in it, and situated this project in that set of undertakings. This study aims primarily at making the following three contributions to that broader agenda. The first is to demystify key dynamics that disable moral capacity for resisting neo-liberal globalization and moving toward alternatives. The second is to uncover and explore ways in which relationship with God indwelling creation may kindle and sustain the requisite moral-spiritual agency. Finally, I intend to locate paths for wresting from faith forebearers guidance toward that moral-spiritual power, that is, guidance toward agency for faithful subversion of structured domination.

The project's secondary aim, a matter of both content and method, is to overcome two dualisms contributing to moral inertia in the globalizing economy. One is the modern constructed dichotomy between spirituality and morality discussed above. The other is the untenable separation of social justice from eco-justice.

Location, Communities of Accountability, and Intended Audiences

Questions, aims, theological presuppositions, methodological principles, and problems and resolutions (elements of method) depend upon socio-ecological location and dis-location. Of my multiple locations, I note three particularly formative in the project's development: my relationship to consumer privilege; communities of accountability; and situation in church, academy, and broader public.

It has been said that three categories of people exist: those who have more than they need, those who have enough, and those who have not enough. As a Euro-American, highly educated, healthy, heterosexual woman with United States citizenship and social access, in a family that includes two adults with earning capacity, I belong to the first category.[20] However, the problem of economic privilege, vis-à-vis sustainable and equitable economic life, is not only *having* and getting but also *consuming/wasting*. To illustrate, I am among the North American population whose average consumption per person produces five hundred times the greenhouse gas emissions than are produced by the average Nepalese.[21] I am one of that population called to radical change in lifestyle, identity, psyche, public citizenship, and socio-ecological structures.

From this location, I also am dis-located—displaced by having stepped into the lives of people brutalized by the economic structures that provide my consumer privilege. Bound to them by having seen and heard their lives, having risked solidarity, and having received their gifts, I am wrenched (rescued?) from solid location in consumer privilege. Commitment in community with others to resist the culture of consumerism, excess, and economic exploitation furthers the dislocation. That commitment often is overshadowed, but never defeated, by multiple structural dynamics including the morally disabling forces discussed in earlier chapters. Thus the theoretical work of this inquiry roots in the experience of location, dislocation, and the struggle to relocate in a land yet untrod.

I experience "accountability" to a vexing configuration of communities ("accountable" in that their voices substantively influence my work, and "vexing" because they often contradict one another): communities of resistance of which I have been a part; feminist and, increasingly, womanist ethicists and theologians; Central Americans and Africans with whom I have lived or worked and whose impassioned critiques of globalization ring in my heart; people in my local congregation and the broader Lutheran communion worldwide; family and friends; and my ancestors.

Finally, my work is located simultaneously and interactively within three sites: academy, church, and broader publics. The implications and ambiguities generated by this multivalent location are many. One concerns language. In academic work, for example, I seek language accessible beyond the academy. And from within Christian traditions I seek to articulate their moral resources in a manner that bears fruitfully on broader publics. Another implication is a dialectic between a hermeneutic (method of interpretation) of suspicion and a "hermeneutic of trust" in relationship to Christian traditions.[22] My sense of Ethics as a practice of Christian faith *within* Christian traditions holds that faithfulness is *not*, if not deeply critical. Thus in turning to Christian traditions as source in Ethics, my informing faith commitments are to seek the song of the living God and, according to the obligation of "faithful disbelief," to disclose where the traditions and their interpreters obscure or distort Her.[23]

Guiding Theoretical Principles

A number of methodological criteria guide and assess this inquiry. They draw upon long-standing and generally accepted feminist and critical theoretical principles, for the tasks of unmasking morally crippling effects of neo-liberal globalization and of recovering the public moral agency effects of relationship with the immanent God. I propose these criteria also for theological ethics, in general, if it is to challenge both the relations of exploitation reinscribed as natural and inevitable by globalization and modernity's privatization of relationality with God. The proposed principles speak to the ongoing methodological dilemma of how we are to do theo-ethical inquiry grounded in experience, when that experience is profoundly limited by the blinders of privilege and by location in the dominant culture and dominant species.

A comment is in order concerning the import of criteria to guide theological reconstruction regarding God's indwelling presence and power. Throughout Christian history, notions of God-human relationship have rationalized regressive political impulses and social exclusion including the exploitation of indigenous peoples, people of color, women, those who are "impoverished," gay and lesbian people, other vulnerable people, and other-than-human parts of creation. Reconstructed notions of relationality with the immanent God, like all theological reconstruction, may fuel either oppressive or liberative forces. More specific to this project, appeals to the indwelling presence of God could empower either the rampage of unaccountable globalization or resistance and alternatives to it. Likewise those appeals could reinforce either the privatization of relationality with God or the recovery of its communal and political dimensions. Thus, criteria to guide this and related theological reconstruction are indispensable.

The following are *working* criteria. That is, they are developing constantly as my work deepens. After identifying the working criteria, I situate my use of "critical theory" in the term's range of referents, and my use of feminist theory in the trajectories of which it is a part. We begin.

FIRST: *Christian ethical reflection on globalization is fatally flawed if that reflection does not begin with—and otherwise privilege—the cries, claims, and constructive proposals of women and all persons whose survival or basic human rights are threatened by globalization and its legacy.* The flaw is both practical and theological. In the first sense, the practical knowledge for generating alternatives is embodied in their lives, rather than in the claims of neo-classical economic theory. As Donna Haraway notes, subjugated standpoints are preferred because they are less prone to denial and they promise "more adequate . . . and transforming accounts of the world."[24] That is, humanity and the planet now *need* the wisdom born on the underside. Theologically, to marginalize the voices of the suffering transgresses "that standing criterion of good Christian Ethics"—that it privilege "where people and the land most suffer."[25] Thus, questions guiding this and any ethical approach to the globalizing economy ought be: "Whose struggles and knowledge are heard and whose are erased by this approach?" "Is the knowledge of economically marginalized women of the Two-Thirds World prioritized?"

SECOND: *Key concepts in any theo-ethical response to globalization ought be honed in the refining fires of feminist and womanist interrogation.* Concepts are the building blocks of social theories and social analyses. Concepts produced by patriarchy, colonialism, and anthropocentric worldviews render analyses and theories ill-equipped to challenge those legacies. Key concepts in my work include "democracy," "the political," and "moral agency," all liberal notions that have been recast in the past two decades by feminist and womanist thought. If a constructive proposal regarding moral agency is not to perpetuate the universalization of white men's agency, then the proposal's central concepts will be shaped by feminist and womanist demands.

THIRD: *Recent feminist theory—pushed by womanists, mujeristas, and other women of color—demands an interstructural account of relations of domination in any context, including the globalizing economy.*[26] Relations of domination may not be reduced to any one universally primary form of oppression. The more fully an analysis of the global economy probes the shifting interaction of race, gender, and class privilege in maintaining and dismantling structures of domination, the more adequate the analysis. Yet no individual project may adequately address all of these complex categories. That impossibility demonstrates the need for "interactive theorizing" and other collaborative work in formats not yet readily available in academic venues.[27] In the meantime, this project is meant to complement other analyses.[28]

FOURTH: *Divine immanence must be embedded in concrete historical trajectories, and the power dynamics at play in globalization must be contextualized in human and ecological history.* Historicizing globalization defies a key tenant of neo-liberalism: the assumption that globalization is inevitable and natural and therefore untranscendable, rather than being humanly constructed and thus transformable. Situating globalization in historical trajectories, including the colonial legacy, undoes a condition that sustains neo-liberalism. That condition is historical amnesia regarding struggles for liberation and survival. Economic ethics concerned with the globalizing political-economy must be an ethics of memory, of history as known from the underside in terms of race, gender, and class.[29] Yet, to historicize the presumed natural—in this case, globalization—from the margins of *human* society is insufficient today. Globalization also must be contextualized ecologically in order to unmask another neo-liberal myth: that social justice and eco-justice are separable spheres. The question of God's immanence, too, is historicized herein, first in Luther's context and then in the contemporary North American middle-strata culture of powerlessness in the face of globalization.

FIFTH: *What is "personal" will be seen also as integrally "political," and vice versa.*[30] This long-standing feminist principle is evident in my intent to challenge the dissociation of personal spirituality from public moral responsibility, and in my thesis that the personal powerlessness of middle-strata North Americans is rooted in the political-economy of globalization. Grounded too in this principle is my refusal to divorce personal economic activity from its concrete political, cultural, and ecological impacts. This move deviates from the pure neo-classical economic model, which does not account for these factors,[31] and from classical liberalism's "autonomy of the so-called public and private spheres of political economy and interpersonal life."[32] Thus, dimensions of economic and faith life commonly privatized (that is, consumption and investment, or "personal relationship with God") are viewed in light of their public ramifications. In fact, a fundamental criterion for assessing economic policy and practice will be their immanently public impact on the sustainability of communities and the "Earth community."[33] A central feature of "the spirit of globalization" is "the praise . . . of everything 'private' and the contempt of everything 'public.'"[34] My insistence on the political, cultural, and ecological impacts of economic activity and on the public moral agency stemming from personal relationality with God undercuts that feature.

SIXTH: *Theory will be in dialectical relationship with practice; theory will both draw upon practice and seek to "crack it open," especially by revealing the social structural roots of problems presumed to be private.*[35] Thus my questions, theses, and arguments are grounded in my experience of struggling to be faithful in a culture of passivity and powerlessness vis-à-vis global economic injustice, and in efforts to hear the experience of people on the underside of globalization. And the theory I develop seeks to disclose structural factors underlying "private" powerlessness in the face of globalization, and to shape practice that confronts those factors.

SEVENTH: *"What has gone uncritically assumed will be problematized."*[36] *In particular, existing orders of power will be suspect.*[37] Applied to the current undertaking, the implications of this critical feminist presupposition are, of course, endless. Noted here are a few examples. This principle coheres with my suspicions regarding the privatization of divine-human relationship, and regarding the "structural relationships between economic control and political power."[38] This principle also grounds a central task of the study: to unmask unacknowledged structures of thought undergirding the neo-liberal model of globalization. Challenged too is the assumption that economics is the purview of professional "experts" alone. In contrast, I hold that economic life is comprehensible to people not formally trained in economics. (In fact, much as faith life is bereft if interpreted solely by trained theologians, so economic life is distorted if interpreted exclusively by trained economists and financiers.)

A FINAL CRITERION: *Grief, anger, awe, and gratitude will lead the way.* Wed to disciplined theo-ethical reflection, they guide the intellect and open channels of compassion and moral power for radical and faithful restructuring of the global political-economy. Rage, grief, gratitude, and awe pave the way for solidarity. In the words of feminist ethicist Beverly Harrison, "Live into your passions. When you live into your passions, you'll find yourself surrounded by a marvelous community of friends."[39] And these passions open space for the empowering feminist dialectic between realistic and utopian vision . . . vision that takes seriously the magnitude of historical evil, and in the face of it, fights for a world in which none are excluded. Again, as taught by Harrison, "We should never make light of our power to rage. . . . It is the root of the power to love."[40]

In sum, according to these criteria, theo-ethics will consider globalization and the indwelling God through the interpretive keys of relationality, power, moral agency, and Earth community. Ethics will ask how power arrangements constructed in the globalizing economic order undermine the relationships, moral agency, and Earth community through which the gift of life is passed on. Only when these and other criteria make critical feminist theory *intrinsic* to theological ethics, can it adequately challenge globalization in its dominant form.

Both feminist theory and critical theory have long and complex genealogies and multiple forms. Here I situate my work in these two theoretical trajectories, beginning with the latter. Different theorists use the terms *critical theory* or *critical social theory* differently.[41] Factors shaping usage include academic discipline, historical era, continental vs. Anglo-American context, and political alignment. Many theorists assume a referent without explaining it, and the result is confusing. To avoid that mistake, I here locate my use of the term *critical theory* in four main referents. From most specific to least, they are as follows:

In its most specific use "critical theory" refers to social theory emanating from the Frankfurt School in the 1930s as a reaction against the reigning trajectory of sociological positivism, and drawing on the work of Kant, Hegel, and Marx. Two distinctions between cultural social theory and positivist sociology developing through Émile Durkheim was the former's understanding of social structures as produced and reproduced by human activity (rather than as "natural"), and critical theory's normative dimension. Critical theory aimed at emancipation from socio-historical processes that produce injustice and misery.

In a second sense, "critical theory" refers to Marxist and neo-Marxist theory, intended originally "to provide a theoretical foundation for interpreting the world in order to change it."[42] While this is not my referent, two factors distinguishing Marx's analysis from classical economic theory pertain to this project. Marxist theory refutes the disassociation of the political from other social spheres (including the economic) so integral to classical economic theory. Secondly, Marxist theory insists on the historical specificity of capitalism and hence the possibility of change and alternatives. Marx "did not take for granted the logic of the capitalist system"; instead, he "challenged the universality of its constitutive categories."[43] Beverly Harrison, identifying these two factors as primary distinctions between radical economic theory and neo-classical economic theory, argues that these characteristics of the former correlate with the needs of a theological economic ethic. Thus they commend critical political-economic theory to theological ethicists.[44]

For some theorists, "critical theory" is a more general term for social theories that "provide radical politics with its chief intellectual tools."[45] Finally, in the term's most general sense, "critical" as opposed to "positivist" social theory refers to social theory that exposes social structures as historically contingent and thus—at least theoretically—subject to human agency, as opposed to natural and inevitable and thereby untranscendable. Critical theory challenges existing power and truth arrangements, rather than presupposing and thus reinscribing them. Instead of assuming an essentialist view of race, class, gender, and other social categories, a critical perspective exposes those categories as productions of power interests. It uncovers "ideological alignments whereby description becomes prescription and the local is represented as universal," thus suspecting rather than presupposing "the self-images of an age."[46] Critical theory looks for and challenges "operations of power," relationships of domination, and how both are concealed. These aims are not ends in themselves but move rather toward empowering people as agents of structural social change.

My use of "critical theory" coheres most closely with the last of these. Yet, in one crucial sense my use of the term critiques all of the above referents. All have been limited historically to "social," failing to acknowledge that social reality is inextricably embedded in a broader web of life. That is, they have assumed that only the social consequences (including political, economic, cultural, psychological) of human decisions and actions count, failing to account for a vast array of consequences beyond the social. Social theories have presupposed that social consequences and causes comprise a closed universe that may be theorized in isolation from the far broader web of life of which the human species is a part. My use of "critical theory" presupposes a corrective, attempting to be critical *socio-ecological* theory. That is, my theorizing seeks to assume human life located in the planetary—if not cosmic—weave of life, and inextricable from it. The verbs ("attempt" and "seek") reveal the difficulty of presupposing a theoretical stance for which language and conceptual frameworks are not readily available in modern Western ethics. The *oikos*, "the ancient vision of the earth as a single public household," offers a theological entry point.[47]

To claim feminist theory as a source of my working methodological principles is to raise an endless array of complex and loaded questions—definitional, categorical, and functional. What, for instance, do I mean by "feminism," "theory," and "feminist theory?" Where do I locate myself in the multiple forms of feminist theory, historical trajectories of feminism, aspects of feminism and feminist theory, and sites of contention in all of these?[48] What are the functions of feminist theory in a theo-ethical critique of globalization and in a constructive response to it? This book *draws on* feminist theory but is not *about* it. My intention here is only to situate succinctly my work in the complex and varied array of feminist theoretical work.

I locate myself in feminist perspectives that acknowledge a three-fold feminist agenda and contribute to some aspect of it. That agenda includes challenging the political, economic, and cultural structures that subordinate some groups of people to others, notably on account of gender, race, ethnicity, sexual preference, and class, with particular attention to the subordination of women and privileging the concerns of those women who are most marginalized.[49] Secondly, the agenda includes disclosing the links between those varied forms of subordination. This means analyzing the philosophical and material common roots of domination in various forms, and their connections to a global capitalist political-economy. The third task is that of bringing forth historical and contemporary struggles for survival, liberation, and flourishing in the face of oppression.

To thus situate myself is to say that I am enormously indebted to various feminist frameworks, land at this time in one which accounts for interstructural analyses and aims, struggle to live up to its standards, and am critical of less inclusive forms.[50] It is to suggest also where I will turn for ongoing theoretical guideposts and development. I will engage more with womanist, *mujerista,* and "Third World" feminist voices; post-colonial feminisms; and eco-feminism. These expand and challenge the epistemological, theoretical, and practical concerns of white Western feminisms.

Depending upon how one conceptualizes both feminist theory and critical theory, either may be seen as a form or subset of the other, or each may be seen as an independent strain influenced by, influencing, and intersecting with the other. My perspective is the latter. Many of the intersections—the loci of critical feminist theory and of feminist critical theory—constitute the methodological criteria guiding this project in general, and the theories that I develop regarding the corrosion and regeneration of moral agency. These ever-developing criteria will guide, too, the constructive work that will follow this project and will be based on it.

Methodological Problems and Working Resolutions

Here I identify methodological problems entailed in thinking critically about the interplay between God's indwelling presence and moral agency in past contexts, for the purpose of unearthing subversive moral agency today. And I suggest working resolutions to those problems. Said differently, I address problems raised by an attempt to seek, in critical encounter with faith forebearers, guidance toward moral-spiritual power for subversive praxis today in the face of public moral crises vastly different from the crises faced by those historical figures. This is an important set of issues for the discipline of Christian Ethics if it is to get on with not only deconstructing Christian traditions' contributions to domination, but also reconstructing and drawing upon ignored, domesticated, or subjugated voices in those traditions, for liberative purposes.

This methodological task is situated in a vast body of epistemological and hermeneutical questions regarding the role of "tradition" in constructive Christian Ethics. How do and ought "pasts" inform current belief and practice? How do and ought current communities appropriate their pasts? How and for what purposes do we listen to the witness of those who went before? My methodological intent is to open that inquiry, with reference to moral-spiritual agency for confronting systemic domination.

Note my presuppositions that contemporary faith communities ought "listen" to the lives of past communities, and that the witness of the past is to be heard critically. The former undercuts both the Enlightenment resolve to strip intellectual activity from "all opinions and beliefs formerly received," and the postmodern rejection of all but particular knowledges.[51] The latter presupposition undercuts "neo-conservative" uncritical adherence to received truth.

The methodological "problems" are myriad. We address a few that seem most vexing, and most foundational to an adequate method. Most of these dilemmas may be identified either in a specific voice as issues entailed in a case-study of Luther, or in a generic voice as issues raised by a constructive encounter with any historical figure or community. I have chosen the former. Thus, in addressing problems raised by the encounter with Luther, I consider issues likely to occur, albeit in varied form, in the attempt to learn moral wisdom from many—if not most—historical figures.

PROBLEM: What is a "good Lutheran" doing focusing on the "indwelling God" in Luther's theology and noting an inseparable link between moral life and salvation? From the perspective of much Lutheran theological tradition, my approach to Luther is not Lutheran and may be suspect.

WORKING RESOLUTION: Mine is a "Luther-an" approach to Luther, called for by the moral passivity historically characteristic of many European and Euro-American Lutheran churches in the face of structural sin. North Atlantic Lutheranism has tended to claim the comfort of justification by faith alone, while eschewing its radical ethical implications.

This predicament of moral passivity has countless social structural and theological roots. One is a persistent theological tendency toward a trinity of reductionism: reduce justification to its forensic dimension, the moral life to the believer's grateful response to justification, and law to the antithesis of gospel. These reductionist tendencies lead Lutheran theology to centralize and sacralize Luther's "answer" (the person is justified by grace alone through faith alone) to a question with which many contemporary Lutherans are not likely to be as tormented as was he. Furthermore, this reductionism obscures certain implications of Luther's "answer." Focus on limited interpretations of responses to burning questions of a bygone context lead us to bypass the questions of our own. Luther pursued questions regarding personal salvation that led directly to the heart of liberation for his time. The Lutheran tendency to sacralize Luther's question and answer distracts us from asking additional questions necessary for liberation in our day.[52] "Moral life as God indwelling creation" leads out of this problem. For it reduces neither justification to its forensic dimension, nor the moral life to the grateful response of the justified. And, while affirming and retaining Luther's conviction that God—not human effort—saves, "moral life as God indwelling creation" decenters the question of personal salvation, making space for other crucial questions of our time and place.[53]

The moral passivity of many Lutheran communities stems also from the theological tendency to disassociate salvation from public moral life. Key elements of that disconnect include the bifurcation of the person as justified individual and the person as historical social being, the dissociation of social righteousness and righteousness before God, the failure to take seriously the social justice effects of justification, and the disconnection of Jesus Christ savior from Jesus Christ transformer of the moral life.

These interrelated dynamics, often associated with Luther's theology, misrepresent him. Luther's notion of the indwelling Christ asserts an indissolvable union between salvation and the public moral life. The saved embody Christ, who, in them, actively serves the widespread good, and especially the well-being of people in need. While much Lutheran tradition has relegated the public moral life to the back burner, Luther keeps it on the front burner.

Finally, I am convinced that the Lutheran tendency to read Luther through the lens of the Augsburg Confession, the Apology of it, and later theological formulations, and to prioritize their authority over that of Luther, has contributed to moral quietude regarding public life. These formulations obscure the nuanced, multidimensional, unsystematic, and mystical character of Luther's soteriology. That character points to the morally transformative power of justification by grace through faith on account of Christ. Thus, in this project, I attempt to hear Luther *not* through the lens of the Augsburg Confession and of later Lutheran theology.

PROBLEM: What is a feminist liberationist theo-ethicist doing appealing to Martin Luther? Let us be frank: Martin Luther demonized Jews, advising Christians "in the name of our Lord Jesus Christ" to burn synagogues, Jewish homes, and holy books. He condemned Anabaptists and weighed in heavily against peasants in their revolt against nobility whose practices Luther himself labeled as oppressive, tyrannical, and at fault in the peasants' rebellion. I will not begin to name the many other problems Luther presents for a contemporary Christian with feminist liberationist sensibilities.

WORKING RESOLUTION: My relationship with Luther is part of a larger paradox: I claim as revelatory and life-giving Christian traditions that for centuries have contributed to domination and exploitation. That legacy has included "normalizing" white, property-owning, heterosexual, male *Homo sapiens*; subordinating "others"; and silencing their voices and collective memories. While I have drunk life from the witness of Christian faith communities throughout the ages, I also have been so horrified by them and ashamed of them that, for some time, I "left" the church. Christian traditions bearing seeds of liberation also have sown the very moral abominations inherent in the globalizing economy.

The theo-ethical task, within that paradox, is to draw upon faith traditions constructively, while simultaneously deconstructing and denouncing ways that they have betrayed God's gracious love for creation by theologically rationalizing structured oppression. To do so from *within* the constellation of Christian traditions—that is, as a person of faith—is to be convinced that faith is *not*, if not critical. My approach juxtaposes critique with reclaiming the traditions for each new time and draws upon faith traditions to critique themselves. Thus I work with two hermeneutics in dialectical relationship, one of "trust" and the other of suspicion (as noted above in my discussion of "location"). According to the former, I draw upon Luther, wresting from him guidance toward moral-spiritual agency rooted in God's indwelling presence. The latter, while implicit in this inquiry throughout, bears fruit explicitly when I argue that, in Luther's case, the subversive moral agency engendered by relationality with the indwelling Christ was undercut—in certain social relationships—by his Constantinian, patriarchal, and anti-Semitic worldview.

Drawing upon historical figures and communities in theo-ethical reflection is, then, a three-fold task: (1) to uncover, expose, and deconstruct where the traditions have obscured or distorted the good news of God's creating, liberating, and sustaining love for all; of who we are; and of how we are to live; (2) to seek out and hear the traditions—especially voices silenced, domesticated, or distorted by dominant streams—where they have proclaimed faithfully the good news and have embodied ways in which human creatures are to live in relationship to God, one another, and the rest of creation; (3) learning both from the betrayals and the faithfulness of faith forebearers, to forge paths of faithful praxis today.

PROBLEM: The capacity to generate moral agency had been crippled in all major post-Enlightenment ethical traditions, until the dawn of various liberationist ethics, by failure to account adequately for the influence of social structures—including institutions, ideologies, systems, policies, and practices—in controlling our lives. More specifically, the role of these forces in limiting moral agency and in mitigating against substantive change in conduct, consciousness, and society are largely "off the screen" in much moral deliberation. This is a dangerous lacuna, especially from a liberationist perspective with its post-Marxian understanding of how systems and structures help shape conduct and consciousness. While this critique pertains to all of the major ethical traditions, classic virtue ethics and more recent character ethics, with their focus on character formation, are most implicated. Morality, proposed in this study as flowing from relationship with the immanent God, is, in some senses, closer to classic virtue ethics than to the other moral traditions. Hence, morality grounded in divine immanence is vulnerable to this weakness unless situated in the larger picture of ethics that I presuppose and prescribe.

The problem of ethics' inadequate attention to social structural factors is raised and exacerbated by an appeal to Luther or to any other premodern figure or community. For, as stated by political philosopher Michael Waltzer, critical appraisal of social structures and organized efforts toward social change "together are aspects only of the modern, that is, the postmedieval political world. . . . the idea that specifically designated and organized bands of men [sic] might play a creative part in the political world, destroying the established order and reconstructing society according to the Word of God or the plans of their fellows [sic]—this idea did not enter at all into the thought of . . . Luther" or other premodern figures.[54] *The contradiction, for our purposes here, is that of appealing to figures for whom the concept of social structural change was not constitutive of reality, in order to help construct an ethic that holds social structural factors as key and social structural change as its aim.*

WORKING RESOLUTION: The problem is two-fold: (1) modern ethics' failure to account for social structural issues, and (2) the appeal to premodern figures to inform an ethic in which social structural factors are central. I address each briefly in turn.

The constructive proposal regarding moral agency developed herein overcomes the first aspect of the problem by a few crucial moves. First, moral inquiry is contextualized in social structural determinants of morality, and especially of moral agency. (This is a task of the study's initial three chapters.) Second, I presuppose that moral power flowing from relationship with "God in all things" is *for the purpose of* directly confronting the social structures that shape life according to the demands of globalization. Third, moral power grounded in divine immanence is seen as an indispensable, but certainly *not sufficient,* dimension of subversive Christian praxis in the globalizing economy. Other dimensions include historical structural analysis of globalization, the crafting of alternatives at multiple levels, and committed collective movement toward those alternatives. (While "indispensable . . . but not sufficient" begins as a presupposition, it becomes a prescription in my discussion of solidarity.)

Regarding the problem's second aspect: I appeal to Luther for what he offers regarding moral power stemming from relationship with God indwelling all of creation. Yet an overall methodological principle is that a constructive appeal necessarily entails a critical and historical inquiry. Thus, I consider factors—including Luther's historically conditioned political worldview—that limited and disfigured Luther's notions of neighbor-love and the scope of the moral universe.

PROBLEM: Luther did not face the moral crises addressed herein. How are we to draw upon him or other distant faith forebearers for response to moral issues discontinuous with the issues they encountered?

WORKING RESOLUTION: Luther himself insists that theo-ethical work is contextual; is experientially based; and draws imaginatively on the conclusions of past teachers but does not necessarily appropriate them directly. Nothing would be more inappropriate than simply to repeat Luther's words in our context and expect them to yield the gospel, moral guidance, or liberation that they yielded in his.

Luther was a thoroughly *contextual* theologian. His theo-ethical and political positions were rooted in his anguished struggle with a burning issue of his context: personal salvation. He wrestled with the Word in relationship to this particular torment, which was related intimately to the dominant ethos of his day. Luther protested "against all who cited him for decisions in cases different from the ones in which his judgment arose."[55]

He was an *experientially based* theologian. His theological discoveries grew out of grappling with his reality, struggles, and bondage. From those struggles, in the light of Christ, he came to theological positions on which he staked his life.

Luther *had no use for the direct application* of past teachers to current situations. Explicitly directing people away from universalizing the authority of his writings, he advises: Let the reader "put them to use as I put the decrees and decretals of the pope to use, and the books of the sophists. That is, if I occasionally wish to see what they have done, or if I wish to ponder the historical facts of the time, I use them. But I do not study them or act in perfect accord with what they deemed good. I do not treat the books of the fathers and the councils much differently."[56]

In line with this methodological heritage, in turning to faith forebearers for moral power to address moral crises they did not face, we neither seek universally applicable theo-ethical deposits from the past, nor reiterate the ancestors' questions and answers. Rather, we seek clues to dimensions of their faith that engendered moral-spiritual power. Then—holding those insights in light of other central theological convictions—we bring those clues to bear imaginatively on the experience of systemic domination in our time and place.[57]

This approach resonates with other feminist theo-ethical projects aimed at drawing upon Luther, notably the work of Mary Solberg. She writes: "I am not interested in proving that Luther would have done what I am trying to do; rather, I am interested in showing how certain of Luther's key notions are quite serviceable in orienting, shaping, limiting, or justifying a project that I believe would have value independently of Luther and his theology."[58]

PROBLEM: Constructive inquiry into the moral landscape of a distant past transgresses two canons of deconstructionist postmodernism by (1) laying claim to a "story" of emancipatory power present in history and yearning to break forth more fully, and (2) failing to consider *all* truth to be contingent and historically particular in every sense.

WORKING RESOLUTION: Regarding the latter, I do not apologize for a method that assumes there is something useful to be said across cultures and historical epochs in the quest for subversive moral wisdom. While I share the deconstructionist suspicion regarding universalizing *descriptive* accounts of the human, I defy the extension of that suspicion to all universalization of *normative* accounts.[59] Regarding the former "transgression," I value the deconstruction of historical meta-narratives in order to disclose their underlying and unacknowledged presuppositions and the ways in which they have underwritten various forms of oppression. Yet the deconstructionist attack on historical narrative per se undermines historical memory including histories of resistance. Historical amnesia—especially regarding legacies of resistance—feeds the myth that globalization as we know it is inevitable. Thus, where this study employs deconstructive strategies, it is not necessarily for the purposes intended by the continental deconstructionists or some of their better known North American followers, from whom I differ in significant ways.

PROBLEM: When Christian ethicists enter the theological and moral terrain of the past bearing contemporary questions, the tendency is to read into historical figures and communities what one hopes to find, to make "history an alibi for our own interests."[60]

WORKING RESOLUTION: This hermeneutical problem, pertinent to historical inquiry in various disciplines, warrants book-length treatment. My provisional conclusion holds that any turn to aspects of a tradition in which one is situated must begin by acknowledging modernity's perceptual lenses and the enormous "strangeness" of the past. My practical guidelines are these: Begin by putting aside (to the extent possible) the motivating questions and hopes, trying to hear the ancestors speak in and to their context.

Only then bring the historical figures into dialogue with contemporary concerns. That is, attend first to the ways in which they, their world, and their ways were radically distant from ours, and then bring them into conversation with contemporary questions. Stay away from identification and empathy as exclusive hermeneutical keys, turning also to otherness for the interpretive key. Avoid easy generalizations. Be wary of definitive and clear interpretations where qualified and vague ones might better represent the historical figures. This all requires studying the historical context "adequately" and asking initially, "Who were these people? How and what did they speak? What historical projects did they intend to serve?"

PROBLEM: "Studying the historical situation adequately" begs a further question. Hearing the voice of a distant past is entry into a foreign culture. A task of Christian moral inquiry is to draw upon the plethora of "foreign cultures" constituent of Jewish and Christian traditions as a source in moral reflection. Appealing to figures of vastly "other" epochs and cultures without having expertise in those historical sites creates multivalent and complex issues. One cannot develop the cultural sophistication required to decipher rhetorical tropes and hidden meanings in multiple cultural contexts. Furthermore, any historical figure must be located within multiple contexts to which may be attached different streams of academic inquiry. What constitutes "adequate" knowledge of historical situations in order to draw—with integrity—from historical figures or movements for moral wisdom today?

WORKING RESOLUTION: This complexity ought not prevent theo-ethical inquiry from appealing to and learning from varied locations in faith heritages. Not to draw upon the legacies—especially upon previously silenced voices or ignored and domesticated aspects of dominant voices—would be to deny and lose the power of their witness. Response to this dilemma exceeds the bounds of this project. Suffice it here to note that the problem illustrates the inherently relational and interdependent character of faith life; we must depend upon the inquiries and knowledge of one another.

In Sum

Taken as a whole, these elements of my method—a "new" ethical question arising from a three-pronged critique of the discipline, social location, communities of accountability, theological starting points, principles of critical and feminist theory and theology, and methodological problems—constitute methodological guideposts for unmasking the morally corrosive effects of globalization, and for drawing upon the wisdom of ancestral faith communities for the sake of faithful response to those effects. The quest is for guidance toward the moral-spiritual agency required to subvert seemingly untranscendable forces of economic globalization that are colonizing our collective consciousness and behavior, and required to cultivate socially just and ecologically sustainable economic life.

Notes

Preface

1. The groups of U.S. citizens included farmers, homemakers, lawyers, physicians, pastors, bishops, journalists, activists, business leaders, tradespeople, unemployed people, mayors, students, and others.

2. I am well aware that "liberationist" may be considered passé in academic discourse today. Yet the vicissitudes of academic jargon do not convince me to discount the ongoing historical significance in the concept—as critiqued and revised especially by feminist and indigenous voices—in communities struggling for liberation.

3. Martin Luther, "The Sacrament of the Body and Blood of Christ—Against the Fanatics," in *Martin Luther's Basic Theological Writings,* ed. Timothy F. Lull (Minneapolis: Fortress Press, 1989), 321; Martin Luther, "Third Sermon for Pentecost Sunday," in *Sermons of Martin Luther*, ed. John Nicholas Lenker (Grand Rapids: Baker, 1983), vol. 3: 316–17.

Introduction

1. Jon Sobrino, a Jesuit priest in El Salvador, once declared in conversation with a delegation: "In El Salvador, poverty spells death." The assertion that globalization exacerbates poverty is contested by some. Proponents of economic globalization in its current form claim that it reduces poverty and serves ecological and cultural well-being. Chapters 1 to 3 acknowledge those claims and test my assertion against them.

2. Daniel Maguire, in *The Moral Core of Judaism and Christianity: Reclaiming the Revolution* (Minneapolis: Fortress Press, 1993), 13, puts it well: "One thing is clear: If current trends continue, we will not . . . we are an endangered species."

3. I presuppose this argument. Scholars who have made it include: Grace Jantzen, *Power, Gender, and Christian Mysticism* (Cambridge: Cambridge Univ. Press, 1995);

Nicholas Lash, *The Beginning and the End of Religion* (Cambridge: Cambridge Univ. Press, 1996); and Sarah Beckwith, *Christ's Body: Identity, Culture, and Society in Late Medieval Writings* (London and New York: Routledge, 1993). The most sustained argument is that of Grace Jantzen, who focuses particularly on gender dynamics in modernity's constructions of mysticism.

4. Luther, "That These Words of Christ, 'This Is My Body,' Etc. Still Stand Firm against the Fanatics," in *Luther's Works* 37, ed. Robert H. Fischer (Philadelphia: Muhlenberg, 1961), 57.

5. The "insulation of privilege" with reference to economic life refers to the perceptive lenses and blinders of many who are relatively secure economically. Although we may have struggled to support families on very sparse budgets, most of us have not been forced to face the terror of possible homelessness or life-threatening poverty and have not become intimately involved in the lives of people who do. As a result of this "privilege," we remain "insulated" from the real life experience of life-threatening poverty, unaware that for many of our sisters and brothers "poverty is death."

6. The term is Michael Harrington's in *The Vast Majority: Journey to the World's Poor* (New York: Simon and Schuster, 1977). Roman Catholic economist Amata Miller notes, "Harrington observed that the people of the United States are among the most generous the world has ever seen, responding with compassion to every kind of disaster afflicting both friend and foe. But . . . in their 'cruel innocence' they do not have the slightest understanding that at the root of the human suffering they deplore is a global system dominated by the U.S. economy." Amata Miller, "Global Economic Structures: Their Human Implications," in *Religion and Economic Justice,* ed. Michael Zweig (Philadelphia: Temple Univ. Press, 1991), 164; Margaret Miles eloquently describes complicity and passivity in the face of urgent and enormous moral crises in *Practicing Christians* (New York: Crossroad, 1988), 3. She speaks of "cultural conditioning to passivity."

7. Seminal or highly influential works in the critique of globalization include Richard Barnet and John Cavanagh, *Global Dreams: Imperial Corporations and the New World Order* (New York: Simon and Schuster, 1994); Jeremy Brecher and Tim Costello, *Global Village or Global Pillage: Economic Reconstruction from the Bottom Up* (Boston: South End Press, 1994); William Greider, *One World Ready or Not: The Manic Logic of Global Capitalism* (New York: Touchstone, 1997); and David Korten, *When Corporations Rule the World* (West Hartford and San Francisco: Kumarian and Barrett-Koehler, 1995). Many additional works are cited in the notes to chapters 1 to 3.

8. In that chapter I establish the range of meaning to which "democracy" and "democratic" refer in the study and situate my use of the terms in critiques of democracy as a norm constructed in and by liberal Western political discourse.

9. I commonly refer to Christian Ethics not as a discipline, but rather as an interdiscipline.

10. This quotation is by Irenaeus of Lyons, *Against Heresies*, 3.17.3, in *The Ante-Nicene Fathers,* vol. 1, ed. Alexander Roberts and James Donaldson (Grand Rapids: Eerdmans, 1952).

11. Luther, "That These Words of Christ," *Luther's Works* 37:57.

12. This point is made by Caryn Riswold in an unpublished paper presented at the Annual Gathering of Lutheran Women in Theological Studies, 1996. Luther's obligation was also to oppose anything that prevented people from hearing the Word.

13. It must be acknowledged that Luther's fear of social disorder and his "social theory" mitigated against this liberative dynamic and toward orderly adherence to a divinely ordained social hierarchy, to the authority of the new theology, and to those political powers that embraced it. Thus, in some arenas, Luther was aligned with dominating powers, which he failed to challenge (as seen most clearly in his devastating denunciation of the peasant uprising and of the "radical" reformers, and his demonizing of Jews). Yet, in the sense and arena with which I primarily am working, he was subversive of dominating powers. This contradiction is acknowledged in chapters 4 and 5 and becomes instructive; it points to factors—especially social theoretical factors—that thwart the subversive potential of relationality with the immanent divine.

14. For example, at issue in the 1519 debate at Liepzig with Eck was whether the papacy was a divine institution (Eck) or a human development (Luther).

15. These dimensions do not correspond *directly* with the six tasks outlined below.

16. I conceptualize "relationship with the indwelling God" as—among other things—a dimension of mysticism. That conceptual logic, however, is not constituent of the argument herein.

17. I already have stated two sets of presuppositions: (1) that the dominant form of economic globalization poses substantive threats and that alternatives are being developed, and (2) that Christian traditions include a historical trajectory in which Divine immanence has underwritten moral agency.

18. Volumes could be written about the different and conflicting constructions of neighbor-love and its moral implications throughout the histories of biblical faith communities.

19. Maguire, *Moral Core,* 220.

20. That neighbor-love implies justice and is the primary norm of faith life according to Scripture is argued by Daniel Maguire in *Moral Core*: "In the main biblical perspective, love and justice are not opposites but coordinates, manifestations of the same affect. . . . The various words for justice and love in both the Hebrew and Greek scriptures are linguistically interlocking" (220). "With Jesus, the very traditional rabbi, active love has a priority over worship. You contact God by loving people; morality, not liturgy, is the sacrament of encounter with God. . . . Lived love is the only holiness" (220–21). This will bear out in my discussion of the sacrament of solidarity as the necessary partner of Eucharist, if Eucharist is to bear its intended fruit.

21. These four "phases of struggle" appear in chapters 5 and 6, specifically in their discussions of "solidarity as sacrament." They cohere with Walter Brueggemann's articulation of "doing justice" according to the Hebrew Scriptures. See Walter Brueggemann, "Voices of the Night—Against Justice," in Walter Brueggemann, Thomas H. Groome, and Sharon Parks, *To Act Justly, Love Tenderly, Walk Humbly* (Mahwah, N.J.:

Paulist Press, 1986). He writes: Doing justice implies "relentless critique of injustice" (7); "envisions a changed social system" (10); and works toward "nothing less than the dismantling of the presently-known world for the sake of an alternative world not yet embodied" (11). More specifically, Brueggemann argues, doing justice, biblically understood, includes "sorting out what belongs to whom and returning it to them" (5).

22. Maguire, *Moral Core*, 211.

23. Ibid., 211; ibid., 208.

24. Janet R. Jakobsen, *Working Alliances and the Politics of Difference: Diversity and Feminist Ethics* (Bloomington: Indiana Univ. Press, 1998), 2. See also Jakobsen's chapter 4.

25. My use of "subversive" in relationship to dominating powers reflects the etymology of the word, "sub" meaning "under," and "verto" (first person singular present tense) or "vertere" (infinitive) meaning "to turn." See *New and Copious Lexicon of the Latin Language*, ed. F. P. Leverett (Boston: J. H. Wilkens, R. B. Carter, C. C. Little, and James Brown, 1840), and *Random House Webster's Unabridged Dictionary*, 2nd ed. (New York: Random House, 1997).

26. Mark U. Edwards refers to Luther's "subversive message" in "Summer Reading: Catch a Few of Martin Luther's Earliest 'Best-Sellers,'" *Accent* (June 1993): 9.

27. Steven Katz in *Mysticism and Religious Traditions* (Oxford: Oxford Univ. Press, 1983), 3–60, reveals that dialectic in his attempt to "reveal the two-sided nature of mysticism" as oscillating between conserving and radically challenging established authority and tradition. His work illumines this dialectic as it pertains also to the role of relationality with the indwelling God.

28. Elizabeth Bounds identifies six distinct yet related current meanings, all responding to a yearning for change, rootedness, and connectedness in the face of dislocation and alienation characteristic of modern social life. See Elizabeth M. Bounds, *Coming Together/Coming Apart: Religion, Community, and Modernity* (London and New York: Routledge, 1997), 2.

29. See Bounds, ibid., and Jakobsen, *Working Alliances,* for critiques of community from two different feminist perspectives.

30. This point is made by Bounds regarding appeals to community by liberal white Protestants in the United States. See Bounds, *Coming Together/Coming Apart*.

31. Larry Rasmussen, *Earth Community, Earth Ethics* (Maryknoll, N.Y.: Orbis Books, 1996).

32. In the words of Catherine Mowry LaCugna, in "God in Communion with Us: The Trinity," in *Freeing Theology: The Essentials of Theology in Feminist Perspective*, ed. Catherine Mowry LaCugna (San Francisco: HarperSanFrancisco, 1993), 86–87: "The radical move of the Cappadocians was to assert that divinity or Godhead originates with personhood (someone toward another), not with substance (something in and of itself). Love for and relationship with another is primary over autonomy. . . . Being-in-relation-to-another was secured as the ultimate originating principle of all reality." LaCugna suggests a Trinitarian "dance" of relationality, noting that a word used by the Cappadocians to describe the relational Trinity, *perichoresis*, etymologically is related to "choreography."

33. Walter Brueggemann, *The Bible Makes Sense* (Atlanta: John Knox Press, 1977), 109; ibid., 110.

34. G. W. H. Lampe traces concepts of God immanent as Jesus Christ and as Spirit, as those concepts developed in various streams of patristic thought, and he illumines the influence of Greek philosophical constructs in that development. See G. W. H. Lampe, *God as Spirit: The Bampton Lectures, 1976* (Oxford: Clarendon Press, 1977).

35. Again, the development of these controversies in varied streams of patristic thought is sketched by Lampe in *God as Spirit*.

1. Introduction to Globalization

1. Larry Rasmussen, "A Different Discipline," in *Union Seminary Quarterly Review: Festschrift for Beverly Harrison* 53:34 (1999): 33.

2. As indicated by the Organization for Economic Cooperation and Development (OECD) in *Open Markets Matter: The Benefits of Trade and Investment Liberalization* (Paris: OECD, 1998), 121, *investment liberalization* refers to the liberalization of both investment and financial services. *Investment* refers both to "physical" or "real" investment (capital expenditure on physical assets), which adds to productive capacity, and to "financial" or "portfolio" investment, which does not, per se, add to productive capacity but transfers ownership of existing assets. *Financial services* refers to the activity of finance institutions (investment banks, commercial banks, brokerage firms, insurance companies, thrifts) and financial markets (money markets and stock exchanges), and the buying, selling, lending, and borrowing of money and other financial instruments (stocks, bonds, bills, etc.).

3. The movement of capital across international borders to acquire assets is referred to as *foreign investment* or *transnational investment*. Private foreign investment has three forms: (1) Foreign direct investment (FDI): capital expenditure on the purchase of physical assets such as plants or equipment, in which investors acquire enough shares of an enterprise to gain control of it; (2) Portfolio investment: financial securities such as stocks and bonds, the payoffs of which are dividends, interest, and appreciation in capital value; (3) International bank lending (debt). In this book, *foreign investment* or *transnational investment* refers to the first two forms. For more detailed discussion, see Doug Henwood, *Wall Street* (London and New York: Verso, 1998), 10–55, 81–86.

4. Sarah Anderson and John Cavanagh, "The Top 200: The Rise of Corporate Global Power" (report by Institute for Policy Studies, Washington, D.C., 1996). This trend is confirmed in the United Nations Research Institute's (UNRISD) *States of Disarray: The Social Effects of Globalization* (London: Banson, 1995), 154.

5. The multiple and highly disturbing political, economic, and ethical ramifications of water privatization are analyzed by Maude Barlow in *Blue Gold: The Global Water*

Crisis and the Commodification of the World's Water Supply (San Francisco: International Forum on Globalization, 2000). The document predicts water as the next "oil" in terms of those ramifications.

6. By *trade in money,* I refer to the buying, selling, lending, and borrowing of money—in the form of various financial instruments—for profit derived from movement in its price. See Henwood, *Wall Street,* 10–55, 91, for discussion of money's varied forms and for definitions of money. *Speculation* refers to the purchase or sale of financial or real assets for the purpose of short-term gain from change in the commodity's price. Clarifying discussions of speculation are offered in Henwood, *Wall Street,* 118–221, and *The Harper Collins Dictionary of Economics* (New York: HarperCollins, 1991), 490–93.

7. For example: Joel Kurtzman, editor of the *Harvard Business Review,* writes, "For every $1 circulating in the productive economy today, 20 to 50 circulate in the world of pure finance." Joel Kurtzman, cited in Henwood, *Wall Street,* 3–4; German Christian ethicist Ulrich Duchrow asserts, "only 5 percent [of the dollars passing through transnational currency markets] are associated with genuine production of goods! The rest goes to speculation." See Ulrich Duchrow, *Alternatives to Global Capitalism: Drawn from Biblical History, Designed for Political Action* (Utrecht: International Books, 1995), 85; The International Chamber of Commerce declares, "Foreign investment . . . has been growing much faster than trade in goods and services and is the driving force behind globalization." See Helmut O. Maucher, "Firm Deadline Now Needed for MAI," *ICC Business World: The Electronic Magazine of the ICC,* available at (http://www.iccwbo.org/home/news_archives/1998/firm_for_mai.asp), 1. These claims are echoed by others including John B. Cobb Jr. and Herman E. Daly, *For the Common Good,* 2nd. ed. (Boston: Beacon Press, 1994), 407–23.

8. One of these dangers is the increasing detachment of money from the goods and services that formerly were money's source of value. See Richard Barnet and John Cavanagh, "Electronic Money and the Casino Economy," in *The Case against the Global Economy,* ed. Jerry Mander and Edward Goldsmith (San Francisco: Sierra Club Books, 1996), 370, and Duchrow, *Alternatives,* 85.

9. According to the International Chamber of Commerce, a primary force behind investment and financial service deregulation, liberalization should "remove obstacles to the provision of cross border financial services. . . . In particular, it should do away with regulations or procedures that inhibit foreign investment."

10. Sangguniang Pambansa Ng Mga Simbahan Sa Pilipinas (National Council of Churches in the Philippines), "Statement on Globalization" (Quezon City: 1999).

11. International Chamber of Commerce and Financial Leaders Group, "Joint Statement on the WTO Financial Services Negotiations" (statement issued September 22, 1997, Hong Kong).

12. This argument is articulated clearly in OECD, *Open Markets Matter,* 40–41: "Market openness brings real and direct economic gains to *all* consumers." 41. Regarding comparative advantage, see ibid., 9–10, 20–21. Regarding efficiency as related to

growth, see ibid., 39. For representative voices assuming or articulating this theory from the private sector, academic economics, and the Christian Right, respectively, see: the International Chamber of Commerce, at http://www.iccwbo.org, and the United States Council for International Business, at http:/www.uscib.org; R. Dornbusch and F. Helmers, ed., *The Open Economy: Tools for Policy Makers in Developing Countries* (Cambridge: Oxford Univ. Press, for the World Bank, 1995); and Michael Novak, *Cultivating Liberty* (Lanham, Md.: Rowman and Littlefield, 1999). This economic argument is not necessarily consistent with *classical* economic theory as expressed by either Adam Smith or David Ricardo.

13. For fuller description of this anthropological theory relative to economic theory, see Amata Miller, "Global Economic Structures: Their Human Implications," in *Religion and Economic Justice*, ed. Michael Zweig (Philadelphia: Temple Univ. Press, 1991), 163–95.

14. Miller, "Global Economic Structures," 169

15. Michael Novak is a vocal articulator of this perspective in the Christian Right. See, for example, his *The Fire of Invention: Civil Society and the Future of the Corporation* (Lanham, Md.: Rowman and Littlefield: 1997). For a more nuanced and moderate appeal to the corporation as social good, see Max Stackhouse, "Christian Social Ethics in a Global Era: Reforming Protestant Views," in *Christian Social Ethics in a Global Era* (Nashville: Abingdon, 1995), 11–74. He argues that the global corporation, depending on how it "gets structured and whether or not it incarnates fundamental moral and spiritual values that help sustain civil society . . . may come to be treated as an instrument of peace, justice, and equity . . . a graceful center of human vocation" (71). "Corporations are not only the chief bearers and generators of technology but the chief sources of jobs, wealth, and hope for material well-being. If they or churches or families fail, civil society will also fail, and many people will die as a result" (73).

16. Max Stackhouse, for example, argues that while corporate globalization renders the working poor more vulnerable in the short run, the global corporation will "bring higher percentages of the world's populations into the middle classes in the long run." Stackhouse, "Christian Social Ethics," 31.

17. Sources used include: Elizabeth Martinez and Arnoldo Garcia, "What Is Neo-Liberalism?" unpublished paper; Ricardo Ribera, "Neoliberalismo y Globalizacion, crisis social para America Latina," *Sentir con la Iglesia* (December 1997): 7–8; *Challenge: Faith and Action in the Americas* 6:1 (winter 1996) and 7:3 (fall 1997), reports published by the Ecumenical Program on Central America and the Caribbean (EPICA), Washington, D.C.; Philip Wheaton, "Unmasking the Powers in Mexico: The Zapatista Prophetic Alternative to the New World Order" (report presented by EPICA, Washington, D.C., 1998). The term *neo-liberal* used in the U.S. has somewhat more varied implications.

18. Nations on which SAPs are imposed must take the following measures: (1) Raise interest rates to cut money supply and consumer spending; (2) Devalue currency to increase exports and decrease imports; (3) Spend less (which generally entails cutting

expenditures for social programs such as health, education, and potable water; abolishing subsidies for food, fuel, and public transportation; raising prices on state-produced goods such as water and electricity; privatizing state-owned enterprises including banks, schools, and industries; and cutting wages or maintaining low wages); and (4) Export more (realizing this measure involves moving from an emphasis on domestic or regional food production to production for export, and attracting transnational corporations by deregulating trade and investment and lowering safety, environmental, and labor standards or maintaining low standards). For excellent discussions of structural adjustment and its impact on social and environmental well-being, see Pamela Sparr, ed., *Mortgaging Women's Lives* (London: Zed Books, 1994); Susan George, *A Fate Worse than Debt* (New York: Grove Weidenfeld, 1990), 171–88; and John Ruthrauff, *An Introduction to the World Bank, Inter-American Development Bank, and International Monetary Fund,* 2nd ed. (Silver Spring, Md.: Center for Democratic Education, 1997), 40–41.

19. This development is discussed in a booklet by Richard L. Grossman and Frank T. Adams, *Taking Care of Business: Citizenship and the Charter of Incorporation* (Cambridge, Mass.: Charter, Ink. 1993).

20. The Due Process clause of the 14th amendment prohibited any state government from depriving any person of life, liberty, or property without due process of law. In 1886 the Supreme Court ruled that a private corporation is a "natural person" under the U.S. Constitution and therefore is entitled to the rights of persons including protection by the Bill of Rights. Over two hundred state laws regulating corporations were ruled to be in violation of due process. When states tried to curb corporate power by passing regulatory legislation, courts tended to invalidate the legislation.

21. For an account of this process, see Harvey Wasserman, *America Born and Reborn* (New York: Collier Books, 1983), 87–182.

22. This deregulation was governed by the argument that global competitiveness required it. United States banks, subject to more regulations than German or Japanese competitors, argued for a levelling of the playing field through deregulation.

23. This development is described by Barnet and Cavanagh, "Electronic Money," 360–73; and by Henwood, *Wall Street,* 56.

24. The Glass-Steagall Act of 1933 mandated the separation of commercial banks from investment banks. Commercial banks were to supply working capital and investment funds to industry. See Barnet and Cavanagh, "Electronic Money," 371.

25. U.S. leadership in the deregulation of international monetary transactions occurred on two pivotal occasions. (European analysts tend to identify these as the beginning of the neo-liberal era.) First was the Nixon Administration's unilateral move in 1971 to undo the Bretton Woods agreement adopted after World War Two establishing fixed exchange rates among currencies and an international dollar standard backed by gold reserves. The value of money was set in increasingly integrated global marketplaces. Foreign exchange traders around the world speculated in currencies and governments lost control over money (Barnet and Cavanagh, "Electronic Money," 368). Second was Paul Volker's decision in 1979, as Chair of the Federal Reserve under

President Carter, to adopt a monetary policy in an effort to control inflation. (Essentially, this meant restricting the supply of money through the standard tool of increased interest rates for commercial banks obtaining dollars from the Federal Reserve Bank.) As a result, interest rates rose everywhere and, together with exchange rates, began to fluctuate wildly. For more discussion of both moves, see Barnet and Cavanagh, "Electronic Money," 360–73, and Duchrow, *Alternatives*, 69–119.

26. See for example: Vandana Shiva, *Biopiracy: The Plunder of Nature and Knowledge* (Boston: South End Press, 1997); Martin Khor, "Global Economy and the Third World," in *The Case against the Global Economy: And for a Turn toward the Local,* ed. Jerry Mander and Edward Goldsmith (San Francisco: Sierra Club Books, 1996), 47–59; and Chief Saul Terry of the British Columbia Council of Chiefs of Tribes, cited in The Council of Canadians, "The MAI Inquiry: Confronting Globalization and Reclaiming Democracy" (Toronto: Council of Canadians, 1999).

27. A summary of that history is, of course, not possible here. It includes the people tortured in Guatemala after U.S.-based fruit companies orchestrated an overthrow of Guatemala's progressive government in 1954, and the Salvadorans tortured in order to undermine their revolt against oligarchies that had stolen land, enslaved peasants to export-oriented plantations, and created a climate conducive to international trade and finance. These peasant peoples are in the story line of the *maquiladora* workers today who become ill or birth babies with severe birth defects because of dangerous and toxic working conditions in "free trade zones," and in the story line of the Zapatistas of Chiapas, Mexico, who initiated their revolt—which cost many Indian lives—to coincide with the beginning of NAFTA. "The free trade agreement," they declared, "is a death certificate for the Indian peoples of Mexico."

28. Shiva, *Biopiracy*, 103.

29. Ibid., 101–5.

30. Terry, "The MAI Inquiry," 17.

31. Khor, "Global Economy," 47–59.

32. Ibid.

33. Kwame Nkrumah, *Neo-Colonialism: The Last Stage of Imperialism* (New York: International Publishers, 1966), ix.

34. Former trilateral commissioner George Ball in "Cosmocorps: The Importance of Being Stateless," *Columbia Journal of World Business* 2:6 (November–December 1967): 26, cited in Holly Sklar, ed., *Trilateralism* (Boston: South End Press, 1980), 9.

35. Council on Foreign Relations, "Memorandum on Methods of Economic Collaboration: Introductory Role of the Grand Area in American Economic Policy" (No. E-B43, Strictly Confidential, July 24, 1941) This memo called also for the creation of "international financial institutions," "a postwar financial structure of the world," "international raw materials controls," "international banking institutions," "development programs [for] 'backward areas,'" and the institutions to deal with the "stabilization of exchanges" and the "role of gold." These recommendations soon were realized in the Bretton Woods institutions.

36. The quote is from David Korten, "The Failures of Bretton Woods," in *The Case against the Global Economy: And for a Turn toward the Local*, eds. Jerry Mander and Edward Goldsmith (San Francisco: Sierra Club Books, 1996), 21. As stated by then–treasurer of Standard Oil of New Jersey in 1946: "American private enterprise is confronted with this choice; it may strike out and save its position all over the world, or sit by and witness its own funeral. . . . We must set the pace and assume the responsibility of the majority stockholder in this corporation known as the world. . . . This is our permanent obligation. . . . Our foreign policy will be more concerned with the safety and stability of our foreign investments than ever before." Cited in Jack Nelson-Pallmeyer, *War against the Poor* (Maryknoll, N.Y.: Orbis, 1989), 52. Tony Clarke reports a telling statement by David Rockefeller, President and CEO of Chase Manhattan Bank, in December 1994 at an event hosted by President Clinton to commemorate the first Summit of the Americas on the expansion of free trade throughout the hemisphere. Present were thirty-two heads of state of the Americas as well as CEOs of many of the world's largest corporations. Two journalists inquired of Rockefeller, "Mr. Rockefeller, you were present in the 1960s during President Kennedy's Alliance for Progress Summit with the leaders of Latin America. Can you tell us what, if anything, has changed since then?" "Well," he replied, "back then business leaders like myself were more or less sitting on the sidelines watching the negotiations unfold. But now we're sitting in the driver's seat and writing many of the documents ourselves." Recounted by Tony Clarke, Director of the Polaris Institute of Canada, in *Silent Coup: Confronting the Big Business Takeover of Canada* (Toronto: James Lorimer and Company; and Ottawa: The Canadian Centre for Policy Alternatives, 1997), 3. Further work on the historical situation of globalization would consider the Trilateral Commission, brought together in 1973 by David Rockefeller and Zbigniew Brzezinski (the Commission's director until 1977). It was comprised primarily of CEOs of large corporations, banks, and media organizations, and a smaller number of chiefs of state and others from Western Europe, North America, and Japan. Critics of the Commission assert that it aimed at continued restructuring of the world economy to create a global free market, which would solve economic problems through economic growth based on mass consumption. This would entail reducing barriers to free trade and investment, "structural adjustments" in economies of developing countries, and reducing the "excess of democracy" evident in many of the Trilateral democracies. The last of these is prescribed in an early report of the Commission entitled "The Crisis of Democracy." See Sklar, *Trilateralism*.

37. In economic terms, the costs are "externalized."

38. Viewing globalization as a historical development invites inquiry into historical resistance to it. While that inquiry is beyond the scope of this project, it is important to note that opposition to globalization has a long history in varied social sectors of many nations. For example, at its founding congress in the Hague in 1915, the Women's International League for Peace and Freedom (WILPF) stated in its "Principles for a Permanent Peace": "Inasmuch as the investment by capitalists of one country in the

resources of another and the claims arising therefrom are a fertile source of international complications, this International Congress of Women urges the widest possible acceptance of the principle that such investment shall be made at the risk of the investor, without claims to the official protection of his government." Cited in WILPF, "Women Define Globalization" (Geneva: WILPF, 1999), 1.

39. Examples of scientists include Indian physicist Vandana Shiva, Canadian geneticist David Sazuki, and British geneticist Mae-Won Ho; examples of economists include Belinda Coote, Herman Daly, Bernard Founou Tchuigoua, and Martin Khor; examples of Christian ethicists and theologians include: Larry Rasmussen, Barbara Rumscheidt, John Cobb Jr., and Ulrich Duchrow; for a World Council of Churches example, see Tony Addy, ed., "The Globalizing Economy: New Risks, New Challenges, New Alliances" (Geneva: World Council of Churches, Unit III, 1999).

40. The data to this effect is readily available. The 1996 United Nations Development Programme's *Human Development Report* (New York and Oxford: Oxford Univ. Press, 1996) states that during the last thirty years (roughly the years of neo-liberalism), the proportion of people with "negative per-capita income growth tripled," and that in "70 countries, average incomes are less than they were in 1980."

41. Belinda Coote, in *The Trade Trap: Poverty and the Global Commodity Markets* 2nd ed. (Oxford: Oxfam UK and Ireland, 1996), unravels how free trade generates poverty; Susan George, in *Fate Worse than Debt*, issues an indictment of debt; and Pamela Sparr, in *Mortgaging Women's Lives*, addresses the impacts of structural adjustment on the impoverishment of women. Free trade, external debt, and SAPs all are implicated in the free trade and investment agenda. See Amata Miller, "Global Economic Structures," for a succinct overview of many aspects of globalization and their impoverishing impact on the poorest. See also UNRISD, *States of Disarray.*

42. Estimates of how many billions vary. One relatively conservative estimate is that 25 billion were transferred each year between 1984 and 1991. See *Challenge: Faith and Action in the Americas* 6:1 (winter 1994): 4.

43. I am not suggesting that globalization is the sole cause of poverty in poor nations. Many internal factors, as well as other external factors, also play a part. Some of these are summarized, in relationship to globalization, by Miller, "Global Economic Structures," 169–71. See for example Adolfo Perez Esquivel, Comments at the "Dialogue between the Peoples of the Americas," October 1995, edited and excerpted in *Challenge: Faith and Action in the Americas* 6:1 (winter 1996): 4–5.

44. The United Nations Development Programme, *Human Development Report 1999* (New York and Oxford: Oxford Univ. Press, 1999), 30–31. The report goes on to say that "gaps in income between the poorest and the richest people and countries have continued to widen" (36). In the words of the Korean People's Action Against Investment Treaties and WTO New Round (KoPA): "In Korea, liberalization deepened the income [inequity] between rich and the poor in spite of improved economic indices" (KoPA, "We Are Here to Say No to the WTO," statement written in 1999 by over twenty-five social, labor, and citizens' movements in Korea). United for a Fair Economy

reports that in the United States, "in 1980 . . . CEOs made a mere 42 times more than average workers. Last year that gap stood at 475 times." See United for a Fair Economy, in *Too Much,* the newsletter of United for a Fair Economy 6:2 (fall 2000): 3.

45. The United Nations Development Programme, *Human Development Report 1998* (New York and Oxford: Oxford Univ. Press, 1998), 29–30.

46. See Musimbi Kanyoro, "Globalization and Its Effect on Women," in *Lutheran World Federation Women Magazine* (August 1999): 8–12. See also Sparr, *Mortgaging Women's Lives.*

47. According to Lester R. Brown et al., in *State of the World 1998* (New York and London: W.W. Norton, 1998): "As the global economy has expanded from 5 trillion of output in 1950 to 29 trillion in 1997, its demands have crossed many of the Earth's sustainable yield thresholds" (58).

48. "[A] continuously expanding global economy is slowly destroying its host— Earth's ecosystem." Ibid., 4.

49. Paul Hawken, *The Ecology of Commerce* (San Francisco: Harper Books, 1993), 22.

50. A 1992 (November 18) "Warning to Humanity" issued by more than 1,600 senior scientists, including a majority of all living Nobel Laureates in the sciences, advises that: "Human beings and the natural world [*sic*] are on a collision course . . . that may so alter the living world that it will be unable to sustain life in the manner that we know." See www.formal.stanford.edu. Larry Rasmussen, in *Earth Community, Earth Ethics* (Maryknoll, N.Y.: Orbis Books, 1996), 4, points out that "the relationship of the human world to the rest of Earth changed fundamentally and dramatically from the outset of the 20th century to its close. Techno-economic power sufficient to destroy the conditions of human and other life is the hallmark of that change, together with the explosion of human numbers and consumption." In the face of this change, Rasmussen asserts, every human activity must be judged by this criterion: its contribution to sustainable Earth community.

51. Brown et al., *State of the World 1998.*

52. Shiva, *Biopiracy,* 103.

53. "One World," *Forbes Magazine* (November 1968), cited in Sklar, *Trilateralism,* 20.

54. Esther Carmac Ramirez, "For a Genuine Peoples's Social Agenda" (address delivered at the International NGO Public Gathering, United Nations World Summit on Social Development, Geneva, Switzerland, June 2000), citing a working group on the United Nations Convention on Biodiversity.

2. Disabling Democracy: Subordinating Political Power to Economic Power

1. Rosemary Radford Reuther, "Thomas Berry's *The Great Work,* Review and Response" (statement presented at panel presentation, American Academy of Religion, Boston, 1999).

2. Other authors also point to this dual referent of the "political." Iris Marion Young, in *Justice and the Politics of Difference* (Princeton, N.J.: Princeton Univ. Press, 1990), contrasts a common narrow meaning of politics as "the activities of government or formal interest group organizations" (9), with her own broader definition of politics as "the critical activity of raising issues and deciding how institutions and social relations should be organized" (240). In like manner, Roberto Mangabeira Unger, in *Social Theory: Its Situation and Its Task* (Cambridge: Cambridge Univ. Press, 1987), clarifies that, "politics seems to have both a narrower and a broader meaning. Politics means conflict over the mastery and uses of governmental power. But it also means struggle over the resources and arrangements that set the basic terms of our practical and passionate relations" (145).

3. This claim that the personal is political, originating in the 1960s with women oppressed by men in radical political movements, has come to assume meanings as varied as strains of feminism. See Anne Phillips, "Public Spaces, Private Lives," in *Engendering Democracy* (University Park, Pa.: Pennsylvania State Univ. Press, 1991), 92–119.

4. Thus the claim of some Christians to disavow politics for an apolitical faith life is misguided. Social life is political; apparent non-participation in political processes constitutes a political stand for whatever "the winners" advocate. Joseph Allen, in *Love and Conflict: A Covenantal Model of Christian Ethics* (Nashville: Abingdon, 1984), argues this point well. He rightly points out also that the empirical and normative relationship of religion to the political, and of faith life to political life, has been understood in highly divergent ways throughout history by theologians and political philosophers. Perspectives range from Aristotle's notion that humans are political by nature, to the Augustinian notion that the political is a divine remedy for human sinfulness, to the classic liberal notion of society as a realm of "individual activity which precedes politics and is apolitical. . . . [and upon which] politics and political institutions intrude" (255).

5. Principal resources for this discussion include: Phillips, "Public Spaces"; Young, *Justice*; Carole Pateman, *The Disorder of Women* (Stanford, Calif.: Stanford Univ. Press, 1989); Carole Pateman, *Participation and Democratic Theory* (Cambridge and Melbourne: Cambridge Univ. Press, 1970); Elizabeth Gross, "Conclusion: What Is Feminist Theory," in *Feminist Challenges: Social and Political Theory*, ed. Elizabeth Gross and Carole Pateman (Boston: Northeastern Univ. Press, 1986).

6. Principal resources for this discussion include: Harry Ward, *Democracy and Social Change* (New York: Modern Age Books, 1940); Samuel Bowles and Herbert Gintis, "The Economy Produces People," in *Religion and Economic Justice*, ed. Michael Zweig (Philadelphia: Temple Univ. Press, 1991); Unger, *Social Theory*; Robert A. Dahl, *A Preface to Economic Democracy* (Berkeley and Los Angeles: Univ. of California Press, 1985); Robert A. Dahl, *Democracy and Its Critics* (New Haven: Yale Univ. Press, 1989); Frances Moore Lappé, *Rediscovering America's Values* (New York: Ballantine, 1989); and C. Douglas Lummis, *Radical Democracy* (Ithaca, N.Y.: Cornell Univ. Press, 1996).

7. See Carole Pateman, "Introduction," in *Feminist Challenges*, ed. Elizabeth

Gross and Carole Pateman (Boston: Northeastern Univ. Press, 1986), 6.

8. Dahl, *Critics*, 5. Dahl adopts the last—democracy as a process—which does not exclude the others but has implications for them.

9. For example, the "ideal" of classical Athenian democracy may be mistaken for the actual life of the *polis* in ancient Athens.

10. As Robert Dahl notes, "A term which means anything means nothing. And so it has become with 'democracy,' which nowadays is not so much a term of restricted and specific meaning as a vague endorsement of a popular idea . . . and an ideological tool." Dahl, *Critics*, 2.

11. Beverly Harrison, in "The Role of Social Theory in Religious Ethics," in *Making the Connections*, ed. Carol Robb (Boston: Beacon Press, 1985), 72, points out that liberalism tends to judge the moral quality of political-economic systems by the presence or absence of formal political rights rather than by human and ecological well-being.

12. Phillips, "Public Spaces," 19. See also Pateman, *Participation*, 1–14. According to the latter, from the 1940s through the resurgence of participatory democracy theories in the mid-1960s, dominant democratic theory reduced participation to voting for leaders, and political equality to universal suffrage. Phillips (10) notes that Rousseau identified the limitations imposed by reducing democracy to periodic elections.

13. Ecumenical Program on Central America and the Caribbean (EPICA), "Democracy and Neo-liberalism," *Challenge: Faith and Action in the Americas* 6:1 (winter 1996): 6.

14. This point is made by Ward, *Democracy*, 6–47; Lappé, *Rediscovering*, 4; and Lummis, *Radical Democracy*, 12. Lummis conceives of democracy as "a principle in human affairs, as distinct from the various institutions or actions through which people seek to realize this principle in practice" (12). According to Ward, democracy is "a living process which must continually change in order to grow" (7).

15. Harrison, "Role of Social Theory," 66.

16. Ellen Meiskins Wood, *Democracy against Capitalism* (Cambridge: Cambridge Univ. Press, 1995), 35. See also 234.

17. Pateman, *Participation*, 17. Deconstructing the notion that democracy and democratic polity have singular universal forms is a principle feminist critique of liberal notions of democracy.

18. The quote is from Pateman, *Participation*, 19. In contemporary theory, limited notions of democratic participation are linked to the limited notion of "the political" noted earlier. This limitation and link is unfolded by Thomas E. McCollough in *The Moral Imagination and Public Life: Raising the Ethical Question* (Chatham, N.J.: Chatham House, 1991).

19. The most notable classical theorist is Jean-Jacques Rousseau, the classical proponent of participatory democracy, whose *Social Contract* provided foundations for later theories of participatory democracy; the quote is from Pateman, *Participation*, 20.

20. Pateman, *Participation*, 105.

21. Bowles and Gintis, "The Economy," 236.

22. Given the many forms of participation, all societies are politically participant in one form or another. Participation may be "either transitive or intrasitive; either moral, amoral or immoral; either forced or free" (Rahnema, 116). It may be token and power-less or actual and effective. For elaboration regarding participation and the manipula-tion of it by economic development institutions, see Majid Rahnema, "Participation," in *The Development Dictionary*, ed. Wolfgang Sachs (Johannesburg: Witwatersrand Univ. Press, and London: Zed Books, 1992), 116–31.

23. For example, Rousseau considered certain economic conditions necessary for political participation that enabled actual impact. According to Pateman, Rousseau's "theory does not require absolute equality as is often implied" (Pateman, *Participation*, 22), but does require that economic inequity not be large enough to result in political inequality. "Liberty cannot exist without [equality]. . . . No citizen shall ever be wealthy enough to buy another, and none poor enough to be forced to sell himself." (Jean-Jacques Rousseau, *The Social Contract and Discourses*, bk. 2 [London: Everyman, 1973], 225). Bowles and Gintis ("The Economy") also point to economic inequity as the antithesis of participation (236).

24. As noted in Young (*Justice, 10*), "participatory democratic theory . . . share[s] with the liberal theory [it] challenges a tendency to suppress difference by conceiving the polity as universal and unified." In contrast, and with Young, I presuppose the ideal of a *heterogeneous* public—or publics—that affirms difference.

25. Following the lead of political scientist Robert Dahl, I use the concept "political equality" with reference to relative equality in political resources and access to influ-ence—in short, the capacity to participate as a relative equal in political process.

26. Many feminist and radical democratic theorists contend that democracy, as a principle guiding the organization of power, must extend beyond the confines of state power to the realm of the economic, or be undone in the former. See, for example, Pateman, *Participation*; Phillips, "Public Spaces"; Wood, *Democracy against Capital-ism*; Bowles and Gintis, "The Economy"; Ward, *Democracy*; Dahl, *Preface*; and Lappé, *Rediscovering*, 203–33. Wood argues that in fact the opposite pertains in capitalist democracies: "The characteristic way that capitalist democracy deals with [the eco-nomic] sphere of power is not to check it but to liberate it . . . in fact not recognizing it as a sphere of power . . . at all. This is, of course, especially true of the market, which is . . . conceived of as a sphere of freedom" (234). Note that the argument *against* extending democracy to economic life, is that so doing blurs the separation of political and economic power, which is, according to this perspective, vital to democracy. According to this line of thought, totalitarianism unites political and economic power, whereas democratic capitalism separates them. See, for example, Robert Benne, *The Ethic of Democratic Capitalism* (Philadelphia: Fortress Press, 1981), 96. See also Rose Friedman and Milton Friedman, *The Right to Choose* (New York: Avon, 1979), xvii: "The free market provides an offset to whatever concentration of political power may arise." See also Milton Friedman, *Capitalism and Freedom* (Chicago: Univ. of Chicago Press, 1962), 16. A problem with this argument is its false presupposition that eco-

nomic democracy would locate economic power primarily in the hands of the state and would be centralized. A second problem is that, while busy warding off the threat of concentrated state power, this argument ignores the threat of concentrated economic power.

27. Exploring the historical conflict in the United States between democracy and property rights, Robert Dahl in *Preface* (65–66) argues that, "From the beginning of our nation's existence, and indeed earlier, the question of the relative priority of democracy and property has received two fundamentally conflicting answers. . . . On the one side, supporters of property held that political equality must finally yield to property rights. . . . Those who supported the goal of democracy insisted, on the contrary, that a person's right to self government, and thus to political equality, was more fundamental than the right to property." He suggests that modern democracy has done relatively well in terms of political liberty, yet not so in terms of political equality, a shortfall attributable in part to the ideology of economic freedom (52–83). Further inquiry from a Christian ethical perspective ought consider the normative question (What *ought* be the relative value assigned economic freedom and political equality?), and the historical descriptive questions (What *has been* the relative value and what *have been* the power dynamics determining that relative value?). That inquiry includes questioning the grounds on which the right to economic freedom has been defended and linked with democracy, and the implications of those grounds for the relative priority of economic freedom and democracy. Dahl notes that, since the inception of this nation, economic freedom has been defended on two grounds—utilitarian and moral—which carry radically different implications for the democratic process (63–83).

28. Dahl summarizes this conflict in *Democracy and Its Critics*, 324–26: In sum, he says, democratic theory and neo-classical economic theory have opposing accounts of the human, of freedom, and of power. Democratic theory sees the human as citizen. According to neo-classical economic theory, the human is primarily *homo economicus* (a "supremely rational consumer forever calculating and comparing precise increments of gain and loss at the margin and acting always to maximize net utilities"). Democratic theory considers freedom as the freedom of "citizens entitled to participate as political equals in making the laws and rules under which they will live together." Freedom, in neo-classical economic theory, is, above all, the freedom of choice in the marketplace. Finally, according to democratic theory, political power—at least theoretically— ought be evenly distributed. "That citizens ought be political equals is . . . a crucial axiom of the moral perspective of democracy." In neo-classical economic theory "relations of power do not exist. . . . Exchanges are freely entered into by rational actors, who are equally rational and equally free.

29. Western liberal societies have tended to conflate democracy with liberalism in spite of the fundamental distinctions between the two. In their early modern forms, liberal theory (defending individual rights) and democratic theory (defending popular rule) were fundamentally opposed in this sense: Locke's theory of liberalism held that humanity's original state of nature included the natural right to life, liberty, and prop-

erty. In contrast, Rousseau, considered the founder of modern democratic theory, held that in humanity's original state there was no private property, and that only in staking off private property did humans develop inequality, domination, and the need for politically organized community. Otherwise said, liberal theory, according to John Locke, defended the natural right to private property while democratic theory saw it as a source of inequality and domination requiring the constraint of political community. The contemporary conflation of liberalism (as neo-liberalism) with democracy must be examined against the historical roots of both.

30. The argument is that capitalism and democracy derive from opposing principles and are therefore inherently antagonistic. In sum, the capitalist principle of capital concentration works against the democratic norm of relatively equal political power, and the capitalist principle of excluding economic power from democratic accountability works against the democratic norm of accountable power. This argument is articulated by Harry Ward and by Eileen Meiskins Wood. Wood argues historically that the notion of capitalist democracy which developed in the United States gave formal political powers (eventually) to all, but retained the power of rule or control through capital in the hands of the propertied elite. Thus, while citizenship was extended (eventually) to all, its power was restricted. Formal democracy could co-exist with social and power inequality intact, and hence worked against rule by the people.

31. I agree with Patricia Mann, who points out that "social theorists tend to use the notion of 'agency' very freely today, its relevance all too apparent, its meaning, however, still quite elusive." Patricia Mann, *Micro-Politics: Agency in a Postfeminist Era* (Minneapolis and London: Univ. of Minnesota Press, 1994), 14–15.

32. That is, my aim at this initial point is not a theory of agency, but a concept. I appreciate Rodney Stark's clear distinction between the two. See Rodney Stark, *The Rise of Christianity* (San Francisco: HarperSanFrancisco, 1997), 23–27.

33. The quote is from Linell E. Cady, "The Intellectual and Effective Critique," *CSSR Bulletin* 27:2 (April 1998): 36. This sort of exclusion is a principal point made by Young.

34. Larry Rasmussen, "A Different Discipline," *Union Seminary Quarterly Review: Festschrift for Beverly Harrison* 53:34 (1999): 38.

35. For elaboration of this norm, please see the introduction to this book. There, the norm's two constituent norms are identified: neighbor-love, and sustainable and regenerative Earth-human relations.

36. Charles Curran develops the significance of christology and soteriology for moral agency. See Curran, "The Person as Moral Agent and Subject," in *Directions in Fundamental Moral Theology* (Notre Dame: Univ. of Notre Dame Press, 1985), 63–97.

37. The relationship of person as moral agent to person as moral subject—the relationship of agency to subjectivity (of doing to being)—is variously construed. See Sandra Lee Bartky, "Agency: What's the Problem," in *Provoking Agents: Gender and Agency in Theory and Practice*, ed. Judith Kegan Gardiner (Chicago: Univ. of Chicago Press, 1995),190; Mann, *Micro-Politics*, 4; Janet R. Jakobsen, *Working Alliances and the Pol-*

itics of Difference: Diversity and Feminist Ethics (Bloomington: Indiana Univ. Press, 1998); Curran, "Person as Moral Agent," 63–65, 231–34; John Macmurray, *The Self as Agent* (New Jersey and London: Humanities Press International, 1957). My working conclusion regarding this set of issues is that agency refers to the capacity to act and the action itself. Subjectivity refers in a more limited sense to the capacity to act. Moral subjectivity is, thus, a dimension of moral agency, the dimension pertaining to disposition, attitudes, qualities of being, and internal dialogue (both conscious and not).

38. Judith Kegan Gardiner, "Introduction," in *Provoking Agents: Gender and Agency in Theory and Practice*, ed. Judith Kegan Gardiner (Chicago: Univ. of Chicago Press, 1995), 1.

39. Susan Hekman, "Subjects and Agents: The Question for Feminism," in Gardiner, *Provoking Agents*, 196.

40. Feminist theories do not produce a single uncontested notion of agency. Rather, they challenge not only traditional liberal notions of agency, but also one another. An example of debates among feminist theorists concerns the impact on women's agency of the feminist and postmodernist decentering of the autonomous individual as locus of agency. Some theorists, while critiquing liberalism's autonomous agent, argue also that, taken too far, that critique disables women's agency, and hence is no friend of feminism. This danger is clearly elaborated by Seyla Benhabib, who argues that in the "strong version of postmodernism," the death of the subject undermines the feminist commitment to women's agency and selfhood, and the death of history undermines women's reappropriation of women's history in the name of an emancipated future. The subject is deconstructed to nonexistence, and hence the possibility of radical political transformation is undone. Seyla Benhabib, *Situating the Self* (New York: Routledge, 1992), 203–241; and in Benhabib, "Feminism and Postmodernism," in Benhabib et al., *Feminist Contentions* (New York and London: Routledge, 1995). This concern also is expressed by Gardiner, "Introduction," 8, and is noted by Jakobsen, *Working Alliances*, 3.

41. As explained by Lawrence Becker, in *Encyclopedia of Ethics*, ed. Lawrence C. Becker (New York: Routledge, 1992), the Kantian models of the autonomous, freely acting, individual moral agency and of "autonomy of the will" as crucial conditions of moral agency are contested by both feminist and communitarian theorists. A communitarian critique holds that the elevation of autonomy obscures the community values and dynamics that shape the moral agent. Many feminists contrast the notion of autonomy as precondition for agency to the impossibility of autonomy for many subjugated peoples. Both argue that focus on autonomy obscures the relational nature of moral agency. The critique of autonomy as necessary to agency is not limited to feminist and communitarian circles. For instance, Charles Curran argues for understanding the moral agent in relational terms. "The Christian person as moral agent and subject should be understood in terms of one's relationship with God, neighbor, world, and self" (Curran, "Person as Moral Agent," 76).

42. Jakobsen, *Working Alliances*.

43. Katie Geneva Cannon, *Black Womanist Ethics* (Atlanta: Scholars Press, 1988).

44. John Macmurray develops the most extended argument against viewing the person "primarily as thinker or knower and only derivatively as agent"(*Self as Agent*, xii). He argues that the problem for contemporary philosophy is the fact that philosophy has prioritized theorizing over acting, and has defined the self primarily as knower/thinker, rather than as actor (xvi, 84). He calls for a radical change in the basis of moral theory, a change to the priority of action. Action, he asserts, entails both thinking and acting.

45. Gardiner ("Introduction," 10) argues that moral agency cannot arise from a single individual source but is always mediated and preceded by other actions and is in relationship to multiple agents. Onora O'Neill, in *Faces of Hunger* (London: Allen and Unwin, 1986), considers standards for ethical reasoning about public crises of global scope. She argues that since many global moral crises require "major economic and political changes that cannot be produced by individual action alone" (33), "if agency is seen as individual, it may also seem that [addressing the crisis], though meritorious, is not obligatory" (34). Where moral problems may be address only with the collaboration of collective agents, she suggests, agency must be conceived in terms of collectivities as well as of individuals.

46. Gardiner, "Introduction," 10.

47. According to a November 5, 1997, letter to President Clinton signed by twenty-five members of Congress, even "Congress was not informed about the MAI" until 1997.

48. Other venues include the Free Trade Area of the Americas (FTAA), the Asia-Pacific Economic Forum (APEC), the Transatlantic Economic Partnership Dialogue (TEP), and the International Monetary Fund (IMF). For each of these, key MAI principles are at the core of negotiations to expand trade liberalization to the liberalization of investment and finance. The MAI is consistent with, but more far-reaching than, the investment clause in the North America Free Trade Agreement (NAFTA). The World Trade Organization was established in January 1995 by the Uruguay Round of the General Agreement on Tariffs and Trade (GATT) to administer and enforce a body of rules governing global trade in goods and, increasingly, in services. It now includes more than twenty agreements including the GATT. In 1996, the WTO established a working group to consider if and how WTO should treat foreign investment.

49. This agenda was contested by a global coalition of civil society organizations seeking to halt new negotiations expanding the WTO's authority, to assess the impact of the WTO's initial five years, and to replace some of its rules with versions elevating the broad public interest (i.e. environmental protection, human and labor rights, and accountable governance) over corporate interests.

50. Both the ICC and the USCIB identify the "liberalization of financial services," or the removal of "restrictions on investment" as primary aims. See http://www.iccwbo. org/home/news_archives/1998/firm_for_mai.asp. The ICC's Commission on International Trade and Investment Policy declares that part of its agenda is "to influence OECD negotiations on a MAI." The USCIB declares the aim of "giving business a seat at the table in promoting an open system of world trade, finance, and investment" (www.uscib.org).

Examples of how that influence is exercised are endless. Note for instance that preceding the WTO ministerial in Seattle, Seattle Host Committee co-chairs Bill Gates and Philip Condit (CEO of Boeing) addressed a letter to over one hundred top level corporate managers, requesting financial support for the Host Committee and promising "the greatest possible interactions" and special briefings with U.S. trade negotiators. They established six classes of donors with accompanying levels of access. (See Tony Clarke, "By What Authority!" [Ottawa: Polaris Institute, 1999], 1.) Note also, for example, that the chairperson of the ICC's Commission on International Trade and Investment Policy is a former Director General of GATT and board member of Nestle, SA.

51. In spring of 1998, over six hundred non-governmental organizations (NGOs) worldwide signed a joint statement against the MAI.

52. Among the MAI-free zones are San Francisco, Oakland, Houston, Denver, Seattle, and Olympia; half of the Canadian Provinces and numerous Canadian municipalities; the Washington Association of Cities; and the Western Governors Association. This pronouncement by the City of Toronto is representative: "Government of Canada be advised that the City of Toronto is opposed to the Multilateral Agreement on Investment and requests that further negotiations cease and desist."

53. The Council of Canadians, "The MAI Inquiry: Confronting Globalization and Reclaiming Democracy" (Toronto: Council of Canadians, 1999), 1.

54. United States Trade Representative, *Multilateral Agreement on Investment (MAI): The Facts* (Washington, D.C.: USTR, 1998), 2. See also OECD, *The Multilateral Agreement on Investment: Frequently Asked Questions and Answers* (Paris: OECD, 1998), 4. The implication that economic "discrimination" against dictatorships ought be eliminated is consistent with the laissez-faire neo-classical economic perspective as articulated by Milton Friedman: "No one who buys bread knows whether the wheat from which it is made was grown by a Communist or a Republican . . . a Fascist, or . . . a Negro or a white. . . . An impersonal market separates economic activities from political views and protects men from being discriminated against." Friedman, *Capitalism and Freedom*, 21.

55. "The Multilateral Agreement on Investment: A Step Backward in International Human Rights," the Human Rights Program of Harvard Law School.

56. The GATT definition of a "good" includes water.

57. Yoon-Jae Chang, "From Mammon of Impoverishment to God of Empowerment: Implications of the Free Market Economy to the Theologies of the Third World," unpublished paper, 1998.

58. OECD, *MAI Negotiating Text*, 59.

59. "Most previous international economic agreements, including the GATT, allow only governments to bring complaints against other governments. NAFTA employs investor-to-state dispute resolution in limited cases, but only applies to three countries." Michelle Sforza, Scott Nove, and Mark Weisbrot, "A Concise Guide to the Multilateral Agreement on Investment—Supporters' and Opponents' Views" (Washington, D.C.: Preamble Center for Public Policy, 1998), 10.

60. See Michelle Sforza, "Preamble Briefing Paper: The Multilateral Agreement on

Investment and the Environment" (Washington, D.C.:Preamble Center for Public Policy, 1998), 13–14.

61. Renato Ruggiero, addressing the UNCTAD Trade and Development Board, October 1996, cited in ibid., 1.

62. Susan George, "A Short History of Neo-Liberalism," (paper presented at the Conference on Economic Sovereignty in a Globalizing World, Bangkok, Thailand, March 1999), 8.

63. The words of President Lincoln, near the end of his life, sound a warning. In the face of emerging corporate power, he commented: "Corporations have been enthroned. . . . An era of corruption in high places will follow and the money power will endeavor to prolong its reign . . . until wealth is aggregated in a few hands . . . and the Republic is destroyed." Cited in Harvey Wasserman, *America Born and Reborn* (New York: Collier Books, 1983), 89–90.

64. Harrison, "Role of Social Theory," 66.

3. Ideological Underpinnings: Neo-Liberalism and Social Amnesia

1. David Korten, *When Corporations Rule the World* (West Hartford, Conn. and San Francisco: Kumarian and Barrett-Koehler, 1995), 68.

2. Frances Moore Lappé, *Rediscovering America's Values* (New York: Ballantine, 1989), xvi–xvii.

3. Janet R. Jakobsen, *Working Alliances and the Politics of Difference: Diversity and Feminist Ethics* (Bloomington: Indiana Univ. Press, 1998), 148.

4. Chris Kramarae and Paula Treichler, *A Feminist Dictionary* (Boston and London: Pandora, 1985), 206.

5. Levi Oracion, "Faith and Ideology: Reflection on the Themes of Buchow," in *Ideologies and Peoples Struggles for Justice, Freedom, and Peace,* ed. Levi Oracion (Geneva: World Council of Churches, 1988), 97.

6 Carol Johnston, *The Health or Wealth of Nations: Transforming Capitalism from Within* (Cleveland: Pilgrim Press, 1998), 93.

7. For representative voices articulating this theory from the private sector, academic economics, and Christian ethics respectively, see: the International Chamber of Commerce, at http://www.iccwbo.org, and the United States Council for International Business, at http:/www.uscib.org; R. Dornbusch and F. Helmers, ed., *The Open Economy: Tools for Policy Makers in Developing Countries* (Oxford Univ. Press for the World Bank, 1995); Michael Novak, *Cultivating Liberty* (Lanham, Md.: Rowman and Littlefield, 1999) and Max Stackhouse, "Christian Social Ethics in a Global Era: Reforming Protestant Views," in *Christian Social Ethics in a Global* Era (Nashville: Abingdon, 1995), 11–74.

8. Organization for Economic Cooperation and Development (OECD), in *Open Markets Matter: The Benefits of Trade and Investment Liberalization* (Paris: OECD, 1998), 39–40; ibid., 25.

9. "The Geneva Business Declaration: Statement by Helmut O. Maucher, President of the ICC" (statement presented at International Chamber of Commerce meeting, Geneva, Switzerland, September 1998), 3–5.

10. We cannot here undertake a full critique of growth theory. For more complete accounts of this critique, see Larry Rasmussen, *Moral Fragments, Moral Community: A Proposal for Church in Society* (Minneapolis: Fortress Press, 1993); Vandana Shiva, "Resources," in *The Development Dictionary*, ed. Wolfgang Sachs (London: Zed Books, 1992), 206–18; John Cobb and Herman Daly, *Sustaining the Common Good*, 2nd ed. (Boston: Beacon Press, 1994); C. Douglas Lummis, *Radical Democracy* (Ithaca, N.Y.: Cornell Univ. Press, 1996), 67–70; Wolfgang Sachs, "Neo-Development: Global Ecological Management," in *The Case against the Global Economy: And for a Turn toward the Local*, eds. Jerry Mander and Edward Goldsmith (San Francisco: Sierra Club Books, 1996), 239–252; and Herman Daly, "Sustainable Growth? No Thank You," in *The Case against the Global Economy*, ed. Mander and Goldsmith, 192–96.

11. Cited by Ted Halstead and Clifford Lobb, "The Need for New Measurements of Progress," in *The Case against the Global Economy*, ed. Mander and Goldsmith, 201.

12. Data compiled by accountant and professor Ralph Estes indicates that the costs corporations externalized in the United States in 1994 in the form of environmental damage, workplace hazards, etc., were roughly five times corporate profits and 37 percent of the GDP. Another example of externalities is the dangerously high levels of toxic waste and other pollution produced by *maquiladoras* on the U.S.-Mexico border. These plants are hailed as model sources of growth. One study indicates that *maquiladoras* on the border could not account for 95 percent of waste generated between 1969 and 1989. Another found high levels of toxins in drainage water outside the plants. Tests conducted in an EPA-certified lab indicated levels of one toxin up to fifty thousand times what is allowed in the United States. See Alexander Goldsmith, "Seeds of Exploitation," in *The Case against the Global Economy*, ed. Mander and Goldsmith, 268–69.

13. United for a Fair Economy, *Too Much: A Quarterly Commentary* (spring 1999): 3.

14. Median household data: ibid.; middle-class wage data is from a Ford Foundation report, *The Common Good: Social Welfare and the American Future: Policy Recommendations of the Executive Panel* (New York: Ford Foundation, 1989), 51, cited in Johnston, *Health or Wealth*, 32; Congressional Budget Office data indicate a 16 percent decrease in after tax income of the poorest 20 percent, compared to a 72 percent increase in after tax income of the wealthiest 1 percent. Cited by Alan Geyer, "Progressive Christianity in Regressive America" (Houston: Interfaith Community Ministry Network, unpublished paper), 2. According to *Business Week,* in 1999 the average compensation of corporate CEOs was 419 times that of production workers. Cited by United for a Fair Economy, *Too Much* (summer 1999): 3.

15. "The Eisenhower Report" (The Milton Eisenhower Foundation, 1999), cited by Geyer, 1.

16. United Nations Development Programme (UNDP), "Progressive Christianity," *Human Development Report 1997* (New York: Oxford Univ. Press, 1997), 88–89. For example, since Mexico liberalized its economy in the mid-1980s, the number of billionaires has increased by 50 percent, pushing growth figures up, thus obscuring the significantly increasing number of people living in absolute poverty. See ibid., 88. The 1998 UNDP report (p. 29) reports that in 1960, the wealthiest 20 percent of the world's population had thirty times the income of the poorest 20 percent. By 1995 that figure had increased to eighty-two times.

17. Mainstream economic theory sets rules determining optimal growth at the micro level (that is, for a business). It is the point of diminishing returns. However, the body of theory has no such rules at the macro level (that is, the planetary level).

18. This claim is epitomized in the statement of then–U.S. Secretary of the Treasury Henry Morgenthau at the opening session of Bretton Woods. He called for embracing the "elementary economic axiom . . . that prosperity has no fixed limits." Cited in David Korten, "The Failures of Bretton Woods," in *The Case against the Global Economy,* ed. Mander and Goldsmith, 21.

19. For example, this point is made by Larry Rasmussen, *Earth Community, Earth Ethics* (Maryknoll, N.Y.: Orbis Books, 1996); Cobb and Daly, *Sustaining*; Herman Daly, *Beyond Growth: The Economics of Sustainable Development* (Boston: Beacon, 1997); Korten, *When Corporations Rule the World*; Paul Hawken, *The Ecology of Commerce: A Declaration of Sustainability* (San Francisco: HarperBooks, 1993); Lummis, *Radical Democracy*; and Lester R. Brown et al., *State of the World 1998* (New York and London: Norton, 1998). According to Brown et al.: "As the global economy has expanded from 5 trillion of output in 1950 to 29 trillion in 1997, its demands have crossed many of the Earth's sustainable yield thresholds. The effects are catastrophic." The report calls for a "restructuring of the global economy." Critics of western "development" models, which are growth-driven, point out that the U.S. economic model, which required exploiting the world's resources, was imposed as the aim of development worldwide without acknowledging the impossibility of replicating it worldwide.

20. In the mid-1980s, international agencies shifted from using Gross National Product (GNP) to GDP as the indicator of economic growth. Although this appeared to be only a change in terminology, the shift was an adjustment in favor of transnational corporations. The old GNP attributed corporate profits to the nation in which the corporation was based. The new GDP attributes profit to the nation in which a corporate operation is located, even if the profit is repatriated to the country in which the company is based.

21. "The case for [free] trade and investment is as robust today as when Adam Smith or David Ricardo first formulated it two centuries ago. Indeed it is even stronger in today's globalizing environment [which] . . . allows the gains from trade and investment

liberalization to reach more people around the world than ever before." OECD, *Open Markets Matter*, 20–21.

22. Adam Smith, in 1776, hypothesized that a theoretical market system free of government regulations would result in optimal allocation of a society's economic resources and growth in wealth. Market forces would over time keep market price (determined by supply and demand) relatively in line with natural price (what a product is worth based on prevailing rates of wages, rent, and profit). Otherwise said: excess supply brings market price down, hence weaker producers leave the market, hence supply goes down, and market price goes up again. Deficiencies lead market price up, and hence more producers enter the market, raising supply and lowering market prices again.

23. I draw upon the work of Carol Johnston, *Health or Wealth*, 11–28.

24. Smith, *The Wealth of Nations* (New York: Modern Library), book 4, chap. 2, 484–85.

25. See, for example, ibid., book 1, chap. 7, 69–70.

26. David Korten, "The Mythic Victory of Market Capitalism," in *The Case against the Global Economy*, ed. Mander and Goldsmith, 186.

27. In the United States, the median wage adjusted for inflation was slightly less in 1999 than in 1973, yet productivity has grown (United for a Fair Economy, *Too Much*, [fall 2000] 3).

28. Smith, *Wealth of Nations*, book 1, chap. 8, 77.

29. Ricardo was the principal classical theoretician of free trade. He developed the concepts of specialization and comparative advantage according to which each country ought to specialize in producing and trading products that it can produce at lower opportunity cost than the same products can be produced by the country's trading partners. Each country would then abandon producing goods and services that could be produced elsewhere at lower opportunity cost. The resulting enhanced efficiency and productivity would increase prosperity. See David Ricardo, *The Principles of Political Economy and Taxation* (1817; rpt., London: Dent, 1965). This theory of international specialization according to comparative advantage is a cornerstone of the argument that "free" trade and investment lead to growth and economic well-being.

30. Herman Daly, "The Perils of Free Trade," in *The Case against the Global Economy*, ed. Mander and Goldsmith, 230.

31. According to the OECD, in *Open Markets Matter*, 42: "The shift of garment assembly to poorer countries . . . the world's 'garment story,' could well be characterized as a continuous search for low-cost production sites by apparel manufacturers."

32. Capital migrates to finance production in countries maintaining low labor costs, to Viet Nam for example, in which forty-seven people may be employed for the price of one in France. (This is noted by James Goldsmith, "The Winners and the Losers," in *The Case against the Global Economy*, ed. Mander and Goldsmith, 173.) Thus, in high-wage countries, people and entire communities lose jobs and suffer the accompanying trauma. In low-wage countries, governments keep wages low to attract investment and labor is exploited, sometimes causing death, in nations in which human rights standards

do not protect the lives of those who resist brutal working conditions and exploitative wages. In addition, capital migrates to finance production in countries that maintain relatively low standards of cost internalization, that is, to countries with low environmental, workplace safety, and land protection standards. For more detailed discussion of Ricardo's theory applied in the contemporary context, see Goldsmith, "Winners and Losers," 171–79; Cobb and Daly, *Sustaining,* 207–35; and Daly, "Free Trade," 229–38.

33. John McMurtry, *Unequal Freedoms: The Global Market as an Ethical System* (West Hartford, Conn.: Kumarian Press, 1998), 87.

34. Ibid., 52.

35. "Geneva Business Declaration," 2.

36. OECD, *Open Markets Matter,* 39; ibid., 31.

37. Franky Schaeffer, "Introduction," in *Is Capitalism Christian?* ed. Franky Schaeffer (Westchester, Ill.: Crossway Books, 1985), xvii, cited in Craig M. Gay, *With Justice and Liberty for Whom? The Recent Evangelical Debate over Capitalism* (Grand Rapids: Eerdmans, 1991), 73.

38. Michael Novak, *On Corporate Governance* (Pfizer Lecture Series [AEI, 1997]), 31.

39. Milton Friedman, *Capitalism and Freedom* (Chicago: Univ. of Chicago Press, 1962), 12. Milton Friedman is a foundational theorist of laissez-faire liberalism or the laissez-faire pole of neo-classical economic theory as developed in the University of Chicago school of economics. His notion of freedom is well summarized by Johnston, *Health or Wealth,* 101–9. He emphasized "freedom as the ultimate goal and the individual as the ultimate entity in the society. . . . [His] definition of freedom defines the economic issues. Friedman defines freedom in purely individualistic terms" (101), and emphasizes freedom as liberty from control by others. While commonly characterized as seeking to dismantle government intervention in the market, he actually "accepts government intervention, but not for the sake of equity" (101). "We do not wish to conserve the state interventions that have interfered so greatly with our freedom, though of course we do wish to conserve those that have promoted it." Friedman, *Capitalism and Freedom,* 6; ibid., 8; ibid., 9.

40. Francis Fukuyama, *The End of History and the Last Man* (New York: Macmillan, 1992), xiii–xiv.

41. TRIPS guarantee ownership rights and legal protection on "intellectual properties" such as ideas, artistic creations, marketing tools, and genetically altered or cloned life forms and microorganisms. For example, patents have been granted on human umbilical cord blood cells. To use them in surgery one must pay royalties. "At the creation of the World Trade Organization in 1994, the most far-reaching multilateral agreement on intellectual property was drawn up: TRIPS . . . and came into effect in 1995 under the WTO. . . . It imposes on all WTO members [the property rights standards] of the industrialized world. . . . Least Developed countries have until 2005 to adjust their laws. . . . If a country does not fulfill its intellectual property rights obligations, trade sanctions can be applied against it—a serious threat" (UNDP, *Human Development Report 1999*), 67.

42. Ibid., 68.

43. Hans Leenders (Former Secretary General of the International Association of Plant Breeders for the Protection of Plant Varieties), "Reflections on 25 years of Service to the International Seed Trade Federation," *Seedmans' Diges*t 37:5, 89 cited in Vandana Shiva, *Biopiracy: The Plunder of Nature and Knowledge* (Boston: South End Press, 1997), 53.

44. Letter from a coalition of Indian individuals and civil society organizations to U.S. Ambassador to India, April 3, 1998.

45. Shiva, *Biopiracy.*

46. Jeff Crosby, quoted in "Our Developing World's Voices," no. 6 (winter 2000): 1, 4.

47. Karen Lehman and Al Krebs, "Control of the World's Food Supply," *The Case against the Global Economy,* ed. Mander and Goldsmith, 126.

48. Alexander Goldsmith, "Seeds of Exploitation," in *The Case against the Global Economy,* ed. Mander and Goldsmith, 269.

49. Bishop Bernardino Mandlate of the Methodist Church of Southern Africa, Mozambique, speaking, in conversation, about the international debt of the most indebted nations.

50. Friedman, *Capitalism and Freedom*, 13.

51. These contrasting notions of freedom are the subject matter of Frances Moore Lappé's *Rediscovering America's Values.* They are discussed well, but in less detail by David Korten, *The Post-Corporate World* (West Hartford and San Francisco: Kumarian and Barrett-Koehler, 1999, 137–50. Kelly Brown Douglas, from a womanist perspective, contributes a theological and multi-dimensional understanding of freedom as wholeness. Freedom as wholeness includes a vision of reality in which all humans "live together in relationships of mutuality and respect," and a "liberation process of struggle toward that vision." See Kelly Brown Douglas, "Freedom," *Dictionary of Feminist Theology*, ed. by Letty Russell and J. Shannon Clarkson (Louisville: Westminster/John Knox Press, 1996), 121–22.

52. Orlando Patterson, *Freedom in the Making of Western Culture* (Basic Books, 1991).

53. "Behind . . . neoliberalism is a concept of the human being that reduces the greatness of men and women to their ability to generate monetary income." Eighteen Provincial Superiors of the Society of Jesus in Latin America, "For Life and against Neoliberalism," rpt. in *Envio* (February/March 1997): 22.

54. Carol Johnston articulates key questions: "Was wealth maximizing already naturally the most powerful human motive, or was it focused on and assiduously cultivated for two hundred years, until today we cannot imagine it as anything but natural? If wealth maximizing really is the most powerful natural human motive, how was it possible for thousands of years of human existence, in very diverse cultures and historical epochs, to keep it from dominating human behavior?" Johnston, *Health and Wealth,* 48.

55. Ibid., 48; ibid., 50.

56. Michel de Certeau, *The Practice of Everyday Life*, trans. Steven Rendall (Berke-

ley: Univ. of California Press, 1984), referenced in William Cavanaugh, "Augustine and Disney on Coercion" (paper presented at the annual meeting of the American Academy of Religion, Orlando, Fla., November 1998), 2.

57. UNDP, *Human Development Report 1998*, 1; ibid., 47.

58. Walter Brueggemann, "The Liturgy of Abundance, the Myth of Scarcity," *The Christian Century* (March 24–31, 1999): 342.

59. "[H]e that incloses Land, and has a greater plenty of the conveniences of life from ten acres, than he could have from an hundred left to Nature, may truly be said, to give ninety acres to Mankind" (12). John Locke, *Two Treatises of Civil Government* (London: J.M. Dent and Sons, 1924).

60. Rasmussen, *Earth Community*, 228. While in much theology, *homo dominans* has been challenged and has given way to human as "steward" of all creation, the ecological consequences of the anthropocentric stewardship paradigm are less questioned.

61. David Ricardo, *Principles of Political Economy and Taxation* (London: J. M. Dent and Sons, 1965), 63.

62. An example from an advocate of globalization is found in Thomas Friedman's notion that globalization is as inevitable as the dawn: "I think it's a good thing that the sun comes up every morning. It does more good than harm. But even if I didn't much care for the dawn, there isn't much I could do about it. I didn't start globalization. I can't stop it—except at a huge cost to human development." Thomas L. Friedman, *The Lexus and the Olive Tree* (New York: Farrar, Straus, and Giroux, 1999), 6.

63. Fukuyama, *End of History*, vx; ibid., xi.

64. Rasmussen, *Moral Fragments*, 48.

65. Gary Becker, Nobel Laureate from the Chicago school of economics, as cited in Rasmussen, *Moral Fragments*, 49.

66. Rasmussen, *Moral Fragments*, 44.

67. Adam Smith, *The Theory of Moral Sentiments*, ed. D. D. Raphael and A. L. Macfie (Indianapolis: Liberty Classics, 1982), 25, 80, and 86 (on 86, he says, "the prevalence of injustice must utterly destroy [society]"); Smith, *Wealth of Nations*, 888; Smith, *Theory of Moral Sentiments*, 9.

68. McMurtry, *Unequal Freedoms*, 43, 62.

69. Ibid., 43.

70. "Liberalism," in theological ethics, may refer to three distinct but related concepts: (1) *Theological liberalism*, which arose in the late nineteenth century as one of Christianity's responses to modernity. It is characterized by use of historical-critical hermeneutical and exegetical methods, acceptance of Darwinian theory, emphasis on the immanence of God, belief in the inevitable progress of history, the notion of sin as ignorance, the quest for the historical Jesus, dependence upon reason, and coherence with scientific understandings of reality. At first, theological liberalism existed in contrast to and was critiqued by fundamentalism; later it was critiqued by neo-orthodoxy; and now it is critiqued by fundamentalism, by feminist and other liberationist perspectives, and by postmodernist deconstructionist theological leanings; (2) *Political liberalism*, known as

the counterpart to conservatism in North American politics, although both are locations in the central part of the political spectrum. Both terms are commonly used to refer to a continuity with the liberalism and conservatism of past generations, although in fact the implications of liberalism and conservatism today differ significantly from their meanings in previous generations; and (3) *Classical Liberalism*, a topic of political philosophy describing the social-political-cultural-economic ethos of the modern democratic western world. My use of liberalism in this project is the third.

71. Originally the theory of human rights pertained only to European men—and according to some theorists—only to European men with property. Yet the notion of "human rights" grounded the expansion of the notion to other social sectors. We do not here touch on the ways in which the rights of humankind have obscured the rights of non-humans, nor on the way in which principles of human rights might, in today's contexts of ecological crisis, undergird notions of rights extending beyond the human species.

72. John Stuart Mill, "On Definition and Method of Political Economy," *The Philosophy of Economics*, ed. Daniel M. Hausman (Cambridge: Cambridge Univ. Press, 1984), 52.

73. Johnston, *Health or Wealth*, 77; ibid., 24.

74. Ibid., 79.

75. Beverly Harrison, "The Role of Social Theory in Religious Ethics," chap. in *Making the Connections*, ed. Carol Robb (Boston: Beacon Press, 1985), 69.

76. Johnston, *Health or Wealth*, 78.

77. William Cavanaugh, "Augustine and Disney on Coercion" (paper presented at the annual meeting of the American Academy of Religion, Orlando, Fla., November 1998), 5.

78. As one employer defending sweatshops in India claimed: "It is a working out of the laws of nature" (McMurtry, *Unequal Freedoms*, 65).

79. Of course other social dynamics also play a role, both in general and in the specific case of neo-liberal ideology. A comprehensive treatment of the latter (far beyond the scope of this project) would include the commodification of relationships, both human-human and human-otherkind.

80. Walter Brueggemann, "The Scandal and Liberty of Particularity" (paper presented at the annual meeting of the American Academy of Religion, San Francisco, November 1997), 4.

81. Brueggemann, "Liturgy of Abundance," 345. Brueggemann turns to faith traditions, as do I, for resources "to generate and authorize liberated 'agents of their own history'" in the face of totalism (Brueggemann, "Scandal and Liberty," 5). "The ideology devoted to encouraging consumption wants to shrivel our imaginations so that we cannot conceive of living in ways that would be less profitable for the dominant corporate structures. . . . But Jesus tells us that we can change the world" (Brueggemann, "Liturgy of Abundance," 345).

82. Cited by Beverly Wildung Harrison in "Feminism and the Spirituality of Late Capitalism," unpublished paper, 1.

4. Martin Luther:
Finite Creatures "Filled to the Utmost with God"

1. The writings of Luther that are included in this volume edited by Timothy F. Lull are cited from it. See *Martin Luther's Basic Theological Writings*, ed. Timothy F. Lull (Minneapolis: Fortress Press, 1989).

2. In addition to the reasons noted previously, my choice to work with Luther stems from fascination with his experiential, contextual, and political theological method; his claims regarding salvation and the living of it in public life; the inseparability of what moderns call morality, spirituality, and theological belief in his expressed understanding of Christian life; the transgressive power born of his knowing the living Christ in Scripture; a mystical element in his theology; and ideological and theological factors that led him to discount neighbor-love in relationship to Jews and to the uprising peasants. Motives for this approach and the method for doing so are discussed in the appendix.

3. Bear in mind also that according to the methodological considerations elaborated in the appendix, my primary hermeneutic (method of interpretation) in reading Luther for this purpose is one of "appreciation," relating dialectically with a "hermeneutic of suspicion." The latter bears fruit explicitly in the last section of this chapter and in the constructive work of chapter 5. Luther's sense of the indwelling Christ and the implications for Christian moral life present myriad serious problems for a feminist liberationist Lutheran of my time and place. That I refrain from addressing them until the end of this chapter and the subsequent chapter is not to minimize those problems, but rather is to steward limited space toward my specific purpose.

4. This suggestion of three possible centerpieces represents my reading of Luther's theo-ethics, rather than the reading of other scholars, who identify the focal point of Luther's ethics in other terms. See, for example, Paul Althaus, *The Ethics of Martin Luther* (Philadelphia: Fortress Press, 1965); Robert Benne, "Perennial Themes and Contemporary Challenges," in *The Promise of Lutheran Ethics,* ed. Karen Bloomquist and John Stumme (Minneapolis: Fortress Press, 1998), 12; Heiko Oberman, "'Iustitia Christi' and 'Iustitia Dei': Luther and the Scholastic Doctrines of Justification," in *The Dawn of the Reformation: Essays in Late Medieval and Early Reformation Thought* (Edinburgh: T. & T. Clark, 1986), 120; and George W. Forell, *Faith Active in Love* (Minneapolis: Augsburg, 1954), 187.

5. In Lutheran theology, the moral life rarely is described as a communal reality. It is the individual made righteous by the grace of God who, in grateful response to that grace, then begins to love God and serve neighbor. See, for instance, George Forell, in *Justification by Faith—A Matter of Death and Life* (Philadelphia: Fortress Press, 1982), 53. A notable exception is Dietrich Bonhoeffer, whose soteriology, by the time of his *Ethics* and *Letters and Papers from Prison,* has communal or collective dimensions.

6. Gustaf Aulen claims that Luther revives the patristic notion of salvation by recalling and expanding the *Christus* Victor theme. Aulen is mistaken in reducing both Patristics' and Luther's doctrine of salvation to *Christus* Victor. Yet he is correct in finding

resonance between the two: Luther's notion of salvation resembles the patristic tendency toward multiple roles of Christ and multiple strands in the doctrine of redemption. These strands are well elaborated in H. E. W. Turner, *The Patristic Doctrine of Redemption* (London: A. R. Mowbray, 1952). For Aulen's claims, see Gustaf Aulen, *Christus Victor* (New York: Macmillan, 1969).

7. I retain Luther's gendered language for God, Christ, and human beings when citing him, and when speaking in his voice. Changing that language would mask its pervasive presence.

8. See for example, Luther, "Confession concerning Christ's Supper—Part III," in Lull, 52; and "Disputation concerning Justification," in Lull, 153.

9. See for example, Luther, "Heidelberg Disputation," Thesis 27, in Lull, 48; "Two Kinds of Righteousness," in Lull, 162 and 164; "Freedom of a Christian," in Lull, 606; and "Sermon on Third Sunday after Epiphany" in John Nicholas Lenker, ed., *Sermons of Martin Luther* (Grand Rapids: Baker, 1983), 2: 74–75.

10. See Luther, "Sermon on New Years Day," in Lenker 6: 288.

11. Tuomo Mannermaa ("Why Is Luther So Fascinating?" in *Union with Christ: A New Finnish Interpretation of Luther,* ed. Carl Braaten and Robert Jenson [Grand Rapids: Eerdmans, 1998] discusses how interpreters of Luther have tried to explain the indwelling Christ and union with Christ in ways that point away from actual union. The Luther Renaissance understood Luther's notion of the indwelling Christ to be contained in the union of the will of God with the will of the believer. Dialectical theology said Luther understood the indwelling Christ to be a community of deed or act in revelation (18). I imagine but do not argue here that modernity's gravitation toward rationalism has been one factor obscuring the theme of "union with Christ" in Luther's soteriology and ethics. Contemporary critique of the domination of Western consciousness by Enlightenment rationalism perhaps widens an opening for this relook at Luther. See Bengt Hoffman in *Luther and the Mystics* (Minneapolis: Augsburg, 1976), 18–21, for his delineation of three-fold censorship regarding the connection between the doctrinal-conceptual and the mystical-experiential in Luther to which Western scholarship has been subjected.

12. The writings of Luther upon which my understanding of "union with Christ" draws most heavily are: "Freedom of a Christian," "The Blessed Sacrament of the Holy and True Body and Blood of Christ and the Brotherhoods," "Two Kinds of Righteousness," "Disputation concerning Justification," "The Heidelberg Disputation" (all found in Lull, *Basic Writings*) and the five sermons cited in this essay (found in Lenker, *Sermons*).

13. Luther, "Third Sermon on Pentecost Sunday," in Lenker, 3: 316–17.

14. Ibid., 317.

15. Luther, "Sermon on the 16th Sunday after Trinity," in Lenker, 8: 279–80.

16. Luther, "Heidelberg Disputation," in Lull, 47.

17. Luther, "The Blessed Sacrament of the Holy and True Body and Blood of Christ, and the Brotherhoods," in Lull, 251.

18. Luther, "Third Sermon for Pentecost," in Lenker, 3: 321. Luther also makes this point in the immediately aforementioned sermon.

19. See Carl Braaten and Robert Jenson, eds., *Union with Christ: A New Finnish Interpretation of Luther* (Grand Rapids: Eerdmans, 1998).

20. My purpose is not to consider the varying implications of these distinct *terms*, but rather to consider certain implications (for moral agency) of this *concept* as a lived faith conviction, expressed by Martin Luther.

21. Stephen Ozment, "Luther and the Late Middle Ages: The Formation of Reformation Thought," in *Transition and Revolution: Problems and Issues of European Renaissance and Reformation History*, ed. Robert M. Kingdom (Minneapolis: Fortress Press, 1974), 109–29.

22. Ibid., 117–19.

23. *"Sermo Lutheri, in Natali Christi, A. 1515," Weimar Ausgabe* 1.28.28, translated by Tuomo Mannermaa in "Why Is Luther So Fascinating?" (17). The "pre-reformation" date of this sermon might render it suspect as a source of Luther's theology, except that the concept we are discussing is so similar to the same concept in multiple later works, including those cited.

24. Luther, "Heidelberg Disputation," Thesis 28, in Lull, 48.

25. Luther, "Heidelberg Disputation," Thesis 18, in Lull, 42.

26. Luther, "Sermon on Sixteenth Sunday after Trinity," in Lenker, 8: 280.

27. Larry Rasmussen, *Earth Community, Earth Ethics* (Maryknoll, N.Y.: Orbis, 1996), 273–74, quoting Rosemary Radford Reuther, *Gaia and God: An Ecofeminist Theology of Earth Healing* (San Francisco: HarperSanFrancisco, 1992), 135.

28. Luther, "Third Sermon for Pentecost," in Lenker, 3: 321. Luther also makes this point in "Sermon on Sixteenth Sunday after Trinity," in Lenker 8: 279–80.

29. Luther, "Heidelberg Disputation," in Lull, 43.

30. Luther, "Two Kinds of Righteousness," in Lull, 158–59.

31. This process is most clear in "Two Kinds of Righteousness" and in "The Blessed Sacrament of the Holy and True Body and Blood of Christ and the Brotherhoods."

32. Kristen Elaine Kvam, "Honoring God's Handiwork: Challenges of Luther's Doctrine of Creation," in *A Reforming Church: Gift and Task*, ed. Charles P. Lutz (Minneapolis: Kirk House, 1995), 177–79.

33. Luther, "The Sacrament of the Body and Blood of Christ—Against the Fanatics," in Lull, 331.

34. Given that prepositions often shape the meaning of a phrase, it is interesting to compare the use of "by" and "through" with reference to faith and grace in justification. Timothy Wengert describes "wrestling" with the meaning of *"durch"* in *"durch den Glauben,"* in his and his co-editors' process of translating and editing *The Book of Concord*. Their conclusion was the same as mine: since *"durch"* translates into English as both "by" and "through," "we [the editors] decided to use both." See Timothy J. Wengert, "Reflections on Confessing the Faith in the New English Translation of *The Book of Concord*," in *Lutheran Quarterly* XIV:1 (spring 2000): 3.

35. Luther, "Two Kinds of Righteousness," in Lull, 155.

36. Luther, "Disputation concerning Justification," in *Luther's Works* 34, ed. Lewis W. Spitz (Philadelphia: Muhlenberg, 1960), 161–62.

37. This notion of "what happens to people when made righteous" differs from some commonly held Lutheran theological assumptions. The tendency in European and Euro-American Lutheran theology is to note only the "first kind of righteousness"—the changed relationship with God—or to give it high priority over the "second kind of righteousness." Otherwise said, the tendency is to prioritize the forensic over the transformative aspect of being made righteous, or to ignore the latter. As Simo Peura notes: "One of the difficult problems to be solved in Lutheran theology concerns the relationship between the forensic and the effective aspects of justification. (See Simo Peura, "Christ as Favor and Gift: The Challenge of Luther's Understanding of Justification," in Braaten and Jenson, *Union with Christ*, 42.) Carl Braaten notes that this tendency is due in part to the Augsburg Confession's emphasis on the forensic aspect of justification. (See Braaten, "Response," in *Union with Christ,* 72–73.) Typically, where the forensic dimension is explained as not standing alone, it is complemented with the justified sinner's grateful response to God's rescue from sin and death, not with the morally transformative element to justification seen in Luther's "second kind of righteousness." When the "second kind of righteousness" is not given due import, Christian morality indeed is only a "response to the gospel." I argue that Christian morality is both a response to and *a part of* the Christian gospel.

38. Luther, "The Blessed Sacrament of the Holy and True Body and Blood of Christ, and the Brotherhoods," in Lull, 251.

39. Luther argued this point based on Scripture and on human experience as it encounters the law and gospel in Scripture. See for example, Luther, "Against Latimus," *Luther's Works* 32: 137–260.

40. Luther, "Lectures on Romans," *Luther's Works* 25, ed. Hilton C. Oswald (St. Louis: Concordia, 1972), 260.

41. "The root and source of all sin . . . is unbelief in the inmost heart." *Luther's Works* 35: 369.

42. *Luther's Works* 32: 224.

43. See "Against Latimus," *Luther's Works* 32: 137–260.

44. Luther, *Weimar Ausgabe*, 2, 413, 27, cited by Forell, *Faith*, 92.

45. Luther, "Disputation concerning Justification," in *Luther's Works* 34: 165; ibid., 161; ibid., 153.

46. Luther, "Heidelberg Disputation," in Lull, 46–47.

47. Luther, "Lectures on Genesis, W.A., 44, 135, 2, cited by Forell, *Faith*, 56. "We should not simply think, 'All I have to do is to believe and everything is taken care of, I do not have to do any good works." No, we must not separate the two. You must do good works and help your neighbor so that faith may shine outwardly in life as it shines inwardly in the heart." Luther, "Sermon on John 6:48," cited by Forell, ibid.

48. Luther, "Freedom of a Christian," in Lull, 625.

49. Luther, in Lenker 7: 68–69.

50. Luther, "The Sacrament of the Body and Blood of Christ—Against Fanatics," in Lull, 331.

51. Luther, "Freedom of a Christian," in Lull, 619; Lutheran theology emphasizes that good works are not necessary for salvation to occur. But the Lutheran focus tends to be on warning against trusting in works for salvation, and not on recognizing or even exploring the effective change toward good works that inheres in salvation according to Luther.

52. Note that other dimensions of Luther's theology yield "subversive" moral power in contexts of domination. This project, focusing only on the moral power issuing from the indwelling God, may not address those other sources. Given my claim that the hegemony of corporate- and finance-driven globalization is underwritten by the presupposition that it is inevitable and divinely sanctioned, of particular import would be Luther's iconoclastic response to a supposedly inevitable and divinely ordained institution of his day, papal supremacy. At issue in Luther's 1519 debate at Leipzig with Johannes Eck was whether the papacy was a divine institution (Eck) or a human development (Luther). Luther argued that this institution seen to be ordained by God, natural, and essential actually was rooted in human history.

53. Luther, "The Sacrament of the Body and Blood of Christ—Against the Fanatics," in Lull, 321. Luther insists that Jesus Christ in both his humanity and his divinity is present not only in the Christian but everywhere.

54. Walter Altmann, *Luther and Liberation: A Latin American Perspective,* trans. Mary M. Solberg (Minneapolis: Fortress Press, 1992), 5–6.

55. That norm is also a function of justification by grace through faith alone, which eliminated the saving power of religious activities.

56. See "Treatise on Good Works," *Luther's Works* 44: 15–114, for Luther's argument against a distinction between secular works and religious works, and against elevating the latter above the former.

57. Rasmussen, *Earth Community,* 274.

58. Luther, "Sermon on Sixteenth Sunday after Trinity," in Lenker, 8: 271.

59. Luther, "That These Words of Christ, 'This is My Body,' etc. Still Stand Firm against the Fanatics," *Luther's Works* 37: 58.

60. Luther, "Confession concerning Christ's Supper," in Lull, 397.

61. Ibid., 387.

62. Ibid., 386.

63. Luther, "The Sacrament of the Body and Blood of Christ—Against the Fanatics," in Lull, 321.

64. See Larry Rasmussen with Cynthia Moe-Lobeda, "Reform Dynamic," in *The Promise of Lutheran Ethics,* ed. Karen Bloomquist and John Stumme (Minneapolis: Fortress Press, 1998).

65. Luther, "The Sacrament of the Body and Blood of Christ—Against the Fanatics," in Lull, 321.

66. This second dimension is most visible in Luther's writings on economic life.

67. Self-sacrifice and servant-love, advocated by people in positions of power, may be used by them to justify the imposed sacrifice or servanthood of those "on the margins" of that power.

68. In "Two Kinds of Righteousness," for instance, Christians are enjoined to live for and only for the well-being of the neighbor, to be concerned only with the needs of the other. "Therefore [the second kind of righteousness] hates itself and loves its neighbor; it does not seek its own good but that of another, and in this its whole way of living consists." Luther, "Two Kinds of Righteousness," in Lull, 157–58.

69. See especially Luther, "The Blessed Sacrament of the Holy and True Body and Blood of Christ, and the Brotherhoods."

70. See, for example, Luther, "Whether One May Flee from a Deadly Plague," *Luther's Works* 43: 115–38.

71. Luther, "Heidelberg Disputation," in Lull, 47.

72. Luther, "Freedom of a Christian," in Lull, 619; ibid., 617.

73. In making the connection between new identity and moral life, I have drawn upon Bruce Birch, "Divine Character and the Formation of Moral Community in the Book of Exodus," unpublished paper. Birch refers not to Luther, but to ancient Israel.

74. Luther, "Freedom of a Christian," 625; ibid., 618; ibid., 619.

75. Luther quoting St. Gregory in "Heidelberg Disputation," in Lull, 48.

76. Luther, "Two Kinds of Righteousness," in Lull, 160; ibid., 157–58.

77. Ibid., 157.

78. Luther, "Sermon on Sixteenth Sunday after Trinity," in Lenker 8: 279.

79. Luther, "Two Kinds of Righteousness," in Lull, 157–58.

80. Luther, "Sermon on Third Sunday after Epiphany," in Lenker 2: 73–74.

81. Luther, "Third Sermon for Pentecost Sunday," in Lenker 3: 316–17.

82. Luther, "Freedom of a Christian," in Lull, 619.

83. Luther, "Disputation against Scholastic Theology," in Lull, 19.

84. These include foundational theological principles, moral norms, and actual judgments.

85. Carter Lindberg, in *The European Reformations* (Cambridge, Mass.: Blackwell, 1996) and in *Beyond Charity: Reformation Initiatives for the Poor* (Minneapolis: Fortress Press, 1993), is an excellent resource regarding Luther and economic ethics. My thinking is indebted to Lindberg's work in these two books.

86. Walther I. Brandt, "Introduction" to "Trade and Usury," *Luther's Works* 45: 238; ibid., 233.

87. Lindberg, *European Reformations*, 114; ibid., 111.

88. Heiko Oberman, *Luther: Man between God and the Devil* (New Haven, Conn.: Yale Univ. Press: 1989), 51.

89. Lindberg, *European Reformations*, 113.

90. For examples of Luther denouncing economic exploitation, see especially Luther's three treatises focusing on economic life: "The Short Sermon on Usury,"

Weimar Ausgabe 6, 1ff.; "Trade and Usury," *Luther's Works* 45: 244–308; "Admonition to the Clergy that They Preach against Usury," *Weimar Ausgabe* 51, 325ff. These were not attacks on usury as such, because the church, state, and public opinion already condemned usury. Rather these were attacks on certain practices which Luther contended were usury but which the papal authorities justified and defended. (See *Luther's Works* 45: 235.) See also Luther's comments on the seventh commandment in the *Large Catechism*. The quote is from Lindberg, *European Reformations*, 118.

91. Luther, "Address to the Christian Nobility of the German Nation," *Luther's Works* 44: 213.

92. The three treatises focusing on economic life are mentioned in note 90. In addition, Luther treats economic life in the following works whose primary focus is not economic life: "The Ninety-Five Theses," "The Blessed Sacrament of the Holy and True Body and Blood of Christ, and the Brotherhoods," "Address to the Christian Nobility of the German Nation," "Ordinance of a Common Chest" (this contains Luther's biblical rationale for social welfare and his descriptions of how a congregation ought organize its social welfare effort.), the "Large Catechism" comments on first, fifth, sixth, seventh, and ninth/tenth commandments (the comments on the seventh contain fierce denunciations of acquiring wealth in ways that burden or oppress the poor), the "Large Catechism" comments on the fourth petition of the Lord's prayer, "On Temporal Authority," and "Treatise on Good Works."

93. Lindberg, *European Reformations*, 111–12.

94. Luther, "The Blessed Sacrament of the Holy and True Body and Blood of Christ, and the Brotherhoods," in Lull, 251.

95. Lindberg, *European Reformations*, 112.

96. This treatise is composed of the "Long Sermon on Usury" (1520) published in 1524 together with a treatise on trade written in that year. See Luther, "Trade and Usury," *Luther's Works* 45: 231–309.

97. "Four" is according to the portion of the treatise composed in 1524. In the 1520 portion, Luther omits the fourth of these.

98. See also pages 247–51, in which Luther argues that the "common rule" and merchants' "chief maxim" ("I may sell my goods as dear as I can") is wrong and against God's commandment. This rule opens "every window and door to hell, for it flies squarely in the face not only of Christian love but also natural law"; it places my own profit over my neighbor's need and well-being. On the basis of this rule, trade "can be nothing but robbing and stealing the property of others." Luther gives a very detailed account of how prices are commonly determined not by costs of production, but by demand: "However high the other will, out of need pay, the good will be priced." He advocates a different standard: "Sell wares at a price equal to the costs of production, labor, and risk." "In determining how much profit you ought to take in your business and labor, there is no better way than by computing the amount of time of labor you have put into it" and take the amount of profit that a "day laborer" earns in that amount of time.

99. In "Temporal Authority: To What Extent It Should Be Obeyed," Luther is even more specific about debt. He admonishes, "you should decide the question of restitution as follows, if the debtor is poor and unable to make restitution, and the other party is not poor, then you should let the law of love prevail and acquit the debtor." See "Temporal Authority," *Luther's Works* 45: 127.

100. Heiko Oberman, "Teufelsdruck: Eschatology and Scatology in the 'Old' Luther," SCJ 19, 444, cited in Lindberg, *European Reformations*, 116.

101. Luther, "Admonition to the Clergy that They Preach against Usury," *Weimar Ausgabe* 51, 367, cited in Ulrich Duchrow, *Alternatives to Global Capitalism* (Utrecht: International Books, 1995), 220–21.

102. Luther, "Trade and Usury," 270; ibid., 271. Luther also denounces the trading companies in his comments on the seventh commandment in the "Large Catechism."

103. As Caryn Riswold points out, for Luther, to erase the practice and memory of sacramental communion with God is to erase knowledge both of who we are and of how we are to live. Luther condemned Rome's doctrine of the mass as sacrifice offered rather than gift received, because that doctrine "quench[ed] the power of baptism . . . in adults, so that now there are scarcely any who call to mind their own baptism . . . so that they might know what manner of men they were and how Christians ought to live." Luther, "The Babylonian Captivity of the Church," *Luther's Works* 36: 58. See Caryn Riswold, "From a Babylonian Captivity to the Otherworld: Martin Luther and Mary Daly" (paper presented at the ELCA's Lutheran Women in Theological Studies Conference, Orlando, Fla., November 1998).

104. David W. Lotz, "The Proclamation of the Word in Luther's Thought," *Word and World* 3: 4 (fall 1983): 344.

105. That resistance was predicated upon recognizing what forces were obscuring or silencing the Word. From his perspective, those forces included the papacy and its hegemonic power to grant or withhold the means of salvation, the resultant control over people's lives through fear of condemnation, the prevailing confidence in the saving power of works, scholastic theology's confidence in human reason and free will, and exploitative economic practices that endangered the souls of oppressors and kept the poor from receiving their daily bread.

106. Leonardo Boff, in "Luther, the Reformation, and Liberation," in *Faith Born in the Struggle for Life: A Re-Reading of Protestant Faith in Latin America Today*, ed. Dow Kirkpatrick, trans. L. McCoy (Grand Rapids: Eerdmans, 1988), 203. Luther's subversive moves were within the arena of religion; his primary intent was not to change social, political or economic structures except where those obscured the Word. Yet, as Boff points out, while Luther's intent was to challenge theological falsehood, his religious convictions had implications in virtually all dimensions of human life. Challenges to the power structure by Luther took many forms. For example: what was held to be salvific, he named oppression and bondage (indulgences, works, poverty and charity); what—other than God alone—was seen as worthy of trust, he named as betrayal (the papacy and salvific works; wealth); what was held to be divinely ordained, he disclosed

as human construct (the papacy); what demanded allegiance and conformity so that allegiance and obedience did not go to Christ alone, he denounced (the pope). In this vein, Luther also challenged civil rulers who called people to arms on behalf of the pope against the Protestants.

107. See especially "On Temporal Authority: To What Extent It Should be Obeyed" and "Treatise on Good Works," *Luther's Works* 44.

108. Luther, "Temporal Authority" in Lull, 659–78.

109. In his first "Letter to Elector Frederick," of 1522, *Luther's Works* 48, Luther attributes to Satan: disruption of society, chaos, and violent rebellion against either church (as was occurring in the case at hand) or state (as Luther feared might happen). Luther is referring to the disturbances at Wittenberg, which Luther attributed to Karlstadt's teaching while Luther was at the Wartburg.

110. Luther, "Temporal Authority," in Lull, 658; ibid.; ibid., 699. See also "Letter to Frederick," in which Luther states: "Human authority is not always to be obeyed, namely when it undertakes something against the commandments of God; yet it should never be despised but always honored."

111. Ibid., 686.

112. "Dr. Martin Luther's Warning to His Dear German People" (*Luther's Works* 47, ed. Franklin Sherman [Philadelphia: Fortress Press, 1971], 3–55) contains one of Luther's strongest statements that where rulers disobey God or call Christians to disobey God, they are to be resisted. "Whoever does obey him [the emperor] can be certain that he is disobedient to God and will lose both body and soul eternally in the war" (30). Here Luther overturns his earlier prohibitions against armed resistance, against self-defense, and against resisting injustice done to self. This treatise was written under extreme circumstances: Emperor Charles was calling people to arms on behalf of the Pope against the Protestants. Luther believed that the gospel itself and the souls of the German people were at stake, jeopardized by the imperial dictate. Luther's alteration in political ideology, theology of temporal authority, and accompanying norms seems to be terribly difficult to him. He says he is "now speaking as if in a dream, as if there were no God" (13). He sounds tormented. My impression is that he is moved to these reversals also by his passionate love for "his dear German people."

113. Luther, in Lenker 8: 275–77.

114. Luther, in Lenker 8: 277, 267, 268, 274, 272, respectively.

115. For Luther the Word of God is "first and foremost" Christself, known in the first place as the preached Word. This point is made by Lotz, "Proclamation," 345.

116. Luther, "Sermon on the Sixteenth Sunday after Trinity," in Lenker, 8: 272. Italics added.

117. Ibid. Italics added.

118. Ibid., 277.

119. Ibid., 280.

120. See *Book of Concord*, ed. Robert Kolb and Timothy J. Wengert (Minneapolis: Fortress Press, 2000), 359.

121. Luther, "Blessed Sacrament of the Holy and True Body of Christ, and the Brotherhoods," in Lull, 260. Obvious examples include the aforementioned economic norms and judgments, and Luther's admonitions against fleeing a deadly plague when one's neighbor is in need. See Luther, "Whether a Christian May Flee a Deadly Plague."

122. His writings on the Christian moral life are inextricable from his theological writings. A prime example is "The Freedom of a Christian." This, "Luther's famous programmatic statement about Christian ethics" (as characterized by Lull, 578), is a theological vision of Christian life.

123. Luther, of course, neither would have used the modern term or concept "social theory," nor would have acknowledged any interaction between it and theology. My post-Troeltschian assumption is that social theory and theology always interact.

124. Luther, "Confession concerning Christ's Supper," in Lull, 54.

125. Steven Ozment, *Protestants: The Birth of a Revolution* (New York: Doubleday, 1991), 3.

126. Forell, *Faith,* 158.

127. See for example his interpretation of the fourth commandment in "Treatise on Good Works" and in the "Large Catechism."

128. Nine works, in particular, reveal the relationship between social theory, theology, ethics, and exegesis in Luther. These nine are the following: the set of three treatises written just before and after the peasant rebellion of 1525; "Confession concerning Christ's Supper"—Part III (delineating the "holy orders and religious institutions established by God"); The "Large Catechism," comments on the fourth commandment; Letters of Martin Luther to Elector Frederick of March 5 and 7, and to Hausmann of March 17, 1522, regarding the disturbances in Wittenberg while Luther was at the Wartburg; "Treatise on Good Works"; "Address to the Christian Nobility of the German Nation" (empowering laity/nobility against ecclesial authority);"On Temporal Authority"; "Dr. Martin Luther's Warning to His Dear German People" (empowering Christians against temporal authority, this time to the point of theologically justifying armed resistance to the emperor if he defies God's Word and his covenant with Christ made at baptism); "On the Jews and Their Lies."

129. For example, in "Two Kinds of Righteousness," "living justly with neighbor" is equated with "love to one's neighbor," and seeking justice on behalf of neighbor is a form of neighbor-love. See "Two Kinds of Righteousness," in Lull, 157–58, 164.

130. Luther, "Admonition to Peace: A Reply to the Twelve Articles of the Peasants in Swabia," *Luther's Works* 46: 39. This is the first of Luther's three tracts addressing the Peasant rebellion. The other two are: "Against the Robbing and Murdering Hordes of Peasants," in *Luther's Works* 46, edited by Robert Schultz (Philadelphia: Fortress Press, 1964), and "An Open Letter on the Harsh Book against the Peasants," in *Luther's Works* 46. See also the Table of Duties in the Small Catechism.

131. Luther, "Admonition to Peace," 46: 39.

132. Ibid., 46: 41; ibid, 46:19.

133. Luther, "Against the Robbing and Murdering Hordes of Peasants," 46: 49–51.

134. Ibid., 52–53.

135. Ibid., 54; Luther, "An Open Letter on the Harsh Book against the Peasants," *Luther's Works* 46: 82–83.

136. Luther, "On the Jews and Their Lies," *Luther's Works* 47: 123–306. In this treatise, Luther claims that Jews curse Christ, pray for the death of Christians, would murder Christians if they could, and are demonic; advocates burning Jewish synagogues, homes, and books "in honor of our Lord, so that God may see that we are Christians," and expelling Jews from the country; and admonishes people to form demonic images of Jews in their minds. This was not the case in Luther's treatise of twenty years earlier, "That Christ Was Born a Jew." There Luther taught that Jews are, humanly speaking, closer to Christ than are Christians; that while Christians ought aim to convert Jews, they ought do so gently; and that Christians ought be guided by the Christian law of love in relationship to Jews. Many theories have been advanced either explaining or minimizing this shift in Luther. See the introduction to the later treatise for a summary of those theories.

5. Subversive Moral Agency Today: God "Flowing and Pouring into All Things"

1. Larry Rasmussen, *Earth Community, Earth Ethics* (Maryknoll, N.Y.: Orbis Books, 1996), 350.

2. I assume here a distinction between "morality" and "ethics." The two often are used synonymously, and with good reason: "ethics" comes from the Greek, and "morality" comes from the word used by Cicero to translate the Greek to Latin. Yet, in modern discourse, there is an important distinction. "Morality" refers to a dimension of life, the dimension that pertains to whether a given way of being and doing is good and right and fitting. "Ethics," on the other hand, denotes the disciplined inquiry into morality. One could say the science of morality, or morality rendered self-conscious.

3. I use "Earth ethics" intentionally rather than "environmental ethics" to suggest a mode of ethics that inherently defies the distinction between "social ethics" and "environmental ethics," or between social justice and eco-justice. By this I do not mean only that the social and the ecological must be held together but also that the construction of these two categories is false. "Earth ethics," as I use it, implies that the Earth is an ecosystem of which the human species is a part.

4. "Expert" here denotes formally trained and credentialed members of church or academy.

5. The validity and relative weight of various sources are contested, but most constructions of sources for Christian Ethics revolve around some version of the Wesleyan quadrangle of scripture, tradition, reason, and experience.

6. One exception, of course, was Max Horkheimer in *Eclipse of Reason* (New York: Seabury Press, 1974). His move was reversed by Jürgen Habermas, a later theorist of the Frankfurt School.

7. See for example, Rasmussen, *Earth Community*, 321.

8. My argument against ethics thus limited does not land me in the camp of "anti-theory" described by Stanley G. Clarke and Evan Simpson in *Anti-Theory in Ethics and Moral Conservatism* (Albany: SUNY Press, 1989). That highly diverse trajectory critiques "normative theory as rationalistic formulation of a set of normative principles governing all rational beings and providing a dependable procedure for reaching definite moral judgments and decision" (4). While I share a critique of the homogenizing tendencies in universal normative formulations, I do so for different reasons and with different consequences than characterize many of the authors identified as "anti-theorists." And I do not reject all forms of universally normative ethical principles.

9. In significant ways, my constructive use of communion is consistent with the 1996 statement on communion issued by the Lutheran World Federation after it had redefined itself (at its assembly in Curitiba in 1990) as a "communion" of churches (as opposed to the previous "association" of churches.) That statement—"The [*sic*] Lutheran Understanding of Communion, A Statement by the Working Group on Ecclesiology of the Lutheran World Federation" (Strasborg, March 5, 1996)—for example, affirms, as do I:

- that communion encompasses God . . . one another . . . and all creation" (6);
- "the wide ranging usage [of communion] . . . from God's inner Trinitarian relationship to economic relationships" (6);
- that communion "must be expressed in tangible spiritual and economic ways" (7) including exposure and critique of unjust and oppressive situations, commitment to transform them, and solidarity with people in need (10);
- that communion is a gift that implies a call to shape life according to it (13).

I explore what this document "challenges" the communion of churches to explore: "what our communion can contribute to alleviating suffering and to transforming our societies," (5) and the consequences for all aspects of life of "understanding ourselves as a communion" (6). However, the significance of the LWF document in relationship to my project lies not in the congruencies but in one incongruence between the two. That difference is a principal point of this book: the LWF document affirms frequently that we are "called" into communion as a gift of God and are "called" to shape our lives as an expression of that communion, but the document does not state (as I believe Luther does) that we also are *empowered* by communion itself to be communion.

10. That "receiving the gift of community and creating it is not how most Christian Ethics has described 'being' and 'doing' in the Christian life" is articulated by Larry Rasmussen as he applauds the influence of Beverly Harrison's feminist insistence to the

contrary. Larry Rasmussen, "A Different Discipline," *Union Seminary Quarterly Review: Festschrift for Beverly Harrison* 53:34 (1999): 44.

11. See Paul Althaus, *The Theology of Martin Luther* (Philadelphia: Fortress Press, 1966), 17.

12. Luther, "Sermon for Pentecost Sunday," in John Nicholas Lenker, ed., *Sermons of Martin Luther* (Grand Rapids: Baker, 1983), 3: 316–17.

13. Luther, "Sermon for Sixteenth Sunday after Trinity," in Lenker, 8: 272.

14. This phrase ("receives loving care from others") is a crucial corrective to the frequent interpretation of Luther's ethics as "faith active in love" for others without recalling that Luther describes and prescribes also receiving the love and support given by others. "As love and support are given you, you in turn must render love and support to Christ's needy ones. . . . See as you uphold all of them, so they all in turn uphold you." Luther, "The Blessed Sacrament of the Holy and True Body and Blood of Christ, and the Brotherhoods," in Timothy F. Lull, ed., *Martin Luther's Basic Theological Writings* [Minneapolis: Fortress Press, 1989), 247.

15. Recall that, according to Luther, people made righteous by God are placed first in a different relationship with God, and then in a different relationship with others—a relationship that has enormous political-economic weight. That relationship, grounded in Christ indwelling and loving in believers, leads to denouncing and disavowing economic activity that places profit over meeting human needs. The use of economic resources, including money, is determined by relationships of self respect, neighbor-love, and public need. All of your resources for making a living "are crying out to you: 'Friend use me in your relations with your neighbor just as you would want one's neighbor to use his [*sic*] property in his relations with you.'" Luther, "Commentary on the Sermon on the Mount," in *Luther's Works* 21: 237.

16. Grace Jantzen and Richard King elaborate this claim. While their focus is on relationship with God as known in mystical traditions, their point that the privatization of relationality with God has served the interests of established powers pertains also to relationship with God as known in God's immanence. See Grace M. Jantzen, *Power, Gender, and Christian Mysticism* (Cambridge: Cambridge Univ. Press, 1995); and Richard King, *Orientalism and Religion: Postcolonial Theory, India, and "The Mystic East"* (London and New York: Routledge, 1999).

17. Larry Rasmussen, "Is Ecology Central to Christian Faiths?" (public lecture at Seattle Univ., Seattle, Wash., July 2000).

18. Thomas Berry, *The Great Work: Our Way into the Future* (New York: Bell Tower, 1999), 104.

19. Mary C. Grey, *Redeeming the Dream: Feminism, Redemption, and Christian Tradition* (London: SPCK, 1989), 86.

20. Mary C. Grey, *Prophecy and Mysticism: The Heart of the Postmodern Church* (Edinburgh: T. and T. Clark, 1997), 29–30; Elizabeth Johnson, *She Who Is: The Mystery of God in Feminist Theological Discourse* (New York: Crossroad, 1994), 67. The theological and philosophical roots of feminist relational theology, as identified by

Mary Grey, include Martin Buber's philosophy of "I and Thou," systems theory, new cosmologies, and process theology. See Grey, *Prophecy and Mysticism,* 26–36.

21. Elizabeth Johnson, *She Who Is,* 69. Johnson goes on to say that "what this revaluation of mutual relationship is bringing to the work of speaking about God is just beginning to be glimpsed" (69).

22. "The final and most important base point for a feminist moral theology is the centrality of relationship." Beverly Wildung Harrison, "The Power of Anger in the Work of Love," in *Making the Connections: Essays in Feminist Social Ethics,* ed. Carol S. Robb (Boston: Beacon, 1985), 15.

23. Janet Jakobson, in a more social theoretical mode, defines moral agency as mutual relationship in alliance. Edith Wyschogrod, *Saints and Postmodernism: Revisioning Moral Philosophy* (Chicago: Univ. of Chicago Press, 1990) working from philosophical ethics and critiquing the "traditional scheme [in which] ethics as a branch of philosophy is 'the investigation of the nomos of conduct'" (xv), revisions ethics as "the sphere of relations between self and Other" (xxi). Systematic theologian Catherine Mowry LaCugna in "God in Communion with Us," in *Freeing Theology: The Essentials of Theology in Feminist Perspective,* ed. Catherine Mowry LaCugna (San Francisco: HarperSanFrancisco, 1993), argues that the fundamental insight of the doctrine of the Trinity is that God lives among us "as a communion of persons" (84). A crucial contribution of the Cappadocians, she argues, was their radical move to make person in relationship rather than substance (in and of itself) the primary ontological category for God (86). Communion, according to this paradigm, underlies being.

24. See for example, Grey, *Redeeming the Dream,* 87: "'Mutuality in relation' implies a reciprocity in relating which may be the ideal, but sadly, is beyond the grasp of most people. Relationships for most people are characterized by a lack of mutuality. Love accepted and returned is sheer grace." See also Rita Nakashima Brock's attention to brokenness as characterizing human relationship, and the presence of the divine as erotic wholeness-making energy [*Journeys by Heart: A Christology of Erotic Power* (New York: Crossroad, 1992)], and Carter Heyward's use of "godding" to describe mutuality in relationship (Isabel Carter Heyward, *The Redemption of God: A Theology of Mutual Relation* (Lanham, Md.: Univ. Press of America, 1982).

25. This affirmation takes varied forms in feminist theology. Cosmic christologies, such as those of Sallie McFague and Grace Jantzen see God as embodied in the universe itself. See Sallie McFague, *The Body of God: An Ecological Theology* (Minneapolis: Fortress Press, 1993); and Grace Jantzen, *God's World, God's Body* (London: Darton, Longman, and Todd, 1984). For Rita Nakashima Brock, the community becomes Christ's body as "Christa-community." See Brock, *Journeys by Heart.* In general, according to Elizabeth Johnson, in feminist perspectives the immanence of God is the embodiment of God, God "indwelling." "Bodiliness opens up the mystery of God to the conditions of history, including suffering and death. She becomes flesh, choosing the very stuff of the cosmos as her own personal reality forever." See Johnson, *She Who Is,* 168.

26. The many examples include Carter Heyward and Sallie McFague, as cited at the

opening of this chapter, and Johnson, who writes in *She Who Is*, "according to the Christian narrative . . . there is a . . . presence of the Spirit of God pervading the world, quickening creation, and working toward the renewal of all creatures, both human beings and the earth" (123). "Sophia as Spirit, Jesus, Mother 'pervades the world to vivify and renew'" (169).

27. See, for example, Beverly Harrison in "Power of Anger," 16. She writes, "All things cohere in each other. Nothing living is self-contained. . . . We are part of a web of life so intricate as to be beyond our comprehension." See also Harrison in "Keeping Faith in a Sexist Church," in *Making the Connections,* ed. Carol Robb, 230.

28. Carter Heyward, *Touching Our Strength: The Erotic as Power and the Love of God* (San Francisco: Harper and Row, 1989), 10.

29. Luther does not claim absolute doctrinal truth in designating only two sacraments: "Never the less, it *has seemed proper* to restrict the name of sacrament to those promises which have signs attached to them. . . . Hence strictly speaking there are but two sacraments in the church of God—baptism and the bread" (*Luther's Works* 36, 124, italics added).

30. Martin Luther, "The Small Catechism," in the *Book of Concord,* ed. and trans. by Theodore G. Tappert (Philadelphia: Fortress Press, 1959), 352. Italics added.

31. Heiko A. Oberman, *Luther: Man between God and the Devil,* trans. Eileen Walliser-Schwarzbart (New York: Image Books, 1992), 156. Italics added.

32. Luther, "The Large Catechism," in *Book of Concord,* 449.

33. I prefer "sensual" to "visible" because, for some people, vision is not possible while other senses may be.

34. Elizabeth Bettenhausen, "Questions Facing the Church" (paper presented at the Annual Gathering of Lutheran Women in Theological Studies, Boston, November 1999).

35. Luther, "The Blessed Sacrament of the Holy and True Body and Blood of Christ, and the Brotherhoods," in Lull, 260.

36. Consider, for example, Luther's lectures on Romans: "We are capable of receiving His works and His counsels only when our own counsels have ceased and our works have stopped and we are made purely passive before God, both with regard to our inner as well as our outer activities" (Luther, "Commentary on Romans," *Luther's Works* 25: 365. See also 364–67). Then the Spirit is with us. Unless we come to this position before God, the Spirit is not with us. When we have become hopeless then the "Spirit helps us in our weakness (Rom. 8:26)" (ibid.).

37. Luther, in Lenker, 3: 321. Larry Rasmussen in "Luther and a Gospel of Earth," *Union Seminary Quarterly Review* 51:1–2 (1997): 111–28, and Elizabeth Bettenhausen in "Questions" refer to Luther's statements about God indwelling creation as his "panentheism."

38. Note Luther's amazement in the wonder of creation: "If you were to search out everything about a kernel of wheat in the field, you would be so amazed that you would die." See Luther, "The Sacrament of the Body and Blood of Christ—Against the Fanatics," in Lull, 323.

39. Luther, "That These Words of Christ, 'This Is My Body,' etc. Still Stand Firm against the Fanatics," *Luther's Works* 37: 57.

40. Ibid., 58.

41. Luther, the *Weimar Ausgabe* 23.134.34, as cited by Rasmussen, "Luther and a Gospel of Earth," 22, citing Paul Santmire, *The Travail of Nature: The Ambiguous Ecological Promise of Christian Theology* (Philadelphia: Fortress Press, 1985), 129.

42. Mary Grey, *Redeeming the Dream*, 87.

43. Nancie Erhard, "Ecological Ethics as Method in Ethics" (exam paper. Union Theological Seminary, New York City, April 2000).

44. Bettenhausen, "Questions," 2.

45. Grey, *Redeeming the Dream*, 88–87; ibid., 86–87; ibid., 84.

46. Jantzen, *God's World*, 157.

47. McFague, *Body of God*, 160; ibid., 134; ibid., 197.

48. Erhard, "Ecological Ethics as Method in Ethics."

49. Grey, *Redeeming the Dream*, 85.

50. McFague, *Body of God*, 207–8; ibid., 212. Italics added.

51. Luther, "Sermon on the Sixteenth Sunday after Trinity," in Lenker 8:276–77.

52. Ibid., 272; 275–76.

53. Elizabeth Bettenhausen, "The Concept of Justice and a Feminist Lutheran Social Ethic," *Annual of the Society of Christian Ethics* (1986): 163–182.

54. Luther, "The Sacrament of the Holy and True Body and Blood of Christ—Against the Fanatics," in Lull, 331.

55. The five statements are from Luther, "The Blessed Sacrament of the Holy and True Body and Blood of Christ, and the Brotherhoods," in Lull, respectively on pages 255, 251, 260, 247, and 250. Italics added.

56. Heyward, *Redemption of God*, 165.

57. Luther, "Treatise on Good Works," *Luther's Works* 44: 52. Italics added.

58. Sri Lankan theologian Tissa Balasuriya asks a similar question: "Why is it that in spite of hundreds of thousands of eucharistic celebrations, Christians . . . who proclaim eucharistic love and sharing deprive the poor people of the world of food, capital, employment, and even land . . . inequities grow, . . . [and] the rich live like Dives in the Gospel story?" (xi–xii). Tissa Balasuriya, *The Eucharist and Human Liberation* (Maryknoll, N.Y.: Orbis, 1979).

59. William Cavanaugh, *Torture and the Eucharist* (Oxford: Blackwell, 1998), 279.

60. Cavanaugh, *Torture*, 279; ibid.; ibid., 2; ibid., 4; ibid.; ibid., 267; ibid., 229.

61. I use "mystery" in the historical sense as related to "sacrament." The Latin *sacramentum* was used in early Christianity to translate the Greek *mystērion*, which referred to the mystery of God—the creating, saving, sustaining love of God—"the ways of God in getting through to us, in opening our eyes to face reality, in bringing us to faith, and hope, and love" (Christopher Morse, *Not Every Spirit: A Dogmatics of Christian Disbelief* [Valley Forge, Pa.: Trinity Press International, 1995], 43).

62. Luther, "The Blessed Sacrament of the Holy and True Body and Blood, and the Brotherhoods," in Lull, 251.

63. The three identified here are not the only problems with solidarity as a norm viewed through feminist and other liberationist lenses. Other "misbegotten" notions of solidarity include notions of solidarity that glorify suffering or the relinquishment of power.

64. Emilie M. Townes, "Women's Wisdom on Solidarity and Differences (On Not Rescuing the Killers)," *Union Seminary Quarterly Review* 53:3-4 (1999): 153–64.

65. Dietrich Bonhoeffer, *Ethics* (New York: Simon and Schuster, 1995), 81–86.

66. Marilyn J. Legge, "Wild Geese and Solidarity: Conjunctural Praxis for a Spirit-filled Ethics," *Union Seminary Quarterly Review* 53:3-4 (1999), 181. Legge, presupposing solidarity as integral to liberative praxis, norms solidarity with "difference" understood not as liberalism's pluralism which falsely equalizes, but rather as difference that dismantles domination.

67. Ibid., 183.

68. Servanthood and self-sacrifice, advocated by people "on the top," may be used by them to justify theologically the imposed servanthood of those "on the bottom."

69. In "Two Kinds of Righteousness," for instance, Christians are enjoined to live for and only for the well-being of the neighbor, to be concerned only with the needs of the other. "Therefore [the second kind of righteousness] hates itself and loves its neighbor; it does not seek its own good but that of another, and in this its whole way of living consists." Luther, "Two Kinds of Righteousness," in Lull, 157–8.

70. See especially Luther, "The Blessed Sacrament of the Holy and True Body and Blood of Christ, and the Brotherhoods," in Lull.

71. "It is striking to think in this connection how much the dramatic plot and sub plots of the gospel accounts, and the Christian liturgies based on them, are shaped by what Jesus is said to have received, and not simply in a one-sided fashion to have given, to those who are more or less presented as outsiders . . . within the cultural context of his ministry." Morse, *Not Every Spirit*, 313.

72. The critique of servanthood as the apex of Christian love levied against Luther is countered also by his many admonishments to self-care, theological presuppositions of self-love, and some of the theological principles underlying his statements that appear to denigrate self.

73. Shawn Copeland, "Difference as a Category in Critical Theologies for the Liberation of Women," *Concilium* 1 (1996): 150, cited in Legge, "Wild Geese," 183.

74. Douglas John Hall, in *Lighten Our Darkness: Toward an Indigenous Theology of the Cross* (Philadelphia: Westminster, 1976), asserts that the authenticity of any faith claim "in which human hope embodies itself is whether its expectations have emerged from the crucible of encounter with human experience in its present, especially in its most degrading, forms" (113).

75. The assertion that solidarity in the globalizing economy takes the form of perceiving and remembering from perspectives of people brutalized by globalization and

heeding those perspectives is almost absurdly complex and wrought with contention. The assertion is rooted theologically in post–Vatican II and Latin American liberation theologies' "preferential option for the poor"; social theoretically in womanist and feminist insistence that fruitful social reconstruction is at the margins of power in struggles for survival, dignity, and liberation; and philosophically in Michel Foucault's call for "an insurrection of subjugated knowledges" (Michel Foucault, *Power/Knowledge: Selected Interviews and Other Writings, 1972–77*, ed. Colin Gordon, trans. C. Gordon, L. Marshall, J. Mepham, and K. Soper [New York and London: Pantheon, 1980], 81.) One aspect of the complexity in the assertion is the inherent challenge it poses to the boundaries of community. For instance, where a given community begins to heed the voices and experiences of "others" who are exploited and excluded by the social arrangements that legitimate and privilege that community, the boundaries of identity surrounding the community will be challenged. See Elizabeth M. Bounds, *Coming Together/Coming Apart: Religion, Community, and Modernity* (New York and London: Routledge, 1997).

76. Simeon Ilesanmi identified as a condition of globalization "the increasing isolation of the economically secure from those whose livelihoods and culture are destroyed by globalization" (Simeon Ilesanmi, panel presentation for Opening Plenary of the Society of Christian Ethics, Arlington, Va., January 2000).

77. Hall, *Lighten Our Darkness*, 110–11. Italics added.

78. Ibid., 113.

79. Ruth Frost, Lutheran pastor.

80. I use the term *moral imagination* to suggest a mix of intellectual, affective, sensual, and artistic work—informed by theology and social theory—that "generates the world of what could be, thereby making moral living possible." See William P. Brown, *The Ethos of the Cosmos: The Genesis of Moral Imagination in the Bible* (Grand Rapids and Cambridge: Eerdmans, 1999), 20.

81. Iris Murdoch, in *Existentialists and Mystics* (New York: Penguin, 1997), describes the morally determinative power of "seeing": "I can only choose within the world I can see. . . . One is often compelled almost automatically by what one can see." She is discussing the moral empowerment derived from "the work . . . of attention, or looking." Crucial "moral choices" are determined, she asserts, by what one has been, over time, seeing or giving attention. Attention or seeing, she says, is "the effort to counteract illusion . . . false pictures of the world" (329). Murdoch goes on to elaborate the ongoing role of attention or seeing in moral action. The "right answer" in moral conundrums depends upon love as an exercise of "really looking. The difficulty is to keep the attention fixed upon the real situation. . . . The background condition of [moral action] is just a mode of vision. . . . It is a task to come to see the world as it is" (375).

82. Harrison, "Power of Anger," 21.

83. Luther, "Blessed Sacrament of the Holy and True Body and Blood of Christ, and the Brotherhoods," in Lull, 251, 260.

84. Carter Lindberg, *Beyond Charity: Reformation Initiatives for the Poor* (Minneapolis: Fortress Press, 1993), 101. Lindberg refers to the "liturgical-sacramental foundation" of Luther's social ethic."

85. Ibid., 110.

86. Luther, "Large Catechism," in *Book of Concord*, 397.

87. Luther, "Trade and Usury," *Luther's Works* 45: 249–50; Luther, "Large Catechism," in *Book of Concord*, 398. Italics added.

88. Luther, "Trade and Usury," *Luther's Works* 45: 270. Luther also denounces the trading companies in his comments on the seventh commandment in the "Large Catechism."

89. Lindberg, *Beyond Charity*, 112.

90. Ibid., 113. Italics added.

91. Ibid., 114.

92. For instance, the obligation to institute social change that furthered preaching and teaching the gospel rendered Luther's judgment that schools ought be provided for all children (including the poor and girls) so that they could read the Bible.

93. Luther, *Weimar Aufgabe*, 10.143.

94. Fritjof Capra, *The Turning Point* (New York: Simon and Schuster, 1982), 77–78.

95. Grey, *Prophecy and Mysticism*, 29.

96. Giving shape to "Earth ethics" (grounded partly and critically in Luther), Larry Rasmussen insists: "We, like all creatures, live utterly dependent on the rest of God's creation for every breath and morsel. Our entire life is a life of gracious indebtedness; we cannot live without borrowing." Rasmussen, "Luther and a Gospel of Earth," 3.

97. This tendency is rooted firmly in the Western philosophical and theological elevation of human being over "nature." As Rasmussen points out, twentieth-century Protestantism (until process theology), grounded in Cartesian notions of the self and Enlightenment cosmologies, divorced nature from history and culture and set human over all else in a relationship of domination and utility.

98. Rasmussen, *Earth Community*, 349.

99. Ibid., 345. In the late 1970s, Beverly Harrison, challenging the nature/culture split pervasive in Western theology and philosophy, warned, "If we do not recover a new respect for our deep interdependence as natural/ historical and cultural beings, understanding our reciprocity with each other and nature as a dimension and condition of our freedom, all of us are doomed." Harrison, "Keeping Faith in a Sexist Church," 230.

100. Rasmussen, *Earth Community*, xii. Note that a Lutheran liturgy already reflects and teaches this norm, when the worshipping community pledges itself in prayer to "the care and redemption of all that God has made." See *Lutheran Book of Worship* (Minneapolis: Augsburg Press, 1978).

101. Useful here is James Gustafson's maxim: "Relate to all things in a manner appropriate to their relations to God." James M. Gustafson, *Ethics from a Theocentric Perspective* (Chicago: Univ. of Chicago Press, 1981).

102. This distinction is drawn from Rasmussen. Drawing on Wendell Berry's term "the Great Economy," Rasmussen elaborates the mismatch between the big economy and the great economy and identifies the moral and practical consequence: "An expanding human economy that issues in a diminishing earth economy commits suicide by increments" (Rasmussen, *Earth Community,* 112).

103. See Brown, *Ethos,* 11 and Nancie Erhard, "The Promise of Ethos in Brown's 'The Ethos of the Cosmos,'" Union Theological Seminary, New York City, May 2000.

104. It is interesting to note that some design sciences are now drawing upon design in "natural" organisms and systems.

105. We have touched only the "tip of the iceberg." The questions go on. For example, if as Luther writes, the God inhabiting Earth is Christ, then the Earth now being "crucified" by human activity is the body of Christ. What questions emerge from this christological development?

106. See Luther, "On the Jews and Their Lies," *Luther's Works* 47: 121–278.

107. Luther, *Weimar Ausgabe*, 2, 413, 27, cited by George W. Forell, *Faith Active in Love* (Minneapolis: Augsburg, 1954), 92.

108. Johnson, *She Who Is*, 133.

109. Luther, "That These Words of Christ, 'This Is My Body,'" *Luther's Works* 37: 58.

6. Invitation

1. Sharon Daloz Parks, "Household Economics," in *Practicing Our Faith,* ed. Dorothy C. Bass (San Francisco: Jossey-Bass Publishers, 1997), 47.

2. "Mud creature" is the term used by Denis Minns to interpret Irenaeus of Lyons' concept of the created human being. I like it. See Denis Minns, *Irenaeus* (Washington, D.C.: Georgetown Univ. Press, 1994).

3. Parks, "Household Economics," 48.

4. Irenaeus of Lyons, *Against Heresies* 3.18.7.

5. "South African NGO Coalition," *NGO Matters* 3:3 (April 2000): 9.

6. Oronto Douglas, "Eco-Justice in the Niger Delta," *YES: A Journal of Positive Futures* 9 (spring 2000): 22–23.

7. *Co-op America Quarterly* 49 (fall 1999): 15.

8. Institute for Policy Studies and United for a Fair Economy, "A Decade of Executive Excess: The 1990s, Sixth Annual Executive Compensation Survey" (Washington, D.C.: Institute for Policy Studies and Boston: United for a Fair Economy, 1999), 11.

9. Bernardino Mandlate, in a presentation to the United Nations PrepCom for the World Summit on Social Development Plus Ten, New York, February, 1999.

10. Rob Hughes, *International Herald Tribune*, December 23, 1998.

11. The information regarding the impact of Bauxite mining in India is drawn from two papers: Orissa Development Action Forum, "An Ethical Response to Globalization—A Christian Perspective," Orissa, India, 2000; and the National Council of Churches in India, "The Land Does Not Belong to Us—We Belong to the Land," Visakhapatnam, India, 2000.

12. Wolfgang Sachs, "Introduction," in *The Development Dictionary: A Guide to*

Knowledge as Power, ed. Wolfgang Sachs (Atlantic Highlands, N.J.: Zed Books, 1992), 2.

13. The phrase is Larry Rasmussen's.

14. Susan George, *A Fate Worse than Debt: The World Financial Crisis and the Poor* (New York: Grove Weidenfeld, 1990), 270–71.

15. The phrase is borrowed from Lisa Stowe Hazelwood.

16. Paul Hawken, *The Ecology of Commerce: A Declaration of Sustainability* (San Francisco: Harper Books, 1993), xiv. Italics added.

17. Such "green taxes," applied progressively over a twenty-year period, would aim at making it "less expensive to use alternatives to carbon-based fuels . . . wind, water, and solar, which provide permanent sources of energy. . . . We can harness more than enough . . . energy that arrives every day from the sun to meet our present and foreseeable future needs, as long as those needs do not continue to involve a runaway, frenetic world of cars, planes, commuting, and travel." Ibid., 180–81.

18. Measure of well-being then shifts from the exclusively macro-economic variables of neo-classical economic theory, to indicators such as those developed by Social Watch: literacy rates, infant mortality and child-health rates, percentage of population with access to adequate health care, education, nutrition, shelter, and so on.

19. Viviene Taylor, *Marketisation of Governance: Critical Feminist Perspectives from the South,* a publication of DAWN (Development Alternatives with Women for a New Era) (Capetown: SADEP, 2000), 164.

20. One can hardly exaggerate the magnitude of change this implies for many industries involved in agribusiness (agri-chemical companies and grain industries).

21. These networks include, for example, Focus on the Global South and a movement of rural Protestant churches in Korea. They are responding to the indebtedness and loss of traditional food crops that have accompanied the focus on export agriculture demanded by structural adjustment policies. The demand and prices of export crops are constantly shifting; corporate grain companies sell seeds requiring chemicals dangerous to land and health; and traditional food crops become scarce, and imported food expensive.

22. United Nations, *Charter of Economic Rights and Duties of States,* Article 2, 2 a-b, General Assembly, Twenty-Ninth Session.

23. Taylor, *Marketisation of Governance,* 163.

24. It is not for me to prescribe or predict where the presence and power of God, living and loving in the beloved, will lead those who dare to know that presence more intimately *and* to see the realities of globalization more clearly. To prescribe one path of response runs the three-fold risk of sanctifying it, truncating creative energies toward other paths, and inciting the fear that may accompany viewing unfamiliar destinations without participating in crafting the way. On the other hand, we cannot go where we cannot imagine, and imagination is fed by the witness of others. Therefore, we view a few possibilities as seen in two communities, one descriptively and the other imaginatively. Most of the possibilities are drawn from actual alternatives in the world today, a few that I have lived and many others that I have encountered. View them as lights to mark paths that exist and pitfalls along the way.

25. "Social mortgage" refers to appreciation in value due to improved infrastructure, services, and community development such as new rapid-transit stations and public recreation facilities.

26. The theory behind "accompaniment" is that international presence offers a modicum of protection against paramilitary and death squad forces.

27. Walter Brueggemann, "Voices of the Night—Against Justice," in Walter Brueggemann, Thomas H. Groome, and Sharon Parks, *To Act Justly, Love Tenderly, and Walk Humbly* (Mahwah, N.J.: Paulist Press, 1986), 11.

28. It does not take long to see that the global warming, species extinction, and clean soil and water depletion that accompany unchecked economic growth jeopardize their own lives. Furthermore, commodification and growth maximization in the global market became evident not only in terms of seed strains in India, women's bodies in Thailand, and water supplies in Cochibamba, but in their homes and lives. Their vegetables contain toxins outlawed in the U.S., but used by U.S.- based corporations elsewhere. The movement of an industrial plant to Mexico leaves some members of the congregation unemployed. A torrent of advertisements is convincing their toddlers to crave name-brand clothing and toys, their teens to spend hours playing electronic games focused on killing, and both to hunger after evermore consumer products. Research indicates that their children will spend far more time being spiritually and morally formed by advertisements than by their church life.

29. For further reading related to various components of this concept, the reader is referred to David Wann, *Deep Design: Pathways to a Livable Future* (Washington, D.C.: Island Press, 1996); Hawken, *Ecology of Commerce*; Rasmussen, *Earth Community, Earth Ethics* (Maryknoll, N.Y.: Orbis, 1996); Michael H. Shuman, *Going Local* (New York: Free Press, 1998); and David Korten, *The Post-Corporate World* (West Hartford and San Francisco: Kumarian and Barrett-Koehler, 1999).

30. Wann, *Deep Design*, xv.

31. Rasmussen, *Earth Community*, 114.

32. See discussions by Shuman in *Going Local*, and by Korten in *The Post-Corporate World*.

33. Irenaeus, *Against Heresies*, 3.17.2

34. The complexity of economic relations means that alternatives to neo-liberal globalization are fraught with moral, theoretical, and practical ambiguity. Right and wrong are not always clear. To claim that moral alternatives are being developed does not claim moral and theoretical certainty, but rather that ambiguity does not preclude moral action. (For discussion of moral commitment in the face of ethical uncertainty, see J. Philip Wogaman, *Christian Moral Judgment* [Louisville: Westminster/ John Knox Press, 1989], 39–58).

35. Luther, "Sermon on Sixteenth Sunday after Trinity," in John Nicholas Lenker, ed., *Sermons of Martin Luther* (Grand Rapids, Baker, 1982), 8: 275–6.

36. Carla Berkedahl, "Dreaming of Green Parishes," in *Earth Letter* (September 1998): 11.

37. Both phrases are from *Lutheran Book of Worship* (Minneapolis: Augsburg Fortress Press, 1978).

38. Text from *With One Voice: A Luther Resource for Worship* (Minneapolis: Augsburg Fortress Press, 1995), 68.

39. These first three elements are consistent with the perspective articulated by an Indian layperson in conversation with me. He has been active for two decades in grassroots organizing amongst Dalits, fisherfolk, and tribal folk of India. I asked what he considered to be the ingredients of resistance and alternatives to globalization. He responded: theological preparation, economic literacy, and actions that prioritize sustainability and justice over profit.

40. Heyward, *Touching Our Strength*, 10; and Luther, in Lenker 8: 272.

41. Luther, "Sacrament of the Body and Blood of Christ—Against the Fanatics," in Timothy F. Lull, ed. *Martin Luther's Basic Theological Writings* (Minneapolis: Fortress Press, 1989), 321.

42. Luther, *Weimar Aufgabe*, 10.143.

43. Hadewijch of Antwerp, *Hadewijch: The Complete Works*, trans. Mother Columba Hart (New York: Paulist Press, 1980), 60.

Appendix

1. See Walter Brueggemann, "Voices of the Night—Against Justice," in Walter Brueggemann, Thomas H. Groome, and Sharon Parks, *To Act Justly, Love Tenderly, and Walk Humbly* (Mahwah, N.J.: Paulist Press, 1986), 17.

2. One of the determinants identified above, theological presuppositions, is not addressed in this appendix, because it was addressed in the introduction.

3. I am not alone in questioning the adequacy of "traditional moral theory" for the moral crises of the late twentieth and early twenty-first centuries, and in proposing that new questions be asked to supplement the traditional questions of ethics. For example, philosopher of religion Edith Wyschogrod (*Saints and Postmodernism: Revisioning Moral Philosophy* [Chicago and London: Univ. of Chicago Press, 1990]) critiques moral theory as "an unsatisfactory way of addressing matters that require action in contemporary life" (xxii). Ethics, she argues, is bound by the "standard canons of reason, the possibility of a totalizing discourse capable of presenting an account of the real" (xvi). The consequences for moral philosophical ethics, she asserts, is its failure to bring about moral conduct in the face of the twentieth century's moral calamities. Wyschogrod, as am I, is seeking to address the gap between moral norms and moral action. Her critique of moral theory is three-pronged, the first of which—a pragmatic criticism of moral theory—is most relevant here: "As Alasdair MacIntyre and others have pointed out, moral theories do not result in moral actions. . . . Moral theory is an instrument that fails to achieve an already predetermined goal: the transformation of moral conduct" (xxv). Her "triple critique of moral theory . . . constitutes the 'argument' or 'justification' for her break with theoretical discourse as the ground for generating moral lives" (xxvi). Her "revisioning [of] ethics entails a move away form moral theory" (xxiv) and toward a postmodern ethic that studies the value of saintly lives in building moral lives today.

4. By "schools of ethics," I refer to deontological, teleological (in both its utilitarian and more classic forms), communitarian, and character/virtue ethics.

5. The problem as failure to hold the two in light of each other is exposed and critiqued by many scholars and activists. They include Mary C. Grey, *Prophecy and Mysticism: The Heart of the Postmodern Church* (Edinburgh: T&T Clark, 1997); Roger S. Gottlieb, *A Spirituality of Resistance* (New York: Crossroad, 1999); Grace M. Jantzen in "Ethics and Mysticism: Friends or Foes?" *Nederlands Theologisch Tijdschrift* 39 (Octo-

ber 1985); Dietrich Bonhoeffer, especially in *Letters and Papers from Prison,* ed. Eberhard Bethge (New York: Macmillan, 1971), 286; and in *Ethics* (New York: Touchstone, 1995); and others. The deeper problem identified in my text, *the distinction* itself, is addressed explicitly by Grey in *Prophecy and Mysticism.*

6. See Bonnie Thurston, *Spiritual Life in the Early Church* (Minneapolis: Fortress Press, 1993).

7. Larry Rasmussen, *Earth Community, Earth Ethics* (Maryknoll, N.Y.: Orbis Books, 1996); Sallie McFague, *The Body of God: An Ecological Theology* (Minneapolis: Fortress Press, 1993); and Carter Heyward, *Touching Our Strength: The Erotic as Power and the Love of God* (San Francisco: Harper & Row, 1989).

8. Rasmussen, *Earth Community, Earth Ethics,* 320. Italics added.

9. Ibid. Italics added.

10. Ibid., xiv.

11. Ibid., 352.

12. McFague, *The Body of God,* 202–3.

13. Ibid, 207.

14. Ibid, 208.

15. Ibid, 212. Italics added.

16. Heyward, *Touching Our Strength,* 10.

17. Ibid., 33.

18. Carter Heyward, *The Redemption of God: A Theology of Mutual Relation* (Lanham, Md.: Univ. Press of America, 1982), 6.

19. Others making this point include Elizabeth Bettenhausen, in "Questions Facing the Church" (unpublished paper delivered at "Lutheran Women in Theological Studies" annual meeting, 1999), who draws, as do I, upon Martin Luther; and Grace Jantzen in *God's World, God's Body* (Philadelphia: Westminster, 1984).

20. In the current economic context, this categorization is questionable. A global economy prioritizing further wealth creation and wealth concentration renders the "middle class" extraordinarily vulnerable to economic decisions that are unaccountable to those affected. The closing of a production site, major downsizing, speculative equity markets, and other common occurrences in the current global economy rapidly may change one who "has too much" into one is economically poor, even homeless.

21. "Why Blame Nature?" *NGO Matters: Newsletter of the South African NGO Coalition* 3:3 (April 2000): 9.

22. Brigitta Kahl grapples with this dialectic (in relationship to Scripture) in "Seeing the Text Anew" (paper presented at Union Theological Seminary, New York City, April 1998), 1. The term *hermeneutic of trust* is hers.

23. The term is from Christopher Morse, *Not Every Spirit: A Dogmatics of Christian Disbelief* (Valley Forge, Pa.: Trinity Press International, 1995), 3–32. He argues that "the truth in Christian doctrine harbors a lie whenever the faithful disbeliefs these doctrines entail go unrecognized."

24. Donna J. Haraway, *Simians, Cyborgs, and Women: The Reinvention of Nature* (New York: Routledge), 191.

25. Larry Rasmussen, "A Different Discipline," *Union Seminary Quarterly Review: Festschrift for Beverly Harrison* 53:3-4 (1999): 35. From my perspective, that criterion is rooted theologically in the church's claim to *be* the body of Christ on Earth, the body of one who suffered torture and execution, and who heard and heeded the suffering people in his midst.

26. Euro-American and European feminists were critiqued rightly by women of color for failing to account for racism and class privilege at practical and theoretical levels. A seminal voice on this point was bell hooks in *feminist theory: from margins to center* (Boston: South End Press, 1984). It is an unrelenting critique of the liberal white feminist movement up to that point, for ignoring categories of class and race. hooks' critique is not an "attempt to diminish feminist struggle but to enrich, to share in the work of making a liberatory ideology and a liberatory movement" (15). The criticism was made also by self-critical white feminists. See, for example, Beverly Harrison in "Theological Reflection in the Struggle for Liberation," in *Making the Connections: Essays in Feminist Social Ethics*, ed. Carol Robb (Boston: Beacon Press, 1985), 235–63. The case for an interstructural account of relations of domination is made by many others. See, for example, Pamela Brubaker, *Women Don't Count: The Challenge of Women's Poverty to Christian Ethics* (Atlanta: Scholars Press, 1994); and by Patricia Hill Collins, "It's All in the Family: Intersections of Gender, Race, and Nation," *Hypatia* 13:3 (summer 1998): 62–82.

27. Maria Lugones, "On the Logic of Pluralist Feminism," in *Feminist Ethics*, ed. Claudia Card (Lawrence: Univ. Press of Kansas, 1991), 35–45.

28. Sallie McFague also points to the impossibility of adequately attending to the interrelating forms of oppression, and to the intended complementarity of her work. See McFague, *Body of God*, ix.

29. In the words of philosopher and social critic Simone Weil: the conquerors account of history will not dismantle the colonial legacy.

30. For a highly readable and succinct introduction to this principle, its historical roots in radical feminism, its contribution to social analysis that leads to empowerment, and its function as a basis of feminist praxis, see Maria Riley, *Transforming Feminism* (Kansas City: Sheed and Ward, 1989), 43–46. An example of this principle applied to liberative education implementing a "Freirean" (per Paulo Freire) method is in Ann Hope and Sally Timmel's *Training for Transformation: A Handbook for Community Workers* (Zimbabwe: Mambo Press, 1984).

31. As Pamela Sparr notes in "The Global Economy: Seeking A Christian Ethic" (New York: Women's Division, United Methodist Church, 1993), 13, the neo-classical economic model holds "that society exists outside of the economy." This notion is one of the reasons that neo-classical economic theory is inadequate for analyzing economic globalization.

32. Brubaker, *Women Don't Count*, 244–45.

33. The term comes from Rasmussen in *Earth Community*. The significance of the term, for our purposes, is this: Notions of morality and community must shift dramatically in light of a fundamental change in "the relationship of the human world to the rest of earth . . . from the onset of the twentieth century to its close" (4). Earth's capacity to regenerate is being destroyed by cumulative human activities. This change calls for concepts of morality and community extending beyond the human to "everything that has life and is necessary to life." (5).

34. Shahra Razavi, "Reply to Jacques Baudot," in *UNRISD News* 21 (December 1999): 24, citing Jacques Baudot, "Poverty and the Spirit of the Time," in *UNRISD News* 20 (November 1999).

35. See Beverly Wildung Harrison, "The Role of Social Theory in Religious Social Ethics," in *Making the Connections*, ed. Robb, 79.

36. Janet Jakobsen, lecture at Union Theological Seminary, New York City, 1998.

37. The import of this criterion for the task of dismantling the widespread political and moral inertia of middle-strata North Americas is demonstrated by Beverly Wildung Harrison, in "The Fate of the Middle Class in Late Capitalism," chap. in *God and Capitalism: A Prophetic Critique of the Market Economy*, ed. J. Mark Thomas and Vernon Visick (Madison: A-R Editions, 1991), 53–71. See especially 54–55.

38. Ibid.

39. Harrison, a conversation at lunch in her honor, Union Theological Seminary, New York City, March 25, 1999.

40. Harrison, "The Power of Anger in the Work of Love," in *Making the Connections*, ed. Robb, 21.

41. For explicit discussion of the term "critical theory" and its varied referents see Seyla Benhabib, *Critique, Norm and Utopia: A Study of the Foundations of Critical Theory* (New York: Columbia Univ. Press, 1986); Joan Cocks, *Oppositional Imagination: Feminism, Critique, and Political Theory* (New York: Routledge, 1989); Roberto Mangabeira Unger, *Social Theory: Its Situation and Its Task* (Cambridge: Cambridge Univ. Press, 1987); Nancy Fraser, "What's Critical about Critical Theory," in *Feminism as Critique: On the Politics of Gender*, ed. Seyla Benhabib and Drucilla Cornell (Minneapolis: Univ. of Minnesota Press, 1987); Guytoon Hammond, *Conscience and Its Recovery: From the Frankfurt School to Feminism* (Richmond: Univ. of Virginia Press, 1993); Jane Braaten, *Habermas's Critical Theory of Society* (Albany, N.Y.: SUNY, 1991), 1–11; Beverly Wildung Harrison, "The Role of Social Theory in Religious Social Ethics," in *Making the Connections*, ed. Robb. "Social theory" too is used variously. For example, the term is roughly interchangable with social scientific theory for Rodney Stark (in sociology) and Roberto Unger (in political philosophy), while Smith divides social theory into three general areas: social science, social ethics, and social polity.

42. Eileen Meiskins Wood, for example, uses the term in this sense in *Democracy against Capitalism* (Cambridge: Cambridge Univ. Press, 1995), 19.

43. Ibid., 3; Ibid., 13.

44. See Harrison, "Role of Social Theory." Eileen Meiskins Wood also identifies these two factors. See Wood, *Democracy*.

45. Unger, *Social Theory*, 1.

46. Russell McCutcheon, "A Default of Critical Intelligence?: The Scholar of Religion as Public Intellectual," *Journal of the American Academy of Religion* 65:2 (1997): 460, cited in Linell Cady, "The Intellectual and Effective Critique," *Bulletin of the Council of Societies for the Study of Religion* 27:2 (April 1998): 36; Joan Cocks, *Oppositional Imagination: Feminism, Critique, and Political Theory* (London and New York: Routledge, 1989), 15.

47. Rasmussen, *Earth Community*, 16.

48. Highly contested areas in recent feminist theory, relevant to this project, revolve around the role of tradition, the character and role of reason, the nature and status of normative criteria, and the relationship of feminism to postmodernism. Regarding all of these see Seyla Benhabib et al., *Feminist Contentions: A Philosophical Exchange* (New York and London: Routledge, 1995).

49. Conceptual clarification is important. "Political, economic, and cultural structures" here refers to institutions, ideologies, policies, power alignments, and practices. "Challenging" implies identifying, bringing to public attention and discourse, analyzing, dismantling, pointing to alternatives—existing, envisioned, and yet to be dreamt— and seeking to practice those alternatives.

50. By "less inclusive forms" I mean the spectrum of feminist frameworks that, while making enormous contributions, limit the scope of critical categories for analyzing the oppression of women. While different theorists identify these frameworks somewhat differently, most cohere loosely with the spectrum identified by Pam Brubaker in *Women Don't Count* (213–42) as "liberal, Marxist, cultural feminist, and socialist feminist frameworks." The first errs by focusing singularly on sex roles and equal rights, and the second by pointing to capitalism as the primary source of women's oppression, failing to recognize adequately the role of patriarchy. The third elevates patriarchy as the singular source of women's oppression, not accounting for the role of capitalism. The fourth attempts to overcome "the ahistorical character of cultural feminism and the sex-blind categories of Marxism by synthesizing cultural feminism and central aspects of Marxist analysis of capitalism," thus identifying women's oppression with capitalist patriarchy. All of these frameworks overlook the critical categories of race and ethnicity.

51. Delwin Brown, *Boundaries of Our Habitations* (Albany: SUNY Press, 1994), 1, citing Descartes.

52. In the words of Richard Shaull (*The Reformation and Liberation Theology* [Louisville: Westminster/John Knox, 1991]), Luther insists that we "resist the sacralization . . . of any achievement of the past, any way of life, or any social structure" (85). This includes the sacralization of Luther's questions or his answers. Elizabeth Bettenhausen makes this point in "The Concept of Justice and a Feminist Lutheran Social Ethic," *Annual of the Society of Christian Ethics* (1986): 163–82.

53. Dietrich Bonhoeffer, firmly rooted in the legacy of Luther, insisted that biblical faith called for decentering questions of "personal salvation" in order to be with the questions of his day regarding right relationships in this world. He writes, "Hasn't the individualistic question about personal salvation almost completely left us?" Dietrich Bonhoeffer, *Letters*, 286.

54. Michael Waltzer, *The Revolution of the Saints: A Study in the Origins of Radical Politics* (Cambridge and London: Harvard Univ. Press, 1989), 1.

55. Larry Rasmussen, "A Community of the Cross," *Dialog* 30:2 (spring 1991): 150.

56. Luther, "Preface to the Wittenberg Edition of Luther's German Writings," in ed. Timothy F. Lull, *Martin Luther's Basic Theological Writings* (Minneapolis: Fortress Press, 1989), 65.

57. Delwin Brown and Gordon Kaufman offer useful insight into the role of theological tradition or inheritance in theological reconstruction for the sake of faithful praxis today. See Brown, *Boundaries,* and Gordon D. Kaufman, *In Face of Mystery: A Constructive Theology* (Cambridge and London: Cambridge Univ. Press, 1993).

58. Mary M. Solberg, *Compelling Knowledge: A Feminist Proposal for an Epistemology of the Cross* (Albany: SUNY Press, 1997), 97.

59. This distinction is made and argued well by Christine Pierce in "Postmodernism and Other Scepticisms," in *Feminist Ethics*, ed. Claudia Card (Lawrence, Ks.: Univ. of Kansas Press, 1991), 60–77.

60. Willi Braun, "Amnesia in the Production of History," *Council of Societies for the Study of Religion Bulletin* 28:1 (February 1999): 5.

Acknowledgments

This work has been nurtured and inspired by too many people to name. Here I offer profound respect and gratitude to Larry Rasmussen and Beverly Harrison: mentors, teachers, friends. I thank too the many colleagues who have shown me the joy to be found in sincere intellectual generosity: Janet Parker, Beryl Ingram, Maylin Biggadike, Karin Case, Toddie Peters, David Wellman, Aana Vigen, Nancy Erhard, Gary Mathews, Ken Estey, and others. Your insistence on authentic support for one another's work, rather than competition, has been a gift of immeasurable worth, a far greater gift than you know. I am grateful to those people who read pieces of this work in progress, or otherwise encouraged me along its way: Martha Stortz, Glen Stassen, Mary Solberg, Karen Bloomquist, Dan Spencer, Pam Brubaker, Marilyn Legge, Liz Bounds. Special thanks to other friends who read pieces and gave comment without the blessing/blinders of academic lenses: Robbie Rohr and Pam Russell. My heartfelt gratitude to Michael West of Fortress Press for believing in this project from the beginning and for giving it a home; to Zan Ceeley, also of Fortress, for your gracious competence and wisdom in seeing the book through to publication; and to Leeann Drabenstott, an astute and insightful copy-editor. Rosemary Harer, for all that you have given me, I offer profound gratitude. I thank the many other magnificent friends in my life. Your support and presence, shared laughter and tears, and refusal to give up on an often absent friend have breathed life into my sometimes weary soul. I am honored to share life's paths with you. This book may not have been finished were it not for the Seattle coffee shops in which I wrote it! Thank you to the kind coffeeshop folk who greeted me warmly and gave me drink. Finally, I thank those to whom this book is dedicated: Suzan, for your constant love; my parents, for your truly boundless support, both emotional and material; and Ron, Leif, and Gabriel. To you three dear ones, I offer my deepest gratitude. You have lived through years of my study, writing, commuting, and teaching. Leif and Gabriel, as you grow, may you know my deep respect for the unique and splendid person that each of you is. And may you know that you are held, always, in the embrace of a loving God. Ron, my love, thank you.

Index